A JOURNEY
INTO PRAYER

A JOURNEY INTO PRAYER

Pioneers of Prayer
in the Laboratory
Agents of Science or Satan?

The Spindrift Research founders, Bruce and
John Klingbeil, discovered relationships
between prayer, conciousness, and healing.
This book explores the controversial scientific
research developed by the father and son team.

Bill Sweet

To order additional copies of this book, contact:
Xlibris Corporation
1-888-7-XLIBRIS
www.Xlibris.com
Orders@Xlibris.com
17686

For those who think to a different drummer

"Bill Sweet makes a significant contribution in documenting an extraordinary hostility to the scientific study of the effects of prayer. Antagonistic reactions are far more common than many people imagine. I expect this book will be seen as an important case study in the decades to come. Anyone interested in research on prayer should read this book."

—George P. Hansen,
Author of *The Trickster and the Paranormal*

CONTENTS

Foreword 11

Acknowledgements 15

Introduction 17

Chapter One: The Awakening 21

Personal experiences of the Spindrift founders
pave the way to research prayer. The research on
prayer in clinical and laboratory environments
approaches the mainstream, which sets the stage
to explain Spindrift's historic role.

Chapter Two: Spindrift Explained 37

How the word *spindrift* is metaphorically applied
is explained followed by the main theories and
concepts behind the experiments.

Chapter Three: Like Minds Meeting 69

The author learned about consciousness and prayer
research from meeting the Klingbeil family.

Chapter Four: Politics and Prayer 102

In 1990, national news coverage publicized
Spindrift when a member of the Board of Directors
of Spindrift ran as the Republican candidate for
governor of Colorado.

Chapter Five: Bible Experiments 110

This chapter examines the experiments in the Bible.

Interlude: Tidbits Learned 120

Speculations about the future are considered.

Chapter Six: The Skeptics 132

Communication with the scientific skeptics about their scientifically testing the Klingbeils while they prayed resulted in barbs back and forth.

Chapter Seven: Agents of Science or Satan? 144

Incidents are described of individuals and groups who opposed Spindrift's experiments with prayer.

Chapter Eight: Mind over Mood 173

The way the experiments were approached is explained which included sorting out the changing mood effects of the human mind's expectations from the organizing effects of the ordering Mind.

Chapter Nine: The Paradigm Shift 184

A positive shift begins toward the Klingbeils' research.

Chapter Ten: All Alone by the Telephone 196

The experiments were beginning to get recognition, but the experiments still clashed with the mind-set that experimenting with holy prayer was heretical.

Chapter Eleven: Science or Fringe Science 224

This chapter addresses scientific concerns about the tests.

Epilogue 235

Since the Spindrift experiments, prayer and consciousness have begun to be recognized as legitimate subjects of scientific inquiry.

APPENDIX

EXAMPLES OF EXPERIMENTS

Appendix: The Botanical Experiments 241

Descriptions are given of several prayer experiments on plants done by the Spindrifters.

Endnotes 297

Index 319

What Others Say 327

THE SPINDRIFT FILES 331

About the Author 375

"Bill Sweet's excellent book *A Journey Into Prayer* offers compelling evidence for the efficacy of healing prayer in the vegetable kingdom. He describes dozens of successful laboratory experiments investigating the growth of plants, yeast, and mold, spanning more than two decades. He also describes the passionate conflict between the researchers at Spindrift and the 'believers,' who feel that prayer is a matter of faith, not to be investigated in the laboratory."

—Russell Targ, physicist and writer,
Co-author of *Miracles of Mind* and *Heart of the Mind*

FOREWORD

By Larry Dossey, M.D.

For most of my life as a physician, prayer was not in my black bag. In my view, it simply didn't rate with drugs and surgical procedures when people were really sick. It's not that I was opposed to prayer. I knew it was a source of great comfort to people, but I felt its benefits were essentially psychological. I'd been trained to believe prayer was a placebo, a medical intervention whose actions were due to suggestion, expectation, and positive thinking.

That was before I stumbled onto the scientific evidence that prayer is associated with healing effects, at a distance, even when the recipient is unaware that the prayer is being offered. During the mid-1980s, a friend told me about a study involving prayer for nearly four hundred heart patients in the coronary care unit at San Francisco General Hospital. The experiment followed the tenets of careful science—a controlled, double-blind test in which no one knew who was receiving prayer and who was not. The prayed-for patients did better on several counts—so much better, in fact, that if the therapy being evaluated had been a new drug, it would have been heralded as a medical breakthrough.

At that time I was extremely skeptical about prayer's benefits, as mentioned, and I did not pray for my patients. This study, therefore, caused me great concern. I frequently had patients with heart attacks in the coronary care unit; should I be praying for them? What if prayer really did make a difference? Was I negligent in not using it? If prayer worked, is it unethical not to pray for one's patients? The more I thought about these questions, the more uncomfortable I became. Finally I decided to investigate this field and see what other evidence I could find. My search took years. I found more scientific evidence favoring prayer than I imagined existed— more than 130 studies, not only in humans but also in animals, plants, and microorganisms. I concluded that prayer had real healing power. I began to pray for my patients and eventually wrote several books about this area.

In my exploration of the science surrounding prayer, I discovered Spindrift and Bill Sweet, Spindrift's former president. Bill showed me that for twenty years Spindrift's father-and-son team, Bruce and John Klingbeil, had asked questions about prayer that others had shunned. They had carried the scientific investigation of prayer into areas I'd never considered. Seeking a simple, repeatable experiment of prayer, they had tested prayer's effects on germinating seeds and the metabolic activities of microorganisms such as yeast cells. After they repeatedly demonstrated through experiments that prayer works, they moved on to other questions. What types of prayer strategies are most effective? Is it best to pray for a specific outcome, or does an open-ended, Thy-will-be-done approach work best? What attitudes or emotions on the part of the pray-ers are important? Is a lot of prayer more effective than a small amount? What are the implications of negative prayers on society?

As I explored the Spindrift experiments, I gained immense respect for Bruce and John Klingbeil. I learned about the difficulties they encountered in their church and the price they paid. I spoke with Bruce several times over the phone about their struggles. He seemed determined, resourceful, dedicated, and passionate.

The Spindrift story is monumentally important. It shows the courage that is required in exploring areas off science's beaten path, and the great risks that are often involved.

Through the Spindrift saga we see that many people, now as throughout history, want to keep religion and science segregated from each other. The Spindrift story reveals the price that is often paid by those who violate these prohibitions. It reveals one of the darker sides of institutionalized religion, and how many religious organizations remain fearful of the revelations of science. The scientific community however behaved no better.

The Spindrift story is not new, of course. Religion and science have often formed an incendiary mixture during the past few centuries, and people have frequently paid with their reputations or their lives when they transgressed the boundaries set up between these two fields. Science's most famous heretic, Galileo, got off light; he was merely confined to house arrest in the seventeenth century during the final years of his life by the Church fathers. Other explorers such as the alchemists of the Middle Ages, who laid the foundations of modern chemistry, were not as fortunate. Untold numbers of them were tortured and killed as heretics. But in our era, when we pride ourselves on being enlightened and tolerant, it is shocking to see scientific investigators treated as heretics by religious institutions. The Spindrift story reminds us that the old hatreds are not dead and that they still exact a terrible toll.

The Spindrift story, however, is much larger than the debate between science and religion. It is an unrelenting search for wholeness, a quest for personal meaning and fulfillment. It is the story of individuals who are not content to segment their lives into the categories of faith and reason, intellect and intuition. The Spindrifters are involved in an archetypal mission—the drive toward Unity—that is enfolded in all the world's great wisdom traditions. Their experience reveals what we often forget—that this search is perhaps the most important ever experienced by humans; that it can involve grave consequences; that it is not to be undertaken lightly.

Today the old divisions between science and religion are crumbling on several fronts. This is most dramatically evident in medicine, where the influence of religious practices and prayer on health have been demonstrated beyond reasonable doubt. Currently, approximately ninety of the 125 medical schools in the U.S. have adopted courses examining the health effects of religious devotion and prayer. By any measure, spirituality and prayer have reentered medicine.

Bruce and John Klingbeil helped set these trends in motion and they deserve our respect and honor. In fact the two major reasons why I entered the field of prayer were the San Francisco hospital study and the Klingbeils' Spindrift studies. So thank you, Bruce and John, for helping to respiritualize medicine. Every physician and patient is in your debt. And thank you, Bill Sweet, for telling the story.

—Larry Dossey, M.D.
Author: *The Extraordinary Healing
Power of Ordinary Things,
Reinventing Medicine,
Be Careful What You Pray For,
Healing Words: The Power of Prayer and the Practice of Medicine,
Prayer is Good Medicine,
Recovering the Soul: A Scientific and Spiritual Search,*
(Spindrift is on p. 54 of *Recovering the Soul.*)
Executive editor, *EXPLORE: The Journal of Science and Healing*

Acknowledgements

My book project began in August, 1994, after I attended a Noetic Sciences conference in Rosemont, Illinois. I noticed that every speaker I met at the conference had a book. Seeing these books inspired me to tell the Spindrift story.

The burdens of writing my Spindrift book were less because of the tireless help of my mother, Alice Sweet, who was able to type endlessly. A former president of Spindrift and an English teacher, Gladys Myers, worked on tedious details of composition. Samantha Fairfax, Ph.D., made corrections and helped with scientific explanations. Ron Burnett's extensive editorial experience helped guide my project. Thanks go to author Theodore Rockwell, a fellow New Trier graduate, for his deep thoughts which helped to pour light on the Klingbeils' unusual concepts.

Author Leigh Fortson applied her skills with words. Barbara Deal worked to place my book with a publisher.

Thanks go out to Dr. Larry Dossey, Dr. Melvin Morse, Joan Borysenko, Ph.D., Cody Sweet, Ph.D., Charles Sweet, Rev. Karl Goodfellow, Sperry Andrews, Cleve Backster (noted in *The Secret Life of Plants*), parapsychologists Rhea White, Dean Radin, George Hansen, and Alexander Imich who is 104 years old. A number of other researchers, Spindrift supporters, and spiritual healers came out of the woodwork to add to the mosaic of Spindrift's history. I thank everyone for the use of their time and talent.

To find the Spindrift website, insert the words *spindrift research* into a search engine or try www.spindriftresearch.org.

"This book describes the work of some original thinkers, supported by over 20 years of meticulous experimental and analytical research of ingenious design. It bears on the nature of prayer and of healing, and of powers of the human mind little appreciated by most people. Because the philosophical background and the experimental work differs from the mainstream, the research and its important implications for all of us has been largely overlooked. Bill Sweet's homely and disarming writing style presents the material in a personal way that is easily accessible to readers of all backgrounds. Read it, enjoy it, and save your judgment until you have finished and pondered it a while."

—Theodore Rockwell, nuclear engineer,
Author of *The Rickover Effect* and *Creating the New World*

Ted Koppel remarked on the government's research of consciousness on ABC's *Nightline* of November 28, 1995.

Imagine how someone a hundred years ago would have reacted to a description of many of the things we take for granted today. Think of telling someone in the 1890's about a flying cylinder that would routinely transport several hundred people at a time . . . from coast to coast. Explain the storage of a small library's worth of information on a silicone chip smaller than your fingernail. [Or try to explain an iPod.]

We live in an age of once-unimaginable miracles, so it would take equal measures of courage and hubris to dismiss as impossible the notion that some people may have certain psychic powers. This may reassure you, it may alarm you, but in fact, for some years now, the U.S. intelligence community has wagered a modest amount of money on the possibility that such powers do exist.

INTRODUCTION

Please Lord, keep my words soft and tender,
for tomorrow, I may have to eat them.
Anonymous prayer

The voyage of discovery is not in seeking new
landscapes but in having new eyes.
Marcel Proust

Who are the Spindrifters? They are a small group of people who have the audacity to believe that the effects of prayer can be measured scientifically in a laboratory test. Their belief in testing prayer has provoked violent reactions. Books have been burned. Church members have been removed from their offices. Supporters have been perceived as cult-members. Hate mail has been received. When a founder of Spindrift lost his church job, he wrote that he "was expelled from his ministry for refusal to recant his belief in scientific proof." Does this expulsion mean testing prayer makes the Spindrifters contributors to science or agents of Satan? People see the Spindrifters as either pioneers in prayer research or as evil heretics.

The author has investigated links between science, religion, and consciousness studies. Most of mankind pray regularly, and I don't know of any culture in history which hasn't practiced prayer. Yet, I felt that prayer as a force of human consciousness had not been studied seriously. When I met Spindrift founders John and Bruce Klingbeil in 1977, my opinion began to change. John and Bruce were performing dozens of scientific experiments of prayer. John and Bruce felt their research scientifically explored how prayer worked, how it interacted with the world. I was thrilled to be associated with the Spindrift research. The annoying problem turned out to be the avalanche of ridicule toward the prayer research and those associated with it, especially the Klingbeils. Why?

The Klingbeils proposed that religious people should participate in prayer experiments. Why religious people? Because, if modern science can't control or duplicate a prayer event, over time science will educate people to deny or dismiss that a prayer event ever happened. The scientific dismissal of prayer as **nothing but brain activity** would be a loss for religion, science, and the healing-arts. *The Klingbeils felt the necessity to do research on prayer because many answers to prayer could be explained by chance, coincidence, the placebo effect, or temporary and spontaneous remissions.* John and Bruce took up the challenge of testing prayer. They had the curiosity to explore how their thoughts and prayers operated in controlled laboratory environments.

I am telling the story of the two men who got involved in the scientific research of healing plants through prayer, of how they did their research, and of what happened to them as a result of their doing it. By testing prayer, Spindrift was breaking boundaries.

Why did I write the book? To tell the Spindrift story and to put on record the experiments. What is important about the Spindrift story? That thought and prayer affect physical systems and create test data compelling enough to warrant further investigation.

The author is a witness to many of the incidents in this book. Some of the incidents during Spindrift's history might seem unbelievable to the reader. These incidents may even remind one of *The X Files*. The Spindrift participants themselves might strike the reader as weird. I would feel the same way about the prayer participants if I were reading about Spindrift's history for the first time. As time has shown, both the startling results of the research and the spikes of scorn for the Klingbeils' research compete for attention.

Billions of people pray. Even terrorists pray. **Prayer is a constant mental input into our world.** Why has the Spindrift effort to explain subtle prayer-healing effects in scientific experiments on plants caused derision and outrage? Read on and decide for yourself.

OPENING THOUGHTS

The more convinced I am that material progress is not only valueless without spiritual progress, it is, in the long term impossible.

Eugene   Holman
Former President Standard Oil

Understanding why the public has generally accepted the existence of psi [psychic phenomena] and why science has generally rejected it requires an examination of the *origins* of science. In exploring this clash of beliefs, we will discover that the scientific controversy has had very little to do with the evidence itself, and very much to do with the psychology, sociology, and history of science.

Dean Radin, Ph.D.,
The Conscious Universe, p. 7

I wonder if we shouldn't start discussing meaningfulness and hope in terms of what seems to be a universal, almost hard-wired belief that there is 'something beyond.' Because it is just this kind of belief that often evokes what we would call the placebo effect, often through such practices as prayers and other religious behaviors.

Herbert Benson, M.D.,
quoted in *The Placebo Effect*, p. 224

Prayer is the act of seeing reality from God's point
of view.

Philip Yancey, *Prayer*, p. 29

The human senses detect only a fraction of
reality: . . . the brain . . . defines the limits of what
we perceive. Human beings see, feel, taste, touch
and smell not the world around them but a version
of the world, one their brains have concocted.

U.S. News & World Report,
January 13, 1997, p. 59

Nobel physicist Brian Josephson of Cambridge
University's Cavendish Laboratory believes there may
be a connection between the causal powers of
consciousness and developments in a field of
fundamental physics that deals with 'nonlocality.'
He proposes that distant, simultaneous, 'nonlocal'
events at the subatomic level may eventually help
explain various nonlocal behaviors of the mind—
events such as telepathy, clairvoyance, transpersonal
imagery, and distant or intercessory prayer. Josephson
suggests that these distant mental connections are
made possible through the unique ability of humans
to find a meaning or a pattern behind our various
perceptions and experiences.

Larry Dossey, M.D.,
Healing Beyond the Body, p. 114

Thinking is an alternative lifestyle.

Gerald Myers, Ph.D., *William James*

A new era does not begin when the old is over,
but long before, for it is the strength and rightness
of the new that causes the old to pass away.

Max Kappeler, Ph.D., Metaphysician

Chapter One

The Awakening

God is the ocean and my prayer is a wave.
the Spindrift researchers

Spirituality is the organizing of consciousness.
Philip Hefner, founder,
the Center for Religion and Science
in Chicago, in the December 1998 *Zygon*

Warm sunshine surrounded the nine year old boy playing with his marbles on the front steps of his country home. Bruce stopped playing and listened. He felt immersed in a spiritual energy in the air around him. This strange perception permeated his consciousness. Bruce waited and felt something good was going to happen.

John Klingbeil tells in his book *The Healer* of his father's first encounter with a guiding presence. "It was not reason that impelled him, nor the pressure of emotion, but an urgency of thought and an action of the body he could not resist. Conscious only of getting on his bicycle, he rode into the depth of quiet that waited beyond the borders of conscious knowledge."[1] As Bruce rode into the corridor of calm, the clover fields, roadside wild flowers, and stones shone with sparkling, vivid clarity.

Bruce felt impelled to get off his bike. He walked through grass that was higher than he was to an abandoned farmhouse. Bruce heard a dog's desperate barks. He followed the sounds of the barking to an old, open well. A tiny puppy was trembling at the bottom.

Speaking softly to calm the puppy, he climbed down and tenderly enfolding the puppy in his arms brought it safely to the sunshine at the top of the well. Bruce felt a sense of goodness and being loved. When he put the puppy down on the glowing grass, the puppy raced across the sparkling meadow to a farmhouse Bruce could barely see.

While peddling back to his home, the vivid, sparkling glow around Bruce vanished. What remained was the feeling of good, of peace and that he was not alone. Some things can't be explained, only felt.[2]

The family sold the small Southern Illinois farm and moved to Chicago. Bruce became involved in the healing work part-time. He was applying the prayer techniques of Christian Science. The Second World War was on. Bruce agonized over killing someone. His church did not approve of one being a conscientious objector. When he went for the physical for the army, the doctors found he had tuberculosis. He was not permitted to go home but had to go directly to a sanitarium. When he came out of the army induction center in the Loop, he was at the foot of LaSalle Street. First, however, Bruce went into the nearby Christian Science Reading Room and prayed.

After three days of testing at the sanitarium, he was given a full release and sent back to the induction center. He was sent to another sanitarium in another part of Chicago. No tuberculosis was again found. The army bureaucracy would not give him a clean bill of health so he was not drafted.

Afterwards his application for listing as a Christian Science practitioner in *The Christian Science Journal* was accepted. *The Journal* contains the list of spiritual healers called practitioners. Now Bruce Klingbeil had an office with his name on the door. As a child, Bruce knew he was gifted as a healer. His work with animals proved that to him. Even back then, however, the elders in the Christian Science Church—

who usually choose prayer in lieu of medical treatment for healing—couldn't accept Bruce's gift since they didn't think he had enough formal training to do what he did. They, apparently, thought healing was a learned trade; Bruce was simply born with the ability to heal.

Bruce's life was going well. He married Gloria, another Christian Scientist, and they had three children. It was a happy time. Bruce made a good living as a practitioner. His primary function was to pray for people to heal. Bruce was contacted to pray for people from all over the world. It was gratifying to help friends and patients overcome their problems. And they did get helped.

Since they did, Bruce became ever more discouraged that chemistry-based technology was taking over the health-care field. Equally disturbing to him was the decline of church membership in America in the 1970's. Bruce was deeply concerned that people were drifting away from a spiritual approach to both healing and life in general. He was also terribly frustrated that the Christian Science church used anecdotal proof instead of the up-to-date scientific laboratory test. Most importantly, Bruce knew how often his prayers did work, and he wanted desperately for the world to know they did. To, in fact, provide credible scientific evidence that prayers were good medicine.

After intense reading and research on what had already been established in scientific circles and the influence of the placebo effect and the effect of prayer and other "paranormal" experiences, Bruce realized the challenge ahead. To convince a drug-minded medical world of his conviction, he would need to use standard medical research techniques. That meant studies that could yield enough repeatable results that anyone with a scientific mind could duplicate.

It also meant keeping things simple. Using human beings as his subjects was too complicated. He could hear in his own mind the arguments from skeptics about how the human subjects were sympathetic to the cause, and so did things—consciously or unconsciously—to generate positive results. Animals were a possibility, but they would be more difficult to manage and maintain in a lab.

A FALLING APPLE

Were there falling apples that suggested plants would make suitable test subjects?

Yes. One falling apple was a falling violet. In the early 1970's, when Bruce Klingbeil was considering ways to pray for rye grass seeds under controlled conditions, he thought back to an incident that occurred years earlier. Bruce's daughter, Deborah, accidentally knocked one of Gloria's African violets into some boiling hot tomato soup. She fished it out of the soup and rinsed it off, but the plant was clearly hurt. Mary, the oldest child, asked her father to pray for the plant to get better. He agreed to do his best for the violet.

Bruce looked at the soup-soaked pulpy plant put back into its flower pot. Bruce had prayed for trees and crops before, but praying for this singular violet had a different feel to it. Within six months, the violet that had fallen into the soup, and that he prayed for, had outgrown and out-bloomed all of Gloria's other violets. **The seed was planted.** Plants would eventually be used for the experiments.

John Klingbeil writes the following about his father's insight during this flash back to the soup-soaked violet. "If his rye grass seeds and the African violet were placed side-by-side, he could know each one's unique identity simply by touching them with his spiritualized thought. It was a new and exciting world!"[3]

Bruce's passion for his research was all consuming. Surprisingly, the Christian Science church admonished him for trying to prove in physical, human terms how God and spirituality works. Friends shunned him. Gloria eventually left him because his ambitions didn't match hers. All three children stayed with Bruce.

John inherited his father's brilliance and vision. Like Bruce, John had a passion for research and an urgency to share what the experiments were showing about how consciousness and prayer interact with the environment.

John graduated from high school in three years and was offered a full math scholarship from Northwestern University. By then, however, John believed completely in his father as both healer and scientist, and was eager to work with him. John refused the scholarship and chose instead to create and develop rigorous scientific methods, backed by computerized technology, to illustrate the scientific effects of prayer on plants and other tests of consciousness.

Later, the father-son team also created Spindrift, a non-profit organization through which their research was conducted. The Klingbeils worked to overcome the criticism and accusations of the skeptics and diligently pursued their passion with the help of courageous, open-minded volunteers. Several Chicago suburban volunteers supported the Klingbeils by participating in the experiments and running Spindrift, Inc.

ORDER IN THE UNIVERSE

We learn something about the spiritual universe by apprehending the spiritual order that underlies what appears to be a physical scene. We appreciate the order of the solar system. We learn from the lilies of the field that a holy power clothes and cares for organisms on earth. These observations point to an underlying spiritual order supporting the physical universe.

PRAYER FORCES TESTED

From *USA Weekend*

Perhaps a sign of the times is that several leading medical schools have announced plans to study the effects of prayer . . . . [Dale Matthews, M.D., said,] "Religion is the big elephant in the room that no one talks about." . . . [Larry Dossey, M.D., said,] "I'm not saying the skeptics have been silenced, but things are definitely loosening up." (4/5-7/96)

Radio commentator Paul Harvey said the following:

This date's most significant news may be this: the healing power of prayer. *USA TODAY* . . . gives page one prominence to medical scientists and to a new book including one hundred thirty separate studies, affirming that prayer is a scientifically verifiable factor in healing, that it benefits those who pray, and *those for whom they pray.* (12/21/93)

Larry Dossey said in *Healing Words* (the book Paul Harvey refers to):

People who achieve success in laboratory experiments utilizing imagery, visualization, or prayer frequently describe a feeling of actually bonding with the object they are trying to influence, whether a machine, animal, or human.

The researchers at Spindrift, Inc., found that feeling of bonding true for plant life as well. The Spindrift organization has done years of prayer research chiefly on plant organisms. The Spindrifters felt they could show a correlation between a person praying and the thing being prayed for. Organisms responded in a measurable way. Other experiments more familiar to the parapsychologists were also researched. As a former president of Spindrift, Gladys Myers, stated, "Spindrift used the modern standard of proof, the scientific laboratory experiment, to study the power of prayer."

Historically there have been few scientific studies of prayer. Whether prayer was beneficial was a matter of opinion. Whether parapsychological effects were real phenomena was left to those looking for the proverbial flying pink elephant. As Louis Rukeyser of Wall Street Week said during the last show of the 1994 year, he would perform what every psychic fears: he would review the last year's predictions.

Precise predictions, paranormal phenomena, and the power of prayer. Trying to prove any of them reminds one of an expression used by President Teddy Roosevelt. "It's like trying to pin jelly to a wall." The debunking mind calls paranormal phenomena patent absurdities. The inquiring mind calls paranormal phenomena scientific anomalies. Convincing proof for psychic and spiritual events occasioned by extending a force field of a person's consciousness across some distance has remained elusive. Such a test of non-physical mental initiations and effects is the dream of most researchers studying anomalous phenomena. They work in an occupation humorously labeled **weird science** and negatively labeled **pathological science**. They study consciousness phenomena that are elusive and not easily explainable.

Can future science substantiate that the forces of prayer play a role in life? Some people have found it distressing to ask what the basis of prayer is. Is it superstition? Is it faith alone? Is it scientific?

The originators of the Spindrift experiments, Bruce and John Klingbeil, felt they had developed new conceptual models of thought and prayer that helped address how consciousness works. The Klingbeils' conceptions helped them design tests that could indicate when prayer and thought were influencing, at a distance, a test organism. **The Klingbeils' quest also shows that some thoughts had quality as well as force.** They postulated that not every thought was the same as every other thought. Thoughts generally fall into two categories. One category of thought is volitional. It is mental force in a particular direction of intent. A second category of thought produces a direction of holy intent which benefits the form it touches. With no intention other than to bless, this second category of thought produces measurable quality, order, and fine tuning for the form needing healing or resolution.

The Klingbeils' plans involved three steps. **Step one** was to develop tests that showed a fairly consistent volitional psychic thought effect. ("I want this or that to happen.") **Step two** was to develop tests that showed fairly consistently that holy prayerful thoughts have a quality healing effect. ("I'll accept what's good for the situation to happen.") **Step three** was to develop improved scientific theories to explain the volitional mechanism of step one and the ordering mechanism of step two. The Klingbeils were **translating** some spiritual experiences and religious language into the scientific language and experiments of our times.

POLITICALLY INCORRECT RESEARCH

Some people reject the testing of sacred prayers. They have essentially asked the Spindrift team, "Give me one good reason why you are perverting prayer by putting it in the laboratory?" Bruce Klingbeil would answer, "Prayer is an abundant reservoir of testable thought. Stepping into the laboratory and praying is not perversion, but a new application." Believers who do not agree with the Klingbeils' tests are likely to be offended by physicist Paul Davies' statement, "science offers a surer path to God than religion." (*God and the New Physics*, Simon and Schuster, 1983) Testing prayer is politically incorrect for some people. *The Albuquerque Journal* (May 3, 1995), carried a story about attempts to stop a federally funded prayer study. Freedom

from Religion Foundation member Annie Laurie Gaylor
said:

> You can't document prayer. It's something you
> take on faith. This is just feeding this general
> superstitious movement of some physicians.

Ms. Gaylor would have to explain away two decades of
scientifically researching prayer by the Klingbeils and the
documenting of prayer by other researchers.

Rev. Barry Lynn who heads Americans United for
Separation of Church and State commented:

> The federal government should not put itself in
> the position of saying, 'We funded a study that
> shows that prayer works or prayer doesn't
> work . . . . ' It's just preposterous.

Barry Lynn's associate, Joseph Conn, questioned:

> It's going to be like on cigarette packages? Are we
> going to have a surgeon general's warning?

Psychology professor William Miller, a researcher working
on the prayer study, remarked:

> I don't understand the argument that one should
> never do research on this topic. This is a significant
> part of human functioning.

**THE SEPARATION OF SCIENCE AND
RELIGION IS ARTIFICIAL.**
                                    John Templeton, investor

Spindrift originally thought it was on safe ground. The Spindrifters prayed for plants and they also prayed for some parapsychology tests. The Spindrifters projected that praying for plants or seeds would not bother people. They were wrong!

People's suspicions of the scientific method applied to religious situations continue. This attitude is changing somewhat, especially since the universe is increasingly seen as a spiritual cosmos. In 1995 mathematical physicist Paul Davies was awarded a million dollars by the John Templeton Foundation for his contributions in finding cosmological connections between religion and science. *Finding connections between religion and science* is what Spindrift's research touches on. The John Templeton monetary prize for progress in religion went to physicist Davies largely because of "his contention that humankind's ability to understand math and science—which in turn allows for comprehension and calculation of the physical universe—evidences *purpose and design* to human existence," according to the John Templeton committee. [emphasis added] The *reason* for Paul Davies' award is encouraging. One attitude critical of doing prayer and consciousness research is "you are dealing with things you can't put your hands on." Paul Davies' argument for design, as well as the fact that scientists are performing prayer and consciousness tests, may start to put "hands on" some of these things. Davies' perception is that the gap between scientists and theologians is small. From his perception "the gap is between theologians and the ordinary believers."

Spindrift has had different experiences than those of Paul Davies. With a few exceptions, theologians and laity alike have felt Spindrift's prayer testing was irreverent, and some even thought it was anti-Christian. Some of the same people who praised Paul Davies' science and religion connections disapprove of Spindrift. How can such schizophrenic thinking be explained? Spindrift has found people can talk about science, argue about it, impress people with it, and say they believe in it; but the *no-no* is to actually *do* science.

It is Spindrift's experience that the doing of science is what causes opposition. Even people who believe in mental and spiritual forces become your enemy when your findings cross over from beliefs and circumstantial evidence to much stronger laboratory evidence. They distance themselves from the tests. For instance, in 1983 when a Spindrift researcher was removed from his church position, the church leadership wrote him about the tests as follows:

> Such attempts to measure the effectiveness of . . . healing . . . are so wholly at variance with the standards expected of practitioners . . . we feel we have no choice but to act . . . . any attempt to 'measure' healing by tests made with seeds and yeast is not in accord with the teachings of [the church].

If Spindrift ever wins the John Templeton Award, there probably will be theological protests.

A November 10, 2003 *Newsweek* article on "Faith & Healing" included several points which parallel points experienced by Spindrift. Claudia Kalb wrote for *Newsweek*:

- How do you measure the power of prayer? Can one person's prayer be stronger—and more effective—than another's? . . . Can prayer be dosed, the way medicines are? Does harder praying mean better treatment by God? In the minds of many, especially theologians, those questions border on the sacrilegious.

- Some scientists, like [Richard] Sloan, believe that religion has no place in medicine and that steering patients toward spiritual practice can do more harm than good . . . . [Dr. Sloan said,] "If you pray for recovery and you don't recover, do you then abandon your faith? It's bad theologically as well as medically."

- So many people already pray for [other people] that scientists cannot establish a control group . . . . This "noise"—the extra prayers of mothers, fathers, sisters, brothers, friends, church members—may taint trial results. (On *ABC News Tonight*, January 8, 2006, Dr. Sloan opined, "There are religious orders out there that pray for all the sick all the time . . . prayer is out of the control of the researchers . . . . We can't test it. It's impossible to test. We can't know.") [That peoples' thoughts taint the results was a reason why the Klingbeils were enthusiastic about testing plants instead of people.]

BUMPS ON THE RESEARCH ROAD

Dr. Richard Sloan's book is *Blind Faith: The Unholy Alliance of Religion and Medicine.* This title encapsulates the long challenge ahead for consciousness and prayer experiments to become competent enough to gain scientific integrity. In 2006, a $2.4 million prayer project reported that prayer didn't help patients who all had the same operation. One group of patients was informed they were receiving prayer. Patients in this informed prayed for group developed more complications than another group of patients who were uncertain if they were going to be prayed for. This uncertain group did receive prayer but fared slightly worse than the control group which didn't receive prayer. Why were the test results the opposite of those anticipated? It's an intriguing question. (For more discussion about the "Ebb and Flow of Success and Failure," see pages 362 and 124.)

Bruce and John Klingbeil appreciated gallant attempts at conventional science. Their viewpoint parallels the sentiment of biologist Thomas Huxley:

> True science and true religion are twin-sisters, and the separation of either from the other is sure to prove the death of both. Science prospers exactly

in proportion as it is religious; and religion flourishes in exact proportion to the scientific depth and firmness of its bases.

I asked John Klingbeil, "Could you tell me a little about the connection between religion and science?"
John said:

> Science has always explained the physical characteristics of our world. But it has never given credence to the fact that we also experience life through feelings, through emotions, through qualities, through what you would . . . say is the quality of life. Music, art, literature, all of these things, have meaning to the individual. But science has never been able to include those kinds of things in their numbers. And because they cannot measure them and put them in their numbers and equations, they take the stance that they are unimportant, and we don't need to look into them.
>
> Religion . . . has taken . . . exactly the opposite stance. [Religion] doesn't care how old the rock is. But religion cares very much about what we would call qualities: holiness, peace, beauty, serenity, all the things that are talked about in the Sermon on the Mount. That sort of thing. But these [two disciplines] are two sides of the same coin. They're both trying to describe the world that we live in . . . .
>
> I think the basic point is that we cannot have a paradigm that truly expresses our world until we have a paradigm that includes both the quantity that the sciences [have] stood for and the quality that religion has stood for. Until you can plug in quality

into the energy equations of the physicists, you're really not going to be able to say this [picture] is our world. This [additional information] is what makes everything go. This [picture] is how everything is put together. Until they start talking to each other and until they start getting experiments that include these things, science is going to be blind, and religion is going to be fairly impotent.

This book is about Spindrift, Bruce and John Klingbeil, and prayer. It covers over twenty years of unconventional working and living. This book encompasses the few normal moments, the paranormal tests, and the abnormal happenings.

INVESTIGATORS OF E. S. P.

Actor James Garner is private investigator, Jim Rockford, on the television show *The Rockford Files*. Jim Rockford is underappreciated, undervalued, and underpaid as a P.I. The fact is, Rockford is a good private investigator. I think of Bruce and John Klingbeil in a similar way. They are underappreciated, undervalued, and underpaid as prayer investigators. In fact, the Klingbeils have done some unique investigations into prayer, consciousness, and the healing process.

If some of the Klingbeils' work is convincingly replicated by other researchers, the present interest in prayer, spirituality, and healing research may become more than a trendish Twenty-first Century fad. Evidence may build to show prayer is a force to legitimately recognize. Why not study prayer the way we do the other forces? Isn't prayer a variation of E.S.P.? **Prayer is Extra Spiritual Perception.**

In a 1996 letter to me, Dr. Larry Dossey commented:

No one has touched on another contribution of the Spindrifters. No one has so courageously probed the impact of prayer research on society as they. The ramifications for theology, science, and culture in general are profound, and they were far out front in considering what these effects might be.

Has any evidence been given that the least little amount of a non-physical phenomenon, a paraphysical proof, even exists in the world today? It is hard enough to prove some things in the physical realm let alone in the consciousness realm. Look at the enormous amount of attention, debate, and scientific evidence in the O.J. Simpson saga. Some people still are not convinced O.J. Simpson is guilty, innocent, or if he committed the two murders alone. There may never be convincing proof for some people. There may never be convincing proof for consciousness research for some people as well.

SUCCESS HAS MANY FATHERS
FAILURE CLAIMS NONE

What about unanswered prayers? I hear about failures of prayer, complaints like "Hey, Bill, the Smith family prayed and look, they died," or "They lost their business," or "Prayer didn't heal their problems." What about when prayer fails to heal someone or some problem, what would counterbalance these discouraging examples of prayer with the positive aspects of prayer? Bruce proposed that *intra personal validation* seems to be one answer. Intra personal validation is agreed-upon evidence seen by several witnesses.

People ask me, "How come prayer didn't work for those sick people?" or "How come God let thousands of people die from the terrorism on 9/11?" or "What kind of peace loving God commands millions of radical Islamic believers to pray to Him for faith to kill non Islamic people and destroy civilization and freedom?" Bruce said that by applying prayer to modest experiments with results that *are validated by several witnesses* seems to be a practical first step toward documenting how **prayer imprints** our human circumstances.

It should be important to society to find out if prayer is a superstitious belief, or a danger to society, or a real healing phenomenon of human life. It seems ironic that so many people opposed the Klingbeils' research when one considers that prayer as behavior is a normal part of human functioning.

REPETITION IS THE MOTHER OF SKILL

Innumerable people believe in practicing prayer. Aren't their prayer-expressive consciousnesses worth investigating? Do the Klingbeil test proposals formulated for showing some forces in prayer stand up to modern standards of proof? Does the Klingbeils' spin on putting testable religious people in the laboratory have a prayer? The Twenty-first Century will give some answers.

These words of composer Ira Gershwin seem to sum up the Spindrift saga:

> They all laughed at Christopher Columbus when he said the world was round.
>
> They all laughed when Edison recorded sound.
>
> They all laughed at Wilbur and his brother when he said that man could fly.
>
> They told Marconi wireless is phony, it's that same old line.[4]

History may recall Bruce and John Klingbeil as experimenters struggling for a greater openness to study prayer research.

The following chapters tell the Spindrift story.

Chapter Two

Spindrift Explained

Prayer is difficult to define, but our attempts to
do so give us insight into its mysterious powers.
Rosemary Ellen Guiley, author,
The Miracle of Prayer, p. vii

The whole of science is nothing more than a
refinement of everyday thinking.
Albert Einstein

Delicious Living magazine editor, Lara Evans, depicted the Spindrift work this way:

A man in a white lab coat stood over the seedlings that had recently broken through the earth. The young shoots were growing straight up, bright green and healthy. Directing a silent prayer for the botanicals, he took a deep breath and focused his thoughts: "Let the seedlings achieve their best state. Let them fulfill their fullest potential. 'Thy will be done.'"

The seedlings' neighbors—in the same shallow container, growing under the same exact conditions and separated only by a string draped across the middle—hadn't yet broken [as far] through the ground. No one was praying for them.

This is a scene one might have witnessed . . . during the first of several experiments conducted by the Spindrift Foundation . . . . While these findings were not well received at the time, today the connection between health and spirituality is gaining attention from serious researchers all over the world. Academia is also taking note. (*Delicious Living*, 12/01, p. 26.)

The original Spindrifters were a father-and-son team, Bruce and John Klingbeil. Their prayer tests on plants have been a *beacon*, lighting opportunities for researchers doing large scale scientific investigations of consciousness, prayer, and healing. The Klingbeils were experienced with prayer, and they took their experience into the laboratory. Has the time arrived for using the scientific method to study prayer? Will the current enthusiasm for prayer and healing science continue? Once an ignored theme, here is the story of what went into producing supporting data for the present popular trend of people admitting they believe in prayer. Bruce and John Klingbeil hoped this trend would continue through the Twenty-first Century. However, they felt there would be resistance and roadblocks. That is why good science will be required. Spindrift's discovery work has pointed out some of the landmarks and laid a foundation based in science. This is Spindrift, the research organization.

I've had people say to me, "Yes, I've heard of that group. What exactly do they do?" To answer that question, here is the shortest speech ever given on Spindrift when I was asked to talk briefly at an annual dinner of fellow ham radio broadcasters.

SPINDRIFT IN SHORT

I am president of a non-profit organization that does one-of-a-kind research. Spindrift does parapsychology experiments. Parapsychology deals with some of the things that science doesn't have the time to explain: anomalies like E.S.P., psychic and spiritual phenomena.

Spindrift, Inc., is unique because its members concentrate mostly on spiritual phenomena produced by prayer. So we have something to measure, we measure the relationship between prayer and healing. We do our prayer and thought experiments on lower organisms such as various kinds of seeds, soybeans, and yeast cells. This way we can really keep the tests simple. The simpler a test, the fewer variables to confuse the data.

Spindrift also has tests that work with the interaction of the mind with electronics. One example is a series of tests of thought on four random number generators. Random number generators are electronic devices which are sensitive to thought. You may wish to do one of our random tests, such as our double loops computer test. This test involves building a random number generator, plugging it in your computer and running a program. The numbers in loop one and loop two should accumulate to about the same amount.

However, we had researchers think about and pray over loop two. Over a long time period loop two begins to show mathematical differences. That is, loops one and two are different. This difference suggests evidence of a mental force affecting a physical occurrence in time.

Spindrift tries to sort out psychic phenomena. Spindrift balances on an intermediate line between the solid believers who **accept everything paranormal** and the skeptics who **reject everything paranormal.**

That Spindrift was looking into consciousness-related phenomena was just great with the audience. Several ham radio operators asked for technical information on our work. Investigating healing was a good idea also. What did not go over well was bringing prayer into the speech. They also heard me say God when I didn't use the word. God and prayer were considered inappropriate. They felt God was a private matter and not a subject for scientific discussion.

TROUBLED WATERS SPIN THE TIPS OF WAVES INTO SPINDRIFT

I did not like the word *Spindrift* chosen by the Klingbeils as the name for their research foundation. I turned out to be wrong. If people don't know anything about the research, they remember the word *Spindrift*. It sticks in the craw of the mind.

The word *spindrift* **refers to whipping and piercing sea spray out at sea that arises during a storm.** It characterizes Spindrift, the research organization. Far from shore, this *intense sea spray* **on wind blown waves is the spindrift.** The fiercer the wind, the rougher the flurries of spindrift blown and thrown over the water. The spray spins and it drifts. Some spindrift flies away from the waves and converts to vapor. Other spindrift hurls back into the water. Like clouds that are beautiful at a distance but turbulent to be in, spindrift is beautiful at a distance but turbulent to be in.

The analogy between Spindrift, a group doing prayer tests on healing, and tips of waves is rich with meaning. The Klingbeils chose the name **Spindrift** for symbolic reasons, one of which was that this research measured the interaction of consciousness with the material world. Dr. Larry Dossey describes the positive aspect of the word in his book *Recovering the Soul* (Bantam, 1989):

> "Spindrift" is a variation of an old Scottish word describing sea spray driven by wind and waves. It

suggests an interface of air and ocean, of the ethereal and concrete, of mind and body.

MORE SYMBOLISM

The spindrift spray is at the cutting edge of the waves. And the Klingbeils' theories and tests are at the cutting edge of psi research. **The ocean depth** symbolizes unconscious thoughts. **The wind** symbolizes the invisible unconscious mind. This unconscious mind drives the ocean into waves. **The surging waves** symbolize agitated unconscious thoughts which are blown by the wind, the unconscious mind. Man's ridicule and controversy provide the turbulence. **The air and the vapor** to which some spindrift water converts symbolizes the invisible realm of Divine Consciousness or Spirit.

Gradually the land which appears on the distant shoreline, (seen by the mind on the horizon), symbolizes **the conscious mind** *emerging out of unconsciousness* showing the body and its environment. The land exhibits the more solid thought formations recognizable to man's every day conscious world.

The Klingbeils' research had implications for science, theology, medicine, and parapsychology, a combination that offended some people. The antagonism and the retaliation it provided were a cross the Spindrifters bore as did those who have been labeled eccentric throughout scientific and religious history.

WHY DO WE PRAY?

I asked Bruce Klingbeil, "What do you think is the purpose of prayer?" Bruce said, "To bless." Prayer that blesses unites our internal and external worlds.

DEFINITIONS OF PRAYER
FOR THE EXPERIMENTS

1. *Holy prayer* is a force that brings increasing evidence of order to its object.—Bruce Klingbeil

2. *Human faith prayer* is a force that projects a list of wants a petitioner thinks should happen to the object of prayer.

SPINDRIFT'S PRESUMPTIONS
ABOUT THE DEFINITIONS

1. What does the form of consciousness we call *holy* prayer do? The Klingbeils said, "Holy prayer is an ordering-power." The presumption is that holy prayer creates occurrences of order (orderly not chaotic functioning) in the organism that is prayed for. So what is recorded in experiments are *subtle incidents of order called ordering-effects.*

2. What is meant by *human faith in prayer?* The word *faith* has many meanings. *Faith* is an umbrella word that can indicate everything on a scale from weak to strong belief, through faith in God, to a mind full of holy consciousness. Pertaining to its tests, Spindrift uses the word *faith* to indicate strong belief or human will. Why? So human will-power as a *faith-force* producing *faith-effects* from one's mind can be measured separately from the *ordering-effects* of one's prayer. One's human faith or belief frequently drives effects in directions that can be distinguished from the ordering-effects of holy prayer. In short, a person's faith or belief produces *a goal-directed force of faith-effects* that is distinguishable from the *ordering-effects* produced by holy prayer.

I will discuss more about the definitions above later.

HERE IS WHAT THE FATHER AND SON DID

Bruce and John Klingbeil developed evidence that prayer forms **"subtle mental imprints"** on the physical world. They studied two intentions in prayer and named them **"goal-directed thought"** and **"non goal-directed thought."** The Klingbeils were first to distinguish and name these two intentions in thought which I discuss later.

WORDS DEFINED

Psi: Psi (for psychic effect) refers to any physical effect apparently caused by consciousness, or intuition, or prayer.

Nonlocal: Nonlocal refers to *no local locality*. Psi (psychic phenomena) are everywhere at once or in a relationship between a healer and a healee.

Healing from a distance: Researchers of psi call healing from a distance *nonlocal healing*.

A PSI BRIDGE TO OTHERS

The Spindrift data gathered during two decades of psi research ties in with thought and prayer research done by the medical profession, religious people, and scientists researching consciousness. Spindrift has been doing prayer experiments in which the effectiveness of healing prayer is measured. Small plant organisms, whose health is easier to measure than humans or animals, are the test subjects. Stress is added to an organism to create a need. Examples of stress are overheating, oversalting the soil, overwatering, and so on. (The organism is prayed for, which reduces the stress, and the need is met. That is, induced stress is reduced by prayer. This reduction of stress for the organism is a measurable phenomenon. For example, the organism under stress that is prayed for prospers faster than the control group organism which is under the same stress.)

MEASUREMENT AND EXPLANATION NEEDED

Is measuring this phenomenon enough science? No. The Klingbeils felt that the time is coming when proofs will win out over beliefs because the beliefs about what prayer does **will require some explanation.** What is beneficial will be separated from what is bogus. If prayer isn't tested, as other types of power are tested, prayer will remain a private matter, a ritualistic practice or belief. If prayer is not tested in our modern age, its inherent beneficial power may be left to speculation, belief, or placebo effects.

ORDERING PURPOSE OF PRAYER

The prayer experiments at Spindrift subtly suggest an implicit order that undergirds the universe. This order is made manifest both in unconscious and conscious thought in recognizable ways. Undulating, unformed, unconscious thought is what holy prayer addresses in the experiments. **The interaction of ordered thought, or prayer, on unordered thought subtly alters material conditions in the direction of order.** Prayer chisels away at unordered thought like a sculptor who chisels away at a non-form until a form is made manifest. (John Klingbeil writes of ordered thought acting on unordered thought in his definition of "interaction" in endnote **1.**)

PRAYER INTERACTS WITH A SYSTEM AND BRINGS ORDER

A *system*, as used here, is anything which is prayed for in life or in a test. Any healee or object of prayer is a system. A system can be a plant, a person, or patterns forming in randomness while tossing dice or guessing cards, and so on. **Prayer interacts with a dis-ordered system to help clarify the order of the system.**[2]

MORE ORDER IS THE NEED

When a need is waiting to be met in a system, prayerful thought, under controlled circumstances, can affirm the *ordering-force*. The ordering-force is a field of intelligence and information. Apparently the ordering-force interacts with a system through *ordering-effects*. This ordering-force brings the general need into congruence with general order. This movement toward order Spindrift calls healing. Healing involves movement away from a need, or disorder, and movement toward fulfillment of that need, or more order, or wholeness, or health. This change from more need to less need is toward more order *or healing*. As order impacts disorder, patterns of normalcy rise up. It is possible to measure this ordering-effect on a system, as I will discuss in a moment.

THE SCIENCE / RELIGION CONFLICT

Emotional nerves are touched when the noun *God* is mentioned or praying and prayer are spoken of directly. The ancient Hebrews were afraid they would be cursed and condemned if they mentioned God's name directly. Fear of addressing God disrespectfully may be part of what has been passed down unconsciously through the ages. There is also the humbling, insecure feeling one may have if he or she has to admit to a pecking order in which God is greater than man. Some people insist there is nothing greater than man. Then there is the age old adage heard around the world, "There is a conflict between religion and science." Where have we heard that before? Spindrift answers, "almost everywhere."

THE SCIENCE / BOTANY CONFLICT

People pray in horticultural situations for flowers, a field of corn in drought, or crops in an early freeze. This praying is considered acceptable, not wrong or bizarre. Why should *praying for germinating seeds or yeast fungi* appear irreverent when many of these same people pray for their flowers and gardens? For the May/June 1991 *New Age Journal* Bruce Klingbeil told the senior editor the following:

> It's better to work with nature, with that cycle, rather than trying to bend the world around us to our own goal-directed end . . . . Which means a gardener who loves his garden and who loves his plants, who goes out and looks at those plants and is grateful for the beauty of them and the joy that they bring—without realizing it—that person is relating to his plants in a way that we would characterize as prayerful in a non goal-directed way. And we find that's very potent. It may do a lot to explain the green thumb phenomenon.

Some plant aficionados worried that the Spindrift researchers were horticultural heretics. These plant aficionados had concerns about Spindrift's subjugation of yeast cells, wheat, rye, bean, and grass-seeds to scientific testing. Three ethical concerns and answers are the following:

> 1) Q. Did we realize that plants are *alive* and *feel* what we are doing to them?

A. Yes, plants are living. Because plants are less conscious, they make decent test subjects. Some plant fans disagree and believe plants are very conscious and even on an equal level with man. If nothing else, it is a lesser of three evils to experiment on plants than on animals or man who are more conscious.

2) Q. Where did we get the right to *add stress* to the feeling plants?

A. Adding stress to test a plant bothers many people. Yet without adding stress, there are few ways to do scientific tests. Why? Because if a subject is not pushed away or deviated from its optimal condition, a measurement back to its optimal condition is not possible. If nothing else, the stress given to the plants is similar to stress they would experience in nature's environment.

3) Q. Did we *ask permission* of the plants to do tests on them?

A. The researchers were sensitive to plants during testing. Working with plant life for so long, sometimes the researchers developed a kinship with plants where individual characteristics of one plant in contrast to another were perceived. In some degree or another, the researchers sought the cooperation of the plants in their prayer-psi testing process. The researchers merely asked that the *interactions* of the psi with the *pray-er* and the plants with the *pray-er* occur harmoniously.

The experimenters made no attempt to control what volunteers thought about during a test. Beyond being informed that they were praying for a plant's need, volunteers were not told what exact thoughts to have or hold or what precisely was the need to pray for during a test. Otherwise, the Spindrift team would be consciously directing the tests, and the researchers were trying to minimize such factors.

I asked Bruce the following question to smooth things over with people. "How can I *concisely* explain what you and John are doing?" Bruce said, "We're exploring the relationship between prayer and healing."

In an interview, Bruce said, **"Our research isolates an ordering-characteristic involved in spiritual healing."** Bruce pointed out that holy prayer affirms the Truth resonating with the pattern of life.

COMBINING
AND COMPARTMENTALIZING

Some people feel that combining science and religion to produce a spiritual science or a scientific religion is joining opposites. For them a scientific religion is an oxymoron. Since Spindrift has tried to find common ground for religion and science, some felt it was taboo and let Spindrift know they disapproved of combining the two. Some people told us it was the Devil's effect, not a prayer effect, showing up in a test.

Psychology and sociology teach that people constantly believe in contrary things in order to cope. To believe in contraries a person would have to compartmentalize his beliefs. We all do it. An historical example was Moses who received the commandment "Thou shalt not kill (original translation is murder)." Still Moses prescribed executions and led a robust army that killed many people.[3] Similarly, people who believe in both religion and science usually find themselves believing some contrary things.

RESEARCH BEGAN IN 1969

In 1969, simple consciousness tests on objects and plants were tried which Bruce designed. For six years before the prayer experiments began full-time in 1975, the Klingbeils put much preparation into defining a **"level playing field"** for applying scientific methods to Christianity, psi, placebo effects, prayer, and healing.

Both religion and science are in search of truths. Men and women in the healing arts are also in search of the truths that heal. Viewed this way, people working in science, theology, and medicine have some common ground.

The need that religion and science have for each other can be made clearer. Scientific methods and protocols by which researchers arrive at objective (though provisional) truths would be helpful to Christianity. Some scientists get stirred up just as religious zealots do. Their emotions can get carried away on certain issues at times, but scientists agree on the scientific method as the medium for determining the most accurate answer. Scientific methods are the *great levelers*. Religion would benefit from this leveling and should not see these methods as unholy or the enemy. Scientific methods are *neutral*. It is how they are used that counts. If religious people would learn to use the scientific methods, they would react less emotionally to science.

Science needs the *moral qualities* of thought that historically have been the province of religion. Some scientists have begun to recognize that moral and spiritual qualities may pertain to scientific research.

Quantity and quantitative analysis are the domain of science. The impact of quality and virtue have not been measurable, scientists have felt. They consider values to be subjective judgments. Scientists would say that they can only deal with those things that are existent and that they cannot make value judgments. Scientists feel there are not good and bad things, right and wrong values, worse, better, and best things. Things are just there and get measured. Scientists do not impute values to it all. Science would say that to impute values to things is the province of religions and philosophies.

QUANTIFYING EFFECTS OF THOUGHT

Spindrift feels that some tests which produce effects from prayer illustrate that quality outcomes can be measured. Bruce said, **"The heart of our findings has been the discovery of a relationship between quality and quantity."** Thought produces subtle changes toward more order in an organism. The fact that thought can produce subtle changes forges a bridge between *qualities of consciousness and quantities of measurement.* Science could benefit from more awareness of the quality of one's thoughts, something usually associated with religion. Also, science would benefit from a sense of ultimate meaning or salvation which has historically been addressed by religion. Except for one quantum physicist's conjecture about "hyperspace supergravity theory" (he theorizes that when our universe ends, mankind will all be suddenly thrown through a "worm hole" into a parallel universe and be saved in some form), the sciences have no description of salvation.

Science excels at describing and quantifying everything in the universe, but where is it all going? Toward a cataclysm or toward an ordered condition? Spindrift supposes that if the qualities and virtues of spiritual thought are not gradually addressed in the equations of science, cataclysm is about all that mankind can expect. Science without spirituality cannot save us.

SOME CHARACTERISTICS OF THOUGHT QUANTIFIED

The reader may feel *any* marriage of science and religion is itself a cataclysm. The cover story of *Time* magazine (12-28-92) on God and science suggests otherwise. One observation is that "God, the creator of the universe, can never be against learning the laws of what he has created." The fact that *Time* did a story on God and science encouraged the Spindrifters. Years earlier Albert Einstein said, "Religion without science is blind. Science without religion is lame." Spindrift says that there are tests of thought and prayer that indicate quality and quantity have some common ground.

QUALITATIVE THOUGHT EXPLAINED

The term *qualitative thought* is synonymous with the holiness in human consciousness which produces order and quality in the world.

Qualitative research is the laboratory study of individual consciousness, how it impacts on the physical realm, and how it produces healing effects of order.

The Klingbeils' research seeks to isolate **ordering-effects** as subtle quality effects of healing. The research supports the idea that people do project qualitative thought.

If the reader is interested in getting a better fix on how Spindrift uses the word *quality* in its research, the book *Zen and the Art of Motorcycle Maintenance: an Inquiry into Values* by Robert M. Persig uses **quality** similarly to Spindrift. In fact in 1975 the Klingbeils decided on using the words *quality thought* and *qualitative research* after digesting Mr. Persig's use of the word *Quality* with a capital **Q**. For example, Mr. Persig writes on page 231, "Quality is neither a part of mind, nor is it a part of matter. It is a *third* entity which is independent of the two." (For other quotes about **Quality** by Mr. Persig, see endnote 4.)

WHAT DO YOU MEAN BY QUALITY EFFECT?

A hint of how the Klingbeils use the words "quality thought" or "the holy ingredient" generated by prayer, can be seen in how the word *virtue* is used in the Bible to describe Jesus Christ producing *ordering or healing* in the disordered conditions of people. For example, the Bible records about Jesus that "the multitude sought to touch him: for there went virtue out of him, and healed them all."[5] When the woman with a blood condition was healed when she touched Jesus, Jesus said, "I perceive that virtue is gone out of me." Virtue poured into her and produced her **renewed order** or healing.[6]

In place of "virtue" the word "power" is used in some Bible translations.[7] The Klingbeils reasoned: if virtue is a type of power, a way can be found to measure that as holiness power.

Expressing the **quality** of spiritual thought in the quantitative terms of science sounds like a nice idea, but can prayer work at all when observed or controlled in a laboratory? The Klingbeils tested prayer to scientifically find out.

PREPARING TO TEST FOR PSI

The saying applies, "If I hold a hammer, every problem I look at, looks like a nail." The Klingbeils felt the need was to put the hammer down, so the problem of quantifying thought could be looked at and pondered in fresh ways.

UNCONSCIOUS PSI BLOCKERS

One question the Klingbeils pursued was, "If psi exists, why isn't more evidence of psi emerging in our everyday world?" Asked another way, "If psychic and spiritual phenomena are occurring around us, why don't we notice the phenomena more often?" The Klingbeils decided to expand on psychology's concept of *defense mechanisms*.

It is accepted in psychology that a person's own mental defense mechanisms block certain information from surfacing in his conscious mind. A person's defense mechanisms keep certain kinds of information about his world hidden from his conscious mind so that he might not notice it.

On the other hand, if a person did not have defense mechanisms against some incoming sensory information, he or she could not concentrate on the narrow band of information needed to survive. Possibly a committee of defense mechanisms might anticipate that our psychic and spiritual natures are too frightening and distracting for us human beings to discover. So we are "defended" and kept safe by the defense mechanisms from finding out about our nonlocal natures.

COVER-UP OF PSI

The Klingbeils theorize that the defense mechanisms in our minds keep us from perceiving the psi activities happening in our everyday life and in the laboratory. Apparently our own defense mechanisms do not want us to know too much about the subtleties of psi and consciousness. A discovery of our psi capabilities would impose a responsibility on us which is scary. The Klingbeils researched ways to *track the cover-up* of the appearances of psi in our lives choreographed by the mind's defense mechanisms. The Klingbeils wrote, "The fact that our minds operate to conceal from us our own natures is thought provoking."[8]

Apparently, defense mechanisms are aware that humans are so constituted that they can give their conscious attention to only one subject at a time. Since being conscious of something *monopolizes* conscious thought, the defense mechanisms remain out of conscious thought so that they will not be detected.

Defense mechanisms may possibly have a connection with brain networks called *neural correlates of consciousness* or NCCs for short. NCCs orchestrate what information from our five physical senses is noticed by a human being. NCCs summarize for the conscious mind the information entering the eyes, skin, ears, nose, and so on. There is such a flood of information coming at the human senses that the NCCs edit most of it. Rightly or wrongly, NCCs may decide that psychic phenomena are too noisy and confusing for a human being to experience regularly. NCCs may feel that we human beings mostly need to concentrate on survival, food, and protecting our families.

The Klingbeil's defense mechanism theory states that a psychic effect is immediately followed by a defense mechanism, thus making life appear as if **nothing unusual happened. Life appears normal to us. Our own minds manipulate our psi perceptions away from our conscious awareness. Our defense mechanisms may deny us noticing experiences we had.** This idea of psi being camouflaged from us may become acceptable to other psi researchers. Why? Because some consciousness researchers are interested in discovering why psi effects are so slippery when sought. Our minds' defense mechanisms filter everything coming into our senses. Perhaps neuroscientists will be able to use PET scans to catch defense mechanisms activating neurons when psi enters our senses. Perhaps the findings of quantum physics, in which conscious observation of a subject is found to precipitate a changed state of matter, could also catch our defense mechanisms in the act of filtering and disguising psi.

Author Theodore Rockwell writes, "To me, the major contribution of the Spindrift work is the idea that there may be both a proactive psi force at work, and an antagonistic defense mechanism trying to hide our scary psi abilities from us."[9]

I'm sure parapsychologist Charles Tart may not have meant a statement the way I have interpreted it, but here goes. Dr. Tart said, **"If an angel holding a triangle is standing in your garden, all you will see is the triangle."** To me, that angel is an illustration of how a paranormal phenomenon can happen right in front of our eyes but is covered-up so we can't see it.

CHOOSING PEOPLE TO TEST

Others who have done parapsychology experiments have used as subjects anybody they could grab—for example, students, graduate students, and people off the street. This selection process probably carries over from experimental psychology. When I was in college I was solicited and taken to a building to do a psychology test where I pushed buttons when lights flashed on. This approach works very well for psychology but generally not too well for parapsychology since most people do not have the ability to manifest their psychic capabilities strongly. Avoidance of this indiscriminate selection, the Spindrift researchers postulated, would improve a psi experiment. Even when professional and professed psychics were taken into a parapsychology lab and tested, many did their own psychic styles of sendings, their mental action-at-a-distance, in different ways from each other. Generally it appears there was not a *consistency of input* in the experiments of psi. Possibly some of the professional and professed psychics could get a result, but figuratively speaking, one psychic was playing baseball, another was playing tennis, and another was swimming. The mental inputs were different. A test's **output** could not be made more stable unless the **input** was made more stable.

This "whoever shows up will be tested" approach was avoided by the Spindrift team when possible. Spindrift approached the selection process in the way in which one would form a basketball team. In forming a team, one would not go out and grab someone off the street. Rather, looking for people who already knew something about the game of basketball and agreed to follow certain procedures would seem more appropriate and advantageous. This way a team would have more similarities than differences. The team members would have more consistency of input.

This method should work for a parapsychology team as well. There were millions of religious people who practice "praying at a distance" in a generally similar way. For Spindrift the team players would be the team pray-ers. For the psi tests there would be more consistent input. (See endnote **10**.)

PRAYER PARTICIPANTS

The Christian Science tradition was where the original Spindrifters prayer experiences had taken place so we started there in familiar territory. At first Christian Scientists were the only ones tested. As some tests started working and we got a second test site, other Christians were tested. Some New Age thinkers also became involved.

When asked to participate in a test, some people turned red in the face or were speechless and would have nothing to do with being tested. Of the Spindrift participants, few volunteered immediately. Having their thoughts and prayers under measurement was a totally novel idea. They had to warm up to the request. Some participants were naturals and prayed as if it was just another setting where they meditated. From this group of natural mediators, some wrote out an outline of the prayer they would follow during a test. This outlining procedure worked well. Glancing at an outline helped the people praying keep their thoughts on track. Even though I didn't have any reluctance about the tests, the first time I was tested I had fear because my thoughts were now partially on display and would reveal if I could get results or not.

Spindrift has not tested many other religions' styles of prayer, but it isn't because it hasn't tried. One example was a group of Orthodox Jews experienced in praying. They were going to be tested, but they backed away from the tests. Another time I mentioned to an Episcopalian bishop and his priests about testing their prayers. The bishop said, "I don't need scientific proof. I have faith." Such rejection is sometimes understandable. (For reasons, see endnote 11.)

THREE EXAMPLES OF TESTS

Of my friends, hardly anyone has been interested in prayer as psi, and most despise the concept of testing prayer. Some friends of mine and others did agree to pray for the tests. For example, one woman from a conservative Christian church produced high prayer scores on the following test.

YEAST TEST

In the yeast test, yeast was under stress and needed relief from the stress. The woman had no idea what to pray about or what specifically the yeast needed. Since her prayers produced such good healing results, we asked her what she was thinking during a test. She said in effect, "I just surrounded that beaker of yeast with love. Whatever that yeast needed, God's love would be right there reaching it." The need was for the beaker of yeast cells to be relieved of the stress they were experiencing. My friend Roy from India also participated in the yeast test. He produced good test scores from his quiet meditations he was giving to the yeast from an adjoining room.

For over two weeks a disciplined young lady drove nearly every day to the Klingbeils' home to pray for the yeast test. She completed a number of yeast tests (John Klingbeil was the lab technician). Her accumulated results were added up: she did very well; she recorded a strong healing prayer effect on the yeast.

I remember Bruce Klingbeil carefully handing her a photographic slide of the graph of her prayer results. She was thrilled to see it and cherished the slide. It was eerie for a group of us to see the effects of her thoughts pictured on a slide. Yet this thought depiction formed from the healing intentions of volunteers was what several of the Spindrift tests could produce.

SOYBEAN TEST

In a soybean test, volunteers prayed for two stressed soybean groups. One group of soybeans was subjected to too much water. The other group was subjected to too much heat. The two soybean groups prayed for returned to normal faster than the control groups. The results of prayer showed that the water drenched soybeans gave off moisture, and the heat soaked soybeans pulled in the moisture they needed. **The same prayer would increase or decrease water retention in the two soybean groups according to the soybean's needs. The Klingbeils theorized that a nonlocal caring intelligence, the ordering-force, knew the needs of each soybean group and channeled prayer-energy for them to relieve their circumstances of too much stress.**

MOLD TEST

In the mold test, an unusual setup was involved. A mold was grown in a petri dish. Alcohol was added. The alcohol acted as a stress which hindered the mold from growing any more rings. A string was placed down the middle of the petri dish which separated the mold into halves. The string separated side A from side B. John Klingbeil prayed *daily* for the mold on one side of the string but not the other side. After many months, the side of the mold that John prayed for daily grew several more rings. The other side of the mold did not grow any rings.

At a Spindrift talk in New York, U.S. astronaut Story Musgrave, Ph.D. and M.D., asked if the proximity of the body heat of those who prayed for the mold could have been a factor in the results. Dr. Musgrave finally agreed that if body heat was a factor, the other side of the mold would have grown rings also.

> Several tests developed by Spindrift are described in detail in "The Botanical Experiments" in the Appendix. Of the approximately seventy different kinds of tests, several dozen were refined, and some are written up as scientific papers.

A NEW THEORY TO TEST A PERSON'S PSI CAPABILITIES

Now more about the definitions and intentions in prayer mentioned earlier. The Klingbeils asked the question, "Are there *different* forms of psi in a person's thought?" The answer became "Yes, there are at least two forms of psi in a person's thought."[12]

The Klingbeils discovered that psi can be divided into *two prayer forces:*

1) a goal-directing force of faith produced by a person's strong beliefs.

2) a non goal-directing force produced by a person's resonating the holy qualities inherent in his thought.

The difference in the two forces of prayer is postulated in the following way:

1) *goal-directed:* the goal-directed force of prayer has faith and visualization to drive it.

2) *need-directed:* the non goal-directed force of prayer is quality driven for openness to whatever is best for the situation prayed for.

The two forces of prayer *produce two distinguishable effects* in the following way:

1) Faith-effects when people pray.

Goal-directed prayer expresses the *faith-force.* Goal-directed prayer produces *faith-effects.* A prayer of goal-directed faith produces effects that may or may not hit the mark of what a plant needs.

In goal-directed prayer, its goal-force is outlined by a person's personal faith, agenda, beliefs, and visualizations about what the prayer should convey to the subject prayed for.[13]

2) Ordering-effects when people pray.

Non goal-directed prayer expresses the *ordering-force* which is a quality promoting force. The ordering-force and the quality-force are the same. Non goal-directed prayer produces *ordering-effects.* A prayer of quality produces subtle ordering-effects that hit the mark of the appropriate norms of what a plant needs.

Non goal-directed prayer is goal-free. Its quality-force is centered by a person's capability to surrender to goals and beliefs other than his or her own. (An attitude of *let go and let God* or *not my way but Thy way.*) A non goal-directed prayer conveys qualities of order, holiness, and blessing to the subject prayed for. The research suggests that when you pray without an agenda in mind (imposing an outcome with your own goals), you are letting the subject prayed for be blessed with natural ordering-effects.[14]

SPINDRIFT COMPARED TO HITLER

In 1985, Bruce Klingbeil had a telephone conversation I set up for him with a physics researcher/professor and Christian, who, I was sure, would be interested in Spindrift's research. Instead, he was appalled by it. Bruce was upset by the phone call and told me the two hours were "wasted." I was upset and could not believe my friend's emotional reaction to the tests and Bruce. One of the comments the physicist said was our prayer experiments reminded him of the type of tests Adolph Hitler's scientists did, especially when science could think it could help determine what was goodness and what was evil. Since I wasted Bruce's time, I sent him twenty dollars to cover the telephone call. To make me feel better, Bruce wrote, "We enjoyed getting your letter today. Don't be the least little bit disturbed about your friend. God has surely revealed these things to babes rather than to the humanly able or prepared. And God's ways are far more abundant than any other, so the road we are walking will be blessed."

That occasion wasn't the only time I heard a reference to Adolph Hitler. In 1989, I attended a weekend seminar on quantum physics in Ganges, Michigan, which was held in a Buddhist monastery. Physicist/author Fred Alan Wolf spoke. Over supper I was telling him about how the data in our tests revealed an "ordering-force" bringing good and normalcy to a test subject, and how the "deviation" from normal we called disrupted good or "disorder." His reply was something like "You think you can determine what is good by results being ordered and what is evil by results being disordered? Why, the most perfect example of order mankind has ever had was Hitler's Third Reich." He wanted to hear no more.

WHAT IS "ORDER"?

It's a critical question. What is Bruce Klingbeil's *concept of order?*

Bruce Klingbeil used the word *order* in a very special way. This is a common practice in the sciences, for example, with such words as *energy, force, mass,* and the like. Each of these words can mean a variety of things in common speech, but they are narrowly defined for science. Bruce used *order* in the Biblical sense of God bringing order out of chaos.

ORDER: THE IDEAL FUNCTIONING OF AN ORGANISM

Metaphorically speaking, if one of us had been around at the time of Creation and had been asked to bring order out of the chaos, we might have tried to line up all the elements according to size, or put all the water in one place, the mountains in another, and the plains in a third. But in creating the first Man, God took quite a different approach to creating a perfect order. Big bones and little bones, muscles and nerves of various sizes and functions, and a wild variety of organs were scattered throughout the body to create an entity of astonishing functionality. This God called *order*, and it is in this sense that Spindrifters use the word.

This definition of *order* can be applied to any living organism. It has nothing to do with "orderliness" in the sense of straightening out a drawer or a closet (putting all the socks together, and separating the blue ones from the brown). **Spindrift's *order* is the arrangement of components that enables the organism to best achieve its intended purpose.** This kind of order can also be applied to a computer device that generates ones and zeros in random order. We might think of orderliness as having all the ones together, and then all the zeros. Or we might suggest a perfect alternation of ones and zeros. But that is not random. There are mathematical tests for randomness: first, there must be a nearly equal number of ones and zeros. Next, there must be just the right number of pairs of ones in sequence, not too many, not too few. And the same for the zeros. There should be an occasional three-in-a-row, but not too many. And so on. If the intended function of the device is to produce random sequences of ones and zeros, then any deviation from true randomness represents a departure from the ideal. Bruce prayed for "a more ideal order of disorder," you might say. A computer's random number generator outputs zeros and ones, more in accord with the generator's function to produce random numbers. **A change in the direction of *true* randomness would be a "healing" change.** This mathematical abstraction of a system is easy to deal with mathematically, and using it, the Klingbeils were able to show some interesting ways in which the healing mind works, as described in the "Botanical Experiments" in the Appendix.

ORDER IN THE SYSTEM

When a person becomes sick or injured, the components of the body are no longer arranged or specified in the original (and intended) order. **Healing involves restoring that disordered structure toward "the intended order."** The closer a person gets to his intended structural order, the more recognizable is his form of identity, function, arrangement, purpose, or pattern of perfect order. Any deviation from a person's intended order is a deviation from ideal functioning.

SUMMARY OF ORDER

The kind of order that Adolph Hitler imposed on his empire was something quite different from Bruce Klingbeil's concept of order. **Hitler's order was not intended to create a situation in which each individual could best achieve his or her individual purpose.** Instead, it was intended to create a situation that maximized the government's control over individuals for purposes defined by that government.

About order Bruce said, "It's one thing to say to people that thought affects things. It's another thing to say that thought has a healing effect on things. It's yet another thing to say that spiritual healing follows in reference to order, to what is best for the context. That's what we're saying." Healing is the restoration of order.

Order follows quality prayer. Quality prayer isn't creating order out of nothing. The order-seeking intelligence in prayer affirms an underlying pattern of normalcy under the circumstances. Quality holy prayer radiates this pattern of normalcy. Order follows.

SYNOPSIS OF ORDER IN 28 WORDS

Any movement of an organism toward *order* means a movement toward *normal functioning*. In the experimental process, Spindrift's theory looks for more order in the data after prayer.

THY WILL BE DONE OR NOT?

Bruce and John carried the Christian Science concept of *Thy will be done* over to their Spindrift experiments. The concept, *Thy will be done*, is resonating with the pattern of life. The Divine Intelligence resonating with *Thy will be done* unfolds the best solutions for the circumstances.

Non goal-directed prayer is *Thy will be done* prayer. *Thy will be done* or having no personal goals is **counter intuitive** of how most people think of prayer. Most people petition for specific things in their prayers. Their presumption is that they know what is best for them or someone else. The Klingbeils' research delineates a better way to pray than just asking for things.

Jesus Christ does tell us to ask and we shall receive, but we often ask selfishly for our goals and things for us alone. Another version of asking askew is **tribalized prayer.** Tribalized prayer is for our tribe alone. The radical Islamic prayers of 9/11 gave the modern world the quintessential example of tribalized prayer.

Spindrift sometimes had to defend its concept of *Thy will be done* because of an alternative interpretation of it. Some people interpret *Thy will be done* to mean, if God wants to slay people or bless them, heal people or let them suffer, it is His choice, *Thy will be done.* A capricious God doling out blessings here and sufferings there on the population of the world would perpetually sabotage researchers from substantiating that prayer has a scientific basis.

An electric battery has a negative and positive charge. Thoughts act like a battery. Thoughts in prayer can be charged negatively or positively. To check the quality of the thoughts we infuse into our prayers, we should answer these questions. Do we pray for the greatest good, or do we pray for the greatest good for us and forget our neighbor? Are our prayers selfish and tribalized, or are we loving our neighbors as ourselves? Do we infuse

harmony or inharmony? The answers to those questions indicate the purity of our subconscious motives in prayer.

ANY SPECULATION ON HOW JESUS PRAYED?

Spindrift's speculation is that Jesus Christ's healing prayers were single-minded because his conveyance of the faith-force and quality-force cooperated in him as a single direction of force. Jesus said, "Not my will, but Thine, be done" which seems to indicate that Jesus directed his human will-force into the same direction the Divine Ordering-Force was flowing.[16] Possibly this single-mindedness is what Jesus Christ meant when he said, "I can of mine own self do nothing . . . because I seek not mine own will, but the will of the Father . . . ."[17]

TO SUMMARIZE PRAYER

Goal-directed prayer has an agenda it targets. Non goal-directed prayer doesn't have an agenda and doesn't dwell on personality.

Experiments were designed to demonstrate that the goal-directed faith-force does *not necessarily* promote growth in an organism which is in the best interest of the organism. The Klingbeils designed test situations where an organism's direction of need was *very different* than what the faith-force anticipated was the organism's need.[15]

In contrast, the quality-force does promote order and growth in an organism which are in the best interest of the organism. In addition, the test results seem to show that when both prayer forces work in the same direction, the quality-force is more effective. **These two forces of quality and faith are a recurring theme in Spindrift's theories and tests of prayer as psi.**

A TASTE OF QUANTUM PHYSICS

The two Spindrift prayer types can be conceptualized from particle and wave theory derived from quantum physics. The analogy of the particle and wave can help us remember our intentions in prayer.

The Klingbeils asked if we observe the particles or the waves in our prayers? The Klingbeils theorized that "particle prayer" describes goal-directed prayer and "wave prayer" describes non goal-directed prayer.

- **Particle prayer** observes more from our physical level of experience. Particle prayer outpictures our personal preconceptions, education, and "goals desired" for how the result should eventually turn out.

- **Wave prayer** observes more from our spiritual level of experience. Wave prayer outpictures the order, patterns, and "norms needed" for how the result should eventually turn out.

- **John Klingbeil said that we often grab the particles in our prayers, but we should learn to catch the waves.** "Thy will be done" is a wave prayer. It catches the rhythm of life. A wave prayer flows with the collective picture of life.

ASKING FOR SPECIFIC RESULTS

For the purpose of contrast, the Spindrift experiments amplify the different effects of goal-directed thought so it can compare with goal-free thought. With goal-directed prayer, we want what we ask for, but our desire may not be what we need or are supposed to have. The Spindrift findings don't mean all wants and heartfelt desires in prayer are bad, but often our wants get entangled in materialistic motives. Petitionary prayer sometimes proceeds from selfishness or from misguided assumptions about how prayer is supposed to get things for us or accomplish what we want.

So the question arises, "Is asking for specific results in prayer good or bad?" That depends upon the **quality** of our desires. If we pray for material things we don't need or for specific outcomes that may not be right, we may create a problem. Looking deeper, if we become aware that what is depicted in the subconscious mind tends to rule our specific desires, we can release these goals to the spiritual template where the Divine Ordering-Force can guide our heartfelt desires in a direction that is natural, good, and balanced. " . . . and He shall give thee the desires of thine heart." (Psalm 37:4)

THE ORDERING-FORCE

Twenty-first Century researchers theorize that consciousness is a physical property produced by the brain. They believe that physical consciousness is another physical law of matter such as gravity and electricity. They deduce that much of this physical consciousness is unconscious thought. Is it possible to test for effects from a spiritual consciousness beyond the supposed physical consciousness? Spindrift thinks so. The Klingbeils have contributed toward the methodology to test for these subtle effects they named *ordering-effects*. Apparently ordering-effects resonate with an intelligent spiritual consciousness. The Klingbeils named this spiritual consciousness the *ordering-force*. The term the *ordering-force* might become an acceptable way to describe a universal God governing order and pattern.

Spindrift theorizes that there is an implicit ordering-force in Divine Consciousness. Divine Consciousness imputes its ordering-force by tincturing human consciousness. More complex forms of organization follow. This theory of the "ordering" of human consciousness by an ordering-force may parallel well with the subtle ordering suggested by evolution theory, complexity theory, chaos theory, and self-organizing systems theory. **These theories occasionally suggest that a subtle principle of order is at work in the unfolding of creation.**

In the next chapter, we learn about the development of these theories by meeting Bruce and John Klingbeil.

Bruce   John

Chapter Three

Like Minds Meeting

The power opposing the experimental work is more sociological than methodological. We are opposed most powerfully by the power of the paradigm.[1]

John Klingbeil

The scientific attitude implies . . . the postulate of objectivity—that is to say, the fundamental postulate that there is no plan; that there is no intention in the universe.

Gauchos Monad, biologist
(explaining part of the paradigm)

Music has been my vocation. Paranormal events and spiritual phenomena have been my avocation. Why I was interested in such a strange subject area I don't know. It must be in the programming.

The exhilarating exposure to others' clear thinking as I was brought up convinced me that if ever I was going to put forth a strange subject like paranormal events which would include spiritual experiences, since I did not have any proof, I'd better find some. Otherwise, I would fail building the argument even before I began. Proof was essential. What kind of proof would come years later.

My family's church background was Baptist and Methodist. During high school I attended Christian Science Sunday School. Christian Science was a radical change in religious interest for my family, especially since several years earlier we were all around the kitchen table when over the radio came a news report that a girl had a serious ailment. The doctors were stopped from treating her by the parents who wanted Christian Science help. The courts were involved. My mother said to us, "Those parents should be thrown in jail." After studying the Christian Science religion, my mother went to a church testimony meeting on a Wednesday night and heard the account of the prayer healing that girl had. The girl sat there and listened while her mother gave the details.

My first Sunday School teacher's brother taught a class at the next table. His Navy pilot experience impressed my memory. In flight with his squadron, the one engine on his jet fighter quit. It was a scary situation as rugged ground was all that lay below. He prayed. One recollection he had was a line of Mary Baker Eddy's: "If Mind is the only actor, how can mechanism be automatic?"[2] He tried to start the engine twice. Another try restarted the engine. After landing, it was discovered that the ground crew had forgotten to connect one fuel pump and the second pump had burned out in flight.

FIRST IMPRESSION STUCK

I was introduced to *The Christian Science Monitor* newspaper in my high school history class. The teacher had everyone subscribe to the *Monitor* for its high quality political coverage.

I assumed Christian Scientists must be believers who combined Christianity and science. Those two words, Christian Science, are an oxymoron to most people, but not to that church. I imagined they got up in church on Sunday morning, sang a hymn, split into small groups and did chemistry experiments looking for proof of God, compared notes, got back together, sang a hymn, and went home.

Maybe it was beginners' luck, maybe it was divine guidance, maybe it was a difference in understanding, but some of the earliest Christian Scientists I knew saw the religion in somewhat the same way I did. Christian Science was a religion that was a science. It was concerned with proving things of the spiritual realm in the physical realm. I thought, that's my kind of church.

One teaching which appealed to me was that eventually the advancement of the sciences would reveal spiritual consciousness as the matrix of existence. Jesus Christ wasn't performing so-called miracles exclusively to establish who he was. Through miracles, Jesus was giving mankind a glimpse of the spiritual nature of reality underlying physical reality which monopolizes mankind's worldview.

Incredibly, the first Christian Science practitioner (a spiritual healer) my family knew was a former M.D., Dr. Frederick Roberts. When Dr. Roberts became a practitioner, his first patient was a cow. A farmer asked him to treat his sick cow with doses of prayer. The cow was healed. Dr. Roberts maintained his medical license all the time he was a church practitioner.

The first time my mother met with Dr. Roberts at his home, one of the people he was helping had baked him a cake. He shared the cake with mom as they talked. Dr. Roberts had a keen sense of the spiritual laws and order inherent in God and man. He got your attention when bringing to conscious awareness that the spiritual laws and order in the atmosphere of Mind, God, included yourself. Here was an exposure to someone who thought scientifically and Christianly.

COHERENT KNOWLEDGE

The Founder of the Christian Science church is Mary Baker Eddy. Mrs. Eddy described herself to Mark Twain as a "Christian Discoverer."[3] Mark Twain described his perception of Mrs. Eddy as ". . . the most daring and masculine and masterful woman that has appeared in the earth in centuries has the same soft, girly-girly places in her that the rest of us have."[4] In a biography, Mrs. Eddy said it was her "life-long task to experiment."[5] Robert Peel, the biographer, writes "Stimulated by . . . ideas [of a magnetic healer Phineas Quimby] and trying to relate them to her own biblical faith, Mrs. Eddy made **some successful experiments** in healing in 1864 which caused that year to stand out for her as a landmark in her development."[6] She wrote in 1888 "Religion, separated from Science, is shockingly helpless." (*CSJ*, Vol. 6, p. 48.)

Here is what Robert Peel said the word *science* meant to Mary Baker Eddy:

> Science, as the word was used in the textbooks which had helped to mold her thought, was just that— knowledge or understanding of truth; the tried, tested, systematic, and liberating knowledge of objective fact. While one could *believe* anything, one could *know* only what was rationally and experimentally verifiable, and that must necessarily be coherent with all other proven knowledge, or science. Since science compelled the admission that behind every phenomenon was a law, must there not be a still undiscovered law behind the healings of Jesus?[7]

Professor and engineer Charles Steinmetz, whose experiments made him the founder of modern electricity, was aware of Mrs. Eddy as a thinker in science. Steinmetz said,

"The best definition of electricity I have seen is on page 293 of *Science and Health* [Mrs. Eddy's book]."[8]

Charles Steinmetz in the *Atlantic Monthly* (date unknown) said, "It is not the province of physics to define the nature of matter ultimately, its origin or end. That is the province of metaphysics, but it is the province of physics to deal with the phenomena as they are observed."

I was surprised to learn that Albert Einstein over many years was interested in some of Mary Baker Eddy's concepts of consciousness, matter, and Spirit. One day when reading a quote of Mrs. Eddy's, I saw that there might be a little correspondence with Einstein's ideas. Mrs. Eddy wrote "The physical universe expresses the conscious and unconscious thoughts of mortals."[9] It became my good fortune to meet two men who were with Einstein when he visited a Christian Science Church.

A biographer of Albert Einstein interpreted Einstein's view of the physical universe. "The whole objective universe of matter and energy, atoms and stars, does not exist except as a construction of the consciousness: an edifice of conventional symbols shaped by the senses of man."[10]

SCIENCE AND SPIRITUAL PHENOMENA

After a few years in the church, I discovered that virtually all the Christian Scientists I was meeting had no interest in *specific examples* of how Christianity and science were related. It was gradually becoming clear that I did not dare bring any scientific experiments into the church. Certainly I should not use observations and mathematics on sacred subjects. Testing was totally wrong to do, and at the very least it was the sin of "tempting the Lord." Thinking about prayer and religion in a scientific way did not bother me though others thought it should.

My suggestion that the scientific method could find things out about spiritual phenomena including prayer drove friends almost berserk. For my incurable curiosity in exploring scientific meanings behind healings and spiritual phenomena, I was expelled from membership in a Christian Science Association. Almost all my friends from the Association have cut off contact with me. A good friend, after this happened, phoned me and said, "Where did you go wrong? Isn't it more important to keep your friends than to think about these science ideas? I feel bad for you." I said, "You mean I should give up my independent thinking to have friends?" He said, "Yes, to have your friends should be more important to you than to continue in such abnormal, far-out thinking about science."

Religious people can state a conviction or claim they had an experience that involved a degree of divine intervention, but seek out a little more information on the scientific basis of the belief or experience, and all emotions break loose. Raising scientific questions must sound like interjecting doubt about God and faith. Just take the claims and experiences as proof. No need for further proof.

Many Christian Scientists aren't aware that they believe in psi phenomena, but they do by accepting the miracles and healings in the Bible. With my Christian Science friends, it was safe to discuss parapsychology and seek further proof of parapsychological experiences as long as the subject was separate from religion. If I brought the subject back into the arena of religion or my church, **that was a no-no.**

The trick was to leave religion out of a discussion. Leaving religion out is strange in itself to me. Why? Because the largest interrelated document of parapsychological phenomena in the history of man is the Bible. There is one paranormal event after another. Yet, the Bible is rarely thought of in that light. If someone hints the Bible is that way, you get accused of having a sacrilegious thought. What is more paranormal than Elisha making an iron axe head float on the water, or St. Peter walking on the water?

See Chapter Five, "Bible Experiments," for examples of paranormal experiences in the Bible.

CURIOSITY NOT CUT OFF

I met a young Christian Science woman who intrigued me with her different insights into thinking, metaphysics, and theology. I mentioned parapsychology with its mental and spiritual phenomena to her. Instead of cutting me off as others have done, she said, "If you are interested in that subject, you should meet my brother and father." Mary's brother and father were Christian Science practitioners. She added in essence, "My brother John is conducting experiments in the parapsychological area by testing his own prayers on various subjects." I was so startled that I still have a visual memory of her telling me. In Schaumburg, Illinois, three towns over from my own, two Christian Science practitioners were doing actual experiments. They were not just spinning theories; they were *doing real experiments.* This conversation with Mary was my first introduction to the founders of Spindrift, John and Bruce Klingbeil.

MEETING JOHN

I met Mary's twenty year old brother, John Klingbeil, first. It was 1977. We were having a party in our home for all the students in the Sunday School. I invited John. That he was a young practitioner was a shock to everyone who visualized only older people in that job. After a meal the guest speaker, a Christian Science military chaplain, talked on issues pertaining to youth. Much good discussion was shared. John's verbal contributions were sometimes show stoppers. There was this moment of silence that said, "What was that he said?" John strained the brain when he spoke. John's comments were not easily appreciated by the group, partly because he explored

unfamiliar territory that sounded uncomfortable and too
different to explore. John proposed that natural science and
Christian Science had the common purpose of exploring how
the world works. In computer terms, John described his
prayer research in effect as *low tech, high concept.*

I remember part of the group discussion. A guest said that,
when you apply a divine law to a personal situation, the law will
work. The spiritual Truth, Life, and Love in the law
acknowledged properly will work. John Klingbeil said in essence,
"Well, it sounds good in theory, but things do not usually pan
out in practice that way. We are grateful to God for direction or
for a healing from applying spiritual laws, but healing is not
being done in a repeatable way. It is a flash of inspiration, and it
is gone. We should have a situation where the results of a law
applied can be more controlled. The fact is parapsychology has
not come up with a controlled repeatable test of thought.
Christian Scientists have not concerned themselves enough with
repeatability either."

John recommended that "To back up our claims, our
thoughts and prayers should be tested and examined." For the
first time, I had heard John mention that parapsychology tests
should be conducted by religious people.

MEETING BRUCE

Later in 1977, a musician friend of mine and I went to
John's townhouse in Schaumburg to meet his father. Bruce
seemed towering, about an inch taller than John's six three. We
four went into a den used for practitioner work. Friendly, with
a professor's personality, Bruce spoke deeply into the subject at
hand. In the backyard Bruce grew some vegetables including
collards and beets.

Bruce and John had an organ in their living room so my
friend played a jazz ballad for them. The signs that creative
types lived in the townhouse were obvious. There were labeled
plant containers, grass seed flats, and bean flats all over the

kitchen and dining room. Piles of scientific papers, graphs, and charts were neatly organized. There was no television set, and that was on purpose. It brought too much distraction into their home for their work. The discussion we had covered many topics including intelligence, spirituality, and some off-the-wall insights. Speaking of his practitioner work, Bruce said, "Since no two individuals have exactly the same problem, the solution to their needs is not a formula. Christian Science is a science that is applied as an art."

Bruce and John felt a feeling of kinship with Apple founders Steve Jobs and Steve Wozniak. Apple Computer started in a family garage. Bruce and John started Spindrift in a family kitchen. I learned that Bruce and John used hand scales to measure the effects of thought and prayer on yeast and various seeds. In late 1977, Bruce and John purchased one of the first Apple II computers. They were proud of its low serial number. Plugged into their Apple computer were two electronic scales which did the measuring automatically of yeast and seeds. The Apple computer also measured how John's consciousness affected electronic circuits. The computer also analyzed how John's consciousness affected the order of zeroes and ones in random number generator experiments. In future decades, the parapsychological community would accumulate **astounding data** from random number generator experiments which support the reality of psychic effects in the physical world.

Later, we spoke of hidden agendas in prayer. Bruce and John laughed when I told them that I heard a friend actually say, "I know a man with two incurable diseases. I want him to know God better so he can get healed. After all, he owes me money."

SCIENTIFIC CURIOSITY

John Klingbeil had innate natural science curiosity and tenacious patience to do careful laboratory work. For example, he counted thousands of beans until his fingers were bloody.

John was curious about the cactus plant, how a cactus grew and survived in a stressful environment. He also looked into praying for animals. For example, a cow had an infection of an udder. Apparently John's prayer effort benefited the cow. The cow returned to normal milk production sooner then expected.

John had experimented with biofeedback. I asked John if different wave states of the human mind recorded by *biofeedback* paralleled well with his plant and prayer research. John said he had "tentative" findings with biofeedback that surprised him a little. John found as he changed from the Beta state, to the Alpha state, or to the Theta state, the wave changes did not appear to affect any differently the outcome of a plant he prayed for. John did not do enough biofeedback to write a scientific paper. He did not have time to do more tests because of other experiments.

John tentatively felt though that as he went in and out of the brain wave states, the effects of prayer at a distance on organisms were the same effects as they were without biofeedback. John tentatively observed that it's more important for a healer to resonate an empathic intention of love and doing good than to be in a specific brain wave state.

John felt that the mind/body connection is benefited by the different mental states of biofeedback. The mind, brain, and their electrical connections to the body, form a *closed circuit system* in the body. John's tests tentatively suggested that *different* empathies of consciousness were involved when one gets his thought *outside* of his mind/brain/body system. John's thought could occasion modest nonlocal healing effects.

Bruce and John told me that there isn't a controversy about healing within the mind/brain/body system. Placebos and faith have produced amazing cures. The controversy is about spiritual healing beyond the body from a healer to a healee.

Bruce had the genius and curiosity for natural science but was not as fond of the tedious details his son John relished. Bruce had a fascination from childhood with gyroscopes and the balances found in nature. In 1969, the same year that man first stepped foot on the moon, Bruce was developing tests for prayer.

Bruce said that when he was a boy, he wanted to be either a Christian Science practitioner, a natural scientist, or a forest ranger. To me Spindrift had all three elements for Bruce to practice.

John Andrews, the project administrator of Spindrift, depicted Bruce this way:

> Prayerfully impelled to find ways of communicating his spiritual convictions with others in the scientific idiom so universal to our century, he began teaching himself laboratory research methods, statistical mathematics, and computer applications. Out of this work has come a body of experimental findings which seem to prove that simple living systems like seeds and yeast cultures . . . function measurably better when treated with [non goal-directed prayer] affirmations of their spiritual identity than they do when such treatment is not applied. (1986)

BIT OF BACKGROUND

John's two sisters, Mary and Deborah, were very animated conversationalists. Later I met the children's mother, Gloria, who immediately expressed some advanced ideas she pondered frequently. Two people who overheard what she said to me did not agree with her *because* they had never heard the ideas before. Gloria was a Christian Science practitioner. In time Mary and Deborah became practitioners. It's exceptional when everyone in the same family becomes a practitioner.

Bruce's father was a college professor and college administrator in Carthage, Illinois. Bruce took college courses during World War II. John Klingbeil completed high school in three years. He was offered a full scholarship in mathematics to

Northwestern University. He and Bruce decided against accepting it because John wanted to learn from his Dad several subjects including how to become a practitioner. Also John told me college would have postponed the experiments for four years. The research was more important than to take four years off for college. His skipping college and a scholarship to Northwestern startled me greatly.

CAUTION! CHILDREN AT WORK

In a conversation I asked Bruce, "What about the criticism that you used and pressured your three children into experimenting with human consciousness and prayer?" Bruce explained as follows:

> My wife and I planned on our children growing up and becoming part of the healing ministry.
>
> The Spindrift concept developed which has involved small healings occurring under controlled conditions.
>
> As an adjunct to the ministry, I have gotten my children involved. I feel the experiments could lead to new lines of prayer work for practitioners [and other healers praying for animals, plants, and scientific situations].
>
> Not only that, the credibility question of spiritual healing occurring in a scientific age is a crucial question to investigate. Without this investigation, spiritual healing could be lost and become a relic of religion. I wanted my children to be part of that investigation.
>
> It hasn't been easy for them, partly because it has caused them problems with the church, and partly

because I have had a great deal of unhappiness for my seeking a testable relationship between prayer and healing.

THE SPINDRIFT FOUNDERS

Preliminary basic tests with prayer and consciousness had been going on since 1969. I met Bruce and John eight years later in 1977. I began working with the Klingbeils in 1978. They were testing some concepts they had been working with as prayer practitioners helping people. One motive for doing the tests was to eventually have tests lend a degree of credibility to the art of helping people through spiritual prayer. Speaking specifically of the job of the Christian Science practitioners, Bruce felt their numbers would dwindle to near zero in the Twenty-first Century unless practitioners could show society some scientific basis to what they did. Bruce's sentiment was "In a modern world, you need modern levels of evidence."

I discovered the Klingbeils were highly intelligent and too single focused on the work ahead to become involved in social activities. An exception was a dinner party Bruce and John attended once a week where they looked forward to simulating conversations and could exchange ideas. They had enthusiasm for the questions and hypotheses they conceived for their experiments. The research made them happy. Visitors to the Klingbeils' home usually sensed that the research was odd, but it was also cutting-edge. I would describe Bruce and John as *polymaths*. A polymath is "a person of great or varied learning."[11]

In 1978, I learned about the seed of the theory behind goal-directed and non goal-directed thought. Bruce Klingbeil glimpsed the bi-dimensional theory of at least two distinct intentions as different agendas in everyones' thoughts when he read a sentence by Mary Baker Eddy. Mrs. Eddy wrote, " . . . it is wise earnestly to consider whether it is the human mind or the divine Mind which is influencing one."

(*Science and Health*, p. 82.) Such a bi-dimensional consideration helps a person decide when to listen to the dimension of his own personal mind and when to listen to the dimension of the broader divine Mind.

A question arose, "Can non goal-directed thought focus directed love and directed compassion and still remain non goal-directed? The reply was "Yes, as long as you don't consciously decide what is best for the healee." A friend said, "You can love the person, but you don't decide what is best for him." Leave **what is best** for *Thy will be done.*

In 1980, at a dinner held in the home of two women Spindrift supporters, John said, "It's time to take the research on the road." With a baffled expression John continued, "But I don't know how to do it." Bruce said, "The research would make its own way."

In 1981, Spindrift incorporated as a non profit foundation in Illinois.

Enthusiastically Bruce said, "If Spindrift can interest scientists and society in doing further research of prayer and consciousness, this exploration would be a great accomplishment."

FROM PONDERING TO PRACTICE

Bruce told me that, in the 1960's, he had studied the progress occurring in the natural sciences, religion, and medicine. Bruce concluded that "Science has shown the most *leadership* of the three disciplines of science, theology, and medicine. The progress in medicine, for instance, has mostly been driven by scientific research. The world today has been informed by science."

For years Bruce Klingbeil had discussed with his family the *interface* between the spiritual *qualities* in prayer and the *quantitative* measurements of science. In 1969 Bruce had devised some tests of thought and prayer. Even so, Bruce and his children spent five to six years pondering the rightness or wrongness of doing tests with prayer. They made lists of the pros and cons. They discussed whether it was ethical or not to test sacred subjects. Much prayer resulted in deep study of scientific journals. Some questions which were prayed and pondered over were the experimenter effect, how the placebo effect worked under controlled conditions, could a way be found to separate the placebo effect from the prayer effect, and how to set up a test where "tempting the Lord" in a lab was eliminated from the project's design. Answers evolved.

Bruce was chuckling about an article in a religious periodical.[12] The title was "A Laboratory Experiment?" Bruce had respect for the writer but pointed out how the writer's preconceived ideas displaced a serious discussion of experimenting with prayer and healing. The writer began the article by saying he would discuss the pros and cons of doing laboratory experiments. Then the writer proceeded to write about only the cons.

Bruce told me he was asked by his church to write a paper on spiritual healing that he would deliver at a medical association of doctors in Chicago. Bruce worked on this paper for almost a year. A few weeks before the medical meeting Bruce was informed he would not be giving the paper. Other than being told someone else was going to speak to the medical group, Bruce was not given any reason why he was taken out. He speculated his beliefs about the scientific method applied to prayer and spiritual healing got him eliminated as the speaker.[13]

IS PRAYER ONLY A PLACEBO OR PRELIMINARY PROOF OF PSI?

Bruce told me that Christian spiritual healing was a subculture practice which could not explain itself credibly to modern society. The practice of spiritual healing through prayer was being categorized as *the placebo effect in religious garb.* New knowledge showed that the placebo effect releases expectations and endorphins which enhance how a person feels and heals. In medicine and in experiments placebo effects can be a distorting factor, especially when one is trying to determine what exactly initiates a healing, because placebos can heal people. The healing produced by placebos suggests to some doctors that writing prescriptions for placebos should be taken seriously.

Could a prayer effect be other than the placebo effect? Could intercessory prayer and spiritual intention be different from self-delusion? Could negative prayer be scientifically distinguished from healing prayer? Could a way be found to test the healing abilities—or lack of them— of those who profess to heal by prayer at a distance and other forms of energy? Do Christians, Muslims, Hindus, etc., produce different results? To measure the psi healing abilities of human beings was a major Klingbeil quest.

Prayer is sometimes regarded by a skeptic as a brain activity that triggers a person's active imagination which feeds on his belief system and then produces the placebo effect. The Klingbeils felt they hypothesized a way to test thought to distinguish the "ordering-characteristic" of holy thought from the healing done by the placebo effect, belief, and expectation.

If preliminary proof of nonlocal healing contrasted with the placebo effect could be presented experimentally, this proof would begin an impact on the prevailing scientific paradigm. The paradigm is that natural science includes only physical knowledge. Intercessory prayer effects are discounted as a person's imagination or outside of science.

In the 1950's, the aerodynamics and foresights which went into the B52 bomber would permit it to fly to year 2037. Like the designers of the B52 bomber, Bruce said that people who make spiritual claims need the foresight to anticipate future scientific challenges to religious experience.

MEATS, NUTS, AND FLAKY EFFECTS

I discovered that John, Bruce, and some other Spindrifters were vegetarians. The Spindrifters not being too keen on eating animals was partly due to what they learned about plants. Perhaps an incident may illustrate. A Christian minister came over to the Spindrift laboratory to pray for the yeast test. Afterwards he made the observation that if the life in plants can respond to prayer, what does this response tell us about the life in animals and eating meat? We are killing conscious life and eating it.

Early on, I told Bruce that people I talked to thought of him as a nut and didn't take his ideas seriously. Bruce said there was a Bible verse which said that Jesus Christ's own brothers and sisters thought Jesus was insane. Bruce must have been referring to St. Mark, Chapter 3, verse 21, (NEB). "When his family heard of this, they set out to take charge of him [Jesus]. 'He is out of his mind,' they said."

I mentioned to Bruce that among the people I knew, most were interested in the huge miraculous healings, the *big* scores, not the *smaller* effects of healing brought out in the Spindrift tests. Bruce told me that the point was "Even though the healing results from our tests are modest [in comparison to so-called miracle healings], once having seen controlled tests of thought and prayer, society might start thinking of reasons to test prayer on healing."

By pursuing a *smaller effect*, Bruce meant a more *subtle* effect which would manifest fairly consistently when the need of an organism stayed within the parameters of a test. I was learning how Bruce and John thought through making a test *controllable*.

About life in general, Bruce believed that smaller healings or changes in life can be important. He said, "Sometimes enormous changes take place in people's lives from experiencing small healings and small changes."

THE BOTANIC BEGINNINGS

What were Bruce and John doing in their kitchen and dining room? *They were applying basic science to botanical systems.* In 1969 research was done part-time. Full-time research began in early 1975.

As mentioned, the Klingbeils hypothesized that there are at least two prayer focuses from one's consciousness: human intention and holy intention. John Andrews of Spindrift described holy intention this way:

> [Bruce and John] call their field of investigation "qualitative research," since it explores the orderly patterning effect of moral and spiritual "qualities" focused upon human experience through prayer and unselfed love. (1986)

Bruce had to withdraw from praying for the tests in 1977. He had reported to the church about the promising results from the tests. The church leadership said he would have to remove his name as a listed Christian Science practitioner while he did the tests. Once the tests were completed, he could reinstate his name. Bruce's first priority in life was his practitioner work, so John did all the tests from then on through 1983. Bruce contributed ideas and mathematical advice.

Bruce's agreement with the church was that he would not pray for the tests, and he didn't. In a phone conversation with an official of the practitioner department at the Mother Church, this official said to Bruce, "I feel sorry for you. I really don't see how you can pray for seeds. As far as I know, seeds don't have minds to prayerfully address."

It was an interesting objection. I would be getting remarks like this as one of the objections in the future to Spindrift's prayer-tests. I asked Bruce for an explanation. His answer was this, "It shouldn't bother Christian Scientists to pray for seeds or even some inorganic things because they regard them all as things of thought, part of God's universe in their real being. It might bother other people, depending on what they believe." Mrs. Eddy writes "Everything in God's universe expresses Him."[14]

TESTING INTANGIBLES

The Klingbeils developed about seventy different tests of thought and prayer. Holy prayers scientifically described as a consciousness sending psychic blessings may be an offensive description of prayer for some believers, but it helps to describe intangible thoughts called prayers.

Even my Webster's dictionary in part defines the word *psychic* as "immaterial, moral, or spiritual in origin or force." It's revealing, but the definition starts with psychic defined as "lying outside the sphere of physical science or knowledge." John and Bruce Klingbeil in tandem with many parapsychologists and anomalies researchers did not accept this "outside the sphere" part of the definition. They were in search of a way to *modify* this cemented prevailing attitude of many physical scientists. What was needed was an experiment of psi that worked fairly consistently beyond chance.

Researchers in the consciousness field had done some experiments, but these experiments *weren't perceived as repeatable enough* for serious physical scientists to shift their attitudes, let alone put their reputations on the line into such fringe scientific inquiries. **Actually, the scientific literature is replete with consciousness data, but it wasn't considered.** The Klingbeils felt they had some tests working repeatedly enough beyond chance to give some evidence for psi and some evidence for normalizing healing-effects as well.

INCREDIBLE COINCIDENCES

There are strange, incredible, and mysterious coincidences that occur in life. Are any of these coincidences paranormal though? A hard lesson for believers in prayer and psychic miracles to swallow is the following: If a good explanation of a few of these strange mysterious coincidences is not accomplished, the only factor making these coincidences real and convincing to a believer, is his personal belief system. The Klingbeils were interested in seeking out better methods of explaining a few of the paranormal coincidences in life which are accepted by many people. Testimonies of spiritual healing and anecdotes about psychic experiences often fall apart as evidence.

One conjecture the Klingbeils conveyed to me about researching some paranormal coincidences of prayer was this: Most psi-actions start in the unconscious mind and are projected out into our conscious world. Thus, if a researcher wants to know about how a personal belief system contrasted with how a person's holy thoughts produce psi-actions, he should explore the unconscious realm.

IMPROVING UNCONSCIOUS THOUGHT

Bruce held that a person's unconscious thought needed addressing when praying. This awareness of addressing the unconscious held for the person praying for himself as well. The *conscious mind* is like a drain. The *unconscious mind* is like a spigot. Addressing the conscious mind was like trying to control water as it flowed down a drain. If you want to control water going down the drain, *you have to control the spigot,* which represents unconscious thoughts and desires. Bruce held that prayerfully addressing the spigot of human thought, the unconscious mind, brought out better quality psi results. Bruce felt that one of Spindrift's important contributions to healing and psi research would come from healers testing their "unconscious awareness" of the healing virtues in their own thoughts. Bruce referred to the awareness of one's unconscious thought as "unknowing knowing." Agatha Christie's Miss Marple said, "I just remembered something I must have known but didn't know I knew."

QUALITY FROM CONSCIOUSNESS

The motivation of *quality, holiness, and virtue,* as producers of order in a person's consciousness and human experience, would be one of the most difficult concepts to explain in years to come. *To quantify some of these quality-effects of prayer is a Spindrift concept.* There are hints that suggest a divine creator in the background matrix of creation: for example, the complexity of creation, the order of creation, the internal witnessing of truth which changes a person from the inside, and the richness and magnitude of creation. Spindrift concentrates on the order in creation guided by a psi template the Klingbeils named the **Universal Ordering-Force.**

Most people would think of prayer as another way to focus energy on a goal, or to focus their intentions, or to petition God with their wish list of desires. These modes are fine. However, discussing a person's **qualitative thought,** a thought pouring forth its spiritual qualities or virtues through a person's consciousness to a healee, would not register clearly with many listeners. The Klingbeils proposed that *a qualitative prayer,* a prayer that generates supportive, holy qualities or virtues of thought, increases the appearance of order in the organism prayed for in a test. John said, "Holiness in prayer brings order to our world, to our environment, and to our personal situations."

A RESEARCH SISTER

Bruce and John Klingbeil told me they were impressed with the work of a nun. Sister Justa Smith lived in upper state New York in a convent. She held a Ph.D. in biochemistry. For her research she isolated enzymes that were involved in the healing process. "In 1967 . . . Dr. Justa Smith conducted tests examining the effects of paranormal healing on enzymes, tests which showed that the enzymes contained in flasks were affected (in terms of their relationship to human health) as if they were in a human body."[15] Sister Smith stressed the enzymes with ultraviolet light. She had healers come in and non-physically affect the enzymes helping them return to their normal state. When compared to the control group of enzymes, the healer's group of enzymes fared much better. During the 1970's the Klingbeils had some contact with Justa Smith.

MOVING FROM SCHAUMBURG TO PALATINE

In 1982, Bruce and John moved from Schaumburg to nearby Palatine, Illinois. They rented an apartment overlooking a forested path.

The first Spindrift board meeting in the apartment was broken up by a woman's scream. We ran out in the hall. A woman had been abused by her husband, and he pushed her into the hall. Bruce said to bring her into his apartment for her protection. The five of us tried to comfort her. I went with her to file a police report. The incident broke up our meeting.

Bruce and John used the living room as a test site for volunteers to pray for the yeast test. A bedroom was used for the soybean tests. One of the sales managers for the Red Star Company, a yeast manufacturer, stopped by the Klingbeils' apartment to deliver yeast and to see the yeast test. He told the Klingbeils something close to the following. "I just sell the stuff. It's unpredictable guys like you in the field we depend on to come up with new uses for it." It is a safe guess that praying for yeast was as unpredictable as it was inventive. How many customers did Red Star have who bought quantities of yeast to pray for? Two.

Once when John was on the elevator holding a 50 pound bag of yeast a man asked him, "What's that for?" John replied, "I do a lot of baking." John told me, "How do you tell your neighbors that you pray for bags of yeast."

NEW LOCATION, NEW CHURCH

Living in a new location, Bruce and John applied for membership in the local Christian Science church. Their interview was in late 1983. The membership committee was aware of the controversial research John and Bruce supported.

The membership committee disapproved and turned down their applications to join. Two comments John and Bruce related to me about their interviews were catchy criticisms. One committee person said to Bruce, "I know what you are *really* trying to do" and then explained that Bruce Klingbeil was starting a group with cult-members. One man said to Bruce that to pray for one group of plants and not another group of plants was unchristian and unloving. He said in effect, "You can't *withhold God's love* from the other plants. God's love is all inclusive." My comment was "I guess that man would not admit, when Jesus singled out one man to pray for and heal at the Pool of Bethesda, Jesus was 'withholding God's love' from the other people, the control group." The objection was a misunderstanding. Love was not withheld from the control group plants. Love was directed towards plants chosen as targets.

GUILTY OF ORIGINAL SPIN

The concern was that prayer was given **exclusively** to some plants to the **exclusion** of other plants. Exclusive prayer was seen as a type of "intentional malpractice" against the plants not receiving any prayer and love. The concern was that holy prayer has to help everything. Otherwise genuine love and holiness are not involved in the prayer. **But this concern about a plant not receiving prayer misses what a control group is. A control group means leaving a plant out of the mental path of a person praying for a test.** The argument against the Klingbeils amounted to love being illegitimate when it's for one child alone, because every other child on earth is being deprived of love.

YOU CAN'T BELIEVE

At the membership interview Bruce made clear John was doing the experiments, but he supported his son's work and gave him advice. Being rejected as members was not enough. The membership committee reported Bruce to the Mother Church in Boston. In two weeks Bruce Klingbeil was notified he was no longer to be recognized as a church practitioner. His name was removed from the *Christian Science Journal* listing of practitioners in late 1983. Bruce was devastated. He was essentially put out of work. His income dropped. After twenty-six years of service to the church, this expulsion was his reward.[16] Bruce did not receive a refund for the fee he just paid for listing in the *Journal*.

Bruce had kept his agreement not to do the experiments. The Mother Church said that agreement was now rescinded. *Bruce was informed that he could not even "believe" in the experiments and remain listed in the _Journal_.* He would not "recant" his belief that prayer could be tested. Bruce was deprived of his listing as a practitioner for his personal beliefs about the scientific method being applied to Christian prayer.

When word of Bruce's expulsion reached the public, John was told how wrong he was to be doing his experiments. John said to me, "I was told that my whole lifework was invalid and was brought to naught! Look at the trouble that your father has caused you and the family." John was upset.

Also John had a friend in the full time ministry who said to him about testing prayer, "John, what if you find out prayer doesn't work?" John was surprised. This man had faith in his prayers, but what would happen to his prayers if they were tested? Would they not work? John did not believe faith in prayer would evaporate under scientific scrutiny. That prayer would fail under examination became a fear for some people.

NEGATIVE REACTIONS

In early 1984, between research and resistance, resistance was quickly mounting. As word got out to local religious communities that two guys were conducting tests and were telling people that they could come over to their home and be tested, the irreverence of testing prayer riled some of them. For example, a man told John Klingbeil that he would get a crowd to picket outside John's home laboratory. The threat didn't materialize. A woman who helped the Klingbeils with their research was told, "More than once you came very close to being excommunicated." She was also told "When the [local] board of directors of your church ran out of things to talk about, they talked about you and Spindrift."

Being associated with the Klingbeils became a social liability for the Spindrift members. I have had several men and women tell me that Bruce was starting his own religion with Spindrift or that Bruce was starting a cult. Others told me that the Klingbeils were engaged in witchcraft. Bruce and John heard similar things including that they required personal counseling or they needed to be censured. All these opinions swirled because people were invited to pray for plants! At different times John and I would laugh, "It seems we have something to offend everyone."

MOVING FROM PALATINE TO SALEM

Bruce's income dropped from forty thousand to six thousand as a result of his loss of listing as a Christian Science practitioner in 1983. Bruce told me that one way Spindrift's work could be stopped was by their running out of money. For financial reasons Bruce and John moved to Salem, Oregon, in the spring of 1984. It was less expensive to live in Salem, Oregon, compared to Illinois and many other states. Would the Klingbeils move to Salem slow the research down? The Klingbeils thought it would but only temporarily.

Moving day was a sad day I would rather forget. All of us band of helpers sending them off to Salem were in some degree or another in tears. The Klingbeils had handed over their worn out car to two helpful Spindrifters. Then Gladys Myers and her husband Bart helped the Klingbeils arrange the buying of a new red truck. Bruce and John drove two trucks, one new and one rented, to Oregon.

This move happened, not because a local church committee turned them down for membership, but because they turned Bruce in to the Boston Church as though he had done something wrong. What Bruce and his son had done was develop hypotheses and try innovative blendings of Christianity and science when it was politically incorrect to do so. The Klingbeils were willing to think unconventionally. The price: loss of reputation, friends, and income.

In the Twenty-first Century it's **politically correct** to research spirituality and prayer. **In 1984, it wasn't politically correct.** For the founders of the Spindrift research to survive financially, they felt they had to move to Oregon. At the time of the move, resistance to doing prayer research was beginning to deeply hurt Spindrift. To make matters worse, when the name of "**Salem**" came up as Spindrift's new location, Salem brought to mind the witchcraft trials in Salem, Massachusetts. **The name *Salem* associated with witchcraft became a public relations nightmare for Spindrift.**

SALEM

The experiments for Spindrift were conducted in the Chicago area until the spring of 1984. After May, 1984, the Klingbeils conducted their research in Salem, Oregon.

As other experiments were developed, Bruce's favorite remained the yeast test. John's favorite experiment tended to be the one he was totally immersed in at the time.

Getting settled in Salem had its struggles. Though these times became the financially lean years and the research was tough to get going again, the Klingbeils did enjoy their new surroundings. Bruce and John rented a townhouse. They liked the weather. They enjoyed visiting the ocean and Oregon's small towns. John enjoyed theaters and cruising computer stores. Sometimes Bruce played catch with a neighbor boy. The Klingbeils' neighbors were not exactly sure what Bruce and John did, but several have commented on what beautiful house plants they had.

Bruce wrote the following from Salem to me on February 20, 1985:

> Spindrift is praying its way now to a sense of identity
> and an evaluation of how to present these ideas.

At the moment John is doing some final work on a second novel, *Mindpatterns*. This tells the story of the development of the yeast test just as *The Healer* told the story of the discovery of the tests themselves.

I had the Apple computer go off in the middle of this letter. It's been doing that lately; looks like we'll need a new power supply unit one of these days.

The swallows have come back to Salem two weeks early which, they say, means an early spring. Weather will be in the sixties over the weekend with sunny skies so Friday we're going to the ocean. Except for a few breaks we've been working hard and getting a lot done. It's been hard to have the tests down for a while, but we're getting that straightened out. All in all things are coming well.

John wrote the following to me on February 29, 1986:

The rhododendrons have their first blooms, the crocus are blooming, the pussy willows are out, the red buds are just starting, and a few other flowers whose names either I forgot or never knew are out. It has been clear so, when I am up on the hill, I can see two huge snow topped mountains behind the smaller range of mountains and then look the other way to the beautiful undulating valley that reminds one of England or Wales. It is so marvelous to live in such a beautiful place. Well, I suppose I'm done. Give my love to your mother and take care of yourself.

TWO SPINDRIFT MEMBERS QUIT

In July 1985, two of the most active Spindrift members jumped ship. They were a husband and wife and sat on the **five member** Spindrift Board of Directors. The husband was president of Spindrift. After the couple quit, the Klingbeils asked Gladys Myers and me to meet with Spindrift's lawyer. He did a legal review of the corporate papers and found that it was legal for Spindrift to have a **three member** board of directors.

The husband and wife's disassociation from Spindrift was a shock. On July third, Bruce called to tell me that the couple would quit at a board meeting on the Fourth of July. On Independence Day the couple declared their independence from Spindrift. They resigned. I gave them their dues back. It was not a happy Fourth of July.

Before their resignations all I knew was the couple was bothered that a recent publicity campaign prepared by them produced only hate mail toward Spindrift.

What led up to their resignations? The Klingbeils had moved from Illinois to Salem, Oregon. The wife had flown out to Salem twice to help with editing and other tasks. The husband and wife even decided to move to Oregon to assist with the prayer research.

The Christian Science church they attended locally called the couple in. They were questioned about their involvement in Spindrift and how they could *reconcile* that behavior with certain church *Manual* by-laws by Mary Baker Eddy. In particular one by-law bothered the couple. They had no answer for it. "Members of this church shall not unite with organizations which impede their progress in Christian Science. God requires our whole heart, and He supplies within the wide channels of The Mother Church dutiful and sufficient occupation for all its members."[17] That by-law was the clincher. The couple were going to lose committee positions, Sunday School teaching positions, and maybe friends. They did not want that loss. The church used the by-law as a means to dissuade the couple from doing any more scientific research with prayer.

The wife told me that, even though Mary Baker Eddy did experiments herself, "Unless I find it in Mrs. Eddy's writings that I can do experiments, I am not going to do them any more." (See endnote **18**.)

We at Spindrift were the couple's friends. The couple never told us they were going to be "called in." They just resigned and told us what happened at the same time. I said, "These by-laws are guidelines. They are not set in cement." I stayed friends, but I am certain the resignation phone call was the last time they ever talked to Bruce and John. Bruce Klingbeil told me, "Are we literalists? What about church members who join organizations like the Veterans of Foreign Wars, or Unions, or country clubs? I guess they have disobeyed that *Manual* by-law, too."

PREVIOUSLY SUPPORTIVE

It was after Bruce's earlier expulsion as a practitioner in Illinois that the husband and wife became closer to the Klingbeils' scientific endeavors. The couple were from the Klingbeils' former Schaumburg church and provided much love, compassion, and support, especially to Bruce. Learning about Spindrift, the couple took on faith to be true what John and Bruce were saying. Though they were very helpful to the research, they admitted not understanding it scientifically. That was how they explained their position to me. When the couple was called in front of their church board and others started telling them the meanings and interpretations of Bruce and John's explanations were theologically skewed, the couple studied for themselves and came roughly to the same conclusion: Christian Science as a spiritual science was just a metaphor. The word *mathematics* was used as a metaphysical metaphor. Mathematics was a symbol of a fixed principle of order. Mathematics was not to be used to measure prayer or things of the Spirit. Using math to measure anything was called a "misinterpretation."

It became an intriguing objection to testing prayer; math is not to be *literally* applied to spiritual things. Math is only to be *figuratively* applied as a metaphor or symbol about spiritual things.[19]

IS MATH ONLY A METAPHOR?

The wife believed the Klingbeils thought mathematics was perfect, like God, when the Klingbeils used mathematics as a tool to gather data. In a sense, she felt that by placing mathematics on a pedestal, the Klingbeils were placing their trust and faith in **Math** instead of **God**. It is true, however, as cosmological inquisitor Paul Davies' reason for winning the John Templeton award for progress in religion in 1995 shows, mathematics may be a window on how God manifests Himself in the universe. It appears mathematics may stand out as the clearest and most perfect mode for expressing a measurable divine order around conscious man. The mix-up over understanding the Klingbeils' usage of math versus the spiritual symbolism of math was a stumbling block for the wife. I asked John to address her problem about how he and his father thought about mathematics. In a letter John failed to clarify to her satisfaction Spindrift's usage of mathematics to measure healing intentions. Two more people were subtracted from the Klingbeils' short list of friends.

MEMBERS MOVE

Two Illinois families did move to Salem, Oregon, to help the Klingbeils. It was a sacrifice for the families to drop everything to help Spindrift. One family was a business man and his wife. The wife was a spiritual healer. The other family moved later: a business owner and her daughter. The daughter ran the Spindrift office in Salem. I was the only member of the board left in Illinois, the state where Spindrift was incorporated.

ACCEPTABLE STRANGENESS

Nearly anyone who lays out evidence for psi is considered a strange person. Evidence for a psi effect or specifically a nurturing, loving, healing prayer produced psi effect would not sit too well with the magician-skeptics or the physical scientists. Presentation and replication proposals in future years gave some evidence that the Klingbeils and what Spindrift did were perceived as strange.

In time, indirectly through the *strangeness* of quantum physics, some physical scientists would reconsider their attitudes toward prayer being a viable force to test. Quantum physics was strange enough. Physicists have a name for strangeness, quantum weirdness. Prayer, having some kind of discernible nonlocal effect, **would not be more bizarre** than what science was learning about quantum physics. One description of quantum physics is this: "Quantum physics is the dreams that stuff is made of." Could prayer be any more astonishing than such a description of quantum physics? No. When our preconceptions yield and the information on how a person's observations affect quantum processes in the real world is absorbed, Spindrift's work will not be seen as strange anymore.

THE TIPPING POINT
OF CIVILIZATION

Is anything practical from the research? In quantum physics, little changes bring large consequences for the world. In human evolution, little changes bring large consequences for mankind. Perhaps the world's balance of harmony versus evil depends on the quality and quantity of the psi we think in our prayers and thoughts. The evidence for both healing prayer and harmful prayer suggests that psi does elicit subtle shifts and changes in physical systems and circumstances. The world is one large physical system that needs our **supportive** prayers.

We may become the **prisoners of prayer** if we don't grasp its psychic potency to infuse good or bad consequences into the world. Even if the scientific evidence for prayer isn't good enough evidence for scientists, should we let radical religious terrorists rule the psychic realm of prayer? Their psychic weapons are hate and the abuse of prayer. **A terrorist's prayer is often to destroy the nonbeliever. A danger of terrorism is that people who aren't members of the tribe become less human and, therefore, acceptable as targets.**

On October 21, 2006, France's Interior Minister Nicolas Sarkozy announced the closing of "seven Islamist, clandestine and illegal prayer rooms" hidden in two airports. Some prayer rooms were underneath runways. Author Philip Yancey writes "Prayer is a subversive act performed in a world that constantly calls faith into question." I interpret that Yancey's point, prayer operating to subvert resistance to God, can refer to **both** good and evil motives driving prayers. (From *Prayer*, page 51.)

Wise men and women are aware that there is a thin veneer protecting civilization from chaos. Are we going to let the terrorists do all the praying for us which might send us into a new Dark Ages, or are we going to pray to keep the thin veneer on civilization? Helping to protect the freedom and creativity of mankind is a practical use of prayer and psi research.

Could there be a tipping point for civilization between order and chaos? There is *some* hope in anthropologist Margaret Mead's words. **"Never believe that a few caring people can't change the world. For, indeed, that's all who ever have."**

Chapter Four

Politics and Prayer

The problem with America today is people's perceptions of reality.

Marianne Williamson,
on *Larry King Live*, 01/96,
Author of *Illuminata: A Return to Prayer*

Satire doesn't have a chance against reality anymore.
Lenny Bruce, comedian

In 1990, Spindrift's prayer experiments became entangled in politics. This entanglement created wild characterizations of Spindrift. John Andrews of Colorado was the president and general secretary of Spindrift. John Klingbeil wrote the following when John Andrews was leaving Spindrift:

> Mr. Andrews leaves because of immense demands on his time. Not only is he President of the Independence Institute, a state-level political think tank, but his church and family obligations and many other activities have drained his available time to the vanishing point. He has done much to steady the course of Spindrift during his years at its head.[1]

John Andrews became Colorado's Republican candidate for Governor. John had been a Nixon/Agnew speech writer and had written great copy for Spindrift. During John's campaign Bruce Klingbeil told a Colorado *Westword* newspaper reporter, "John Andrews left Spindrift because it posed potential problems with his political life . . . . He made a logical and wise decision by leaving Spindrift. It was the only sensible thing for him to do, considering the career path he was on." An opponent to John's candidacy told the reporter he admitted Spindrift's tests were "weird, weird, weird. They lead to a larger question—does John Andrews have a firm grip on realty?"[2] I wonder what this critic of John Andrews' "grip on reality" would say about a sentence by quantum physicist Nick Herbert. "One of the best-kept secrets of science is that physicists have lost their grip on reality."[3]

An *Associated Press* news story did move Spindrift's name across the land. After years of being ignored, Spindrift was being written up in *The New York Times*, *The Washington Post*, *The Denver Post*, and so on. I got to be on several talk shows. I defended Spindrift for testing prayer and consciousness on plants. It was a pleasure.

The stories made Spindrift's work look foolish, but so what? People were asking questions about prayer and consciousness research. The sudden attention was welcome. Here is the September 23, 1990, copyrighted article from *The Daily Sentinel* by Bob Silbernagel that broke the news of John Andrews' connections to Spindrift:

Andrews tied to experiments
Organization studied power of
prayer over mung beans, yogurt

Gubernatorial candidate John Andrews in 1987 served on the board of an organization that prayed over mung beans, yogurt, and a handmade dresser in experiments designed to scientifically prove the power of prayer.

Spindrift, Inc., is an organization that studies parapsychology, a discipline Andrews described

as "a recognized field on the edge of exploring new knowledge."

Scientists at Duke and Princeton universities are involved in parapsychology experiments, he noted.

On Friday, Andrews down played his involvement with the organization, saying it "didn't command a high priority with me," and he decided to spend his time on higher priorities "like public policy in Colorado."

Andrews, a 45-year-old Republican, said he became involved with the group in an effort "to help some friends do some networking." He said he thought he could help them find grants and ways to evaluate their experiments. "All I was doing was using my experience in marketing and research."

He also said his intellectual curiosity and Christian background made him interested in the efforts to scientifically validate prayer. Andrews is a Christian Scientist, but Spindrift isn't a church-sponsored group.

"I believe the expansion of useful knowledge and relief of human suffering are better served when no questions are out of bounds," he said.

Andrews said he got out of the organization when "it seemed to me the results were not conclusive, and there was not a climate where proponents and opponents could agree on what was being done."

"Also, some of the ideas appeared to me to be somewhat off the wall," he added.

Records from the Illinois Secretary of State, where Spindrift was incorporated as a not-for-profit group in 1981, show Andrews was general secretary of Spindrift in 1987 and 1988.

A 1987 press release from Spindrift listed Andrews as the organization's contact and named him as its project administrator.

Spindrift also sought to win an $11,000 reward from a San Francisco-based group of scientists called the Bay Area Skeptics, which offered the money for any demonstration of paranormal phenomena under controlled circumstances.

Kent Harker, who was editor of the Skeptics' newsletter at the time, said no test was ever done because no agreement could be reached with Spindrift about how to conduct the tests.

But, Harker also said, he dealt almost entirely with Andrews during the discussion. "He was quite heavily involved," Harker said. "He was the project administrator, if I remember."

Harker also said Andrews got "quite exercised" when Harker questioned the validity of the experiments.

Spindrift's goal is to "explain the relationship between prayer and healing through the experimental test," said Bill Sweet, of Mount Prospect, Ill., the current president of the group. "People for thousands of years have believed in the power of prayer, but they've had no proof."

"Compared to the gamut of groups out there, we're the most normal of the weirdos," Sweet added. "We're talking about a few bean sprouts, not reincarnation."

In one experiment, 14,000 mung beans were divided into two groups. One was prayed over and the other was not.

According to a Spindrift brochure, the beans were put in a saline solution for 24 hours, and nine days later their sprouts were counted. Spindrift said nearly twice as many sprouts were counted in the prayed-for group as in the group that wasn't prayed over.[4]

In another experiment, listed in a book called *Cathedral of the Mind*, which Sweet said outlined the Spindrift experiments, trays of rye grass were correlated with jars of yogurt and potted plants.

"The plants were promised . . . more light and the yogurt was promised milk if more of 'their' seeds germinated better than control seeds did," the book said. "And their seeds did do better than control seeds."

A different experiment attempted to connect constructed items with the thoughts of those who made them.

"Thus, a drawer was removed from a handmade dresser and the intention (mentally) formed to replace it if correlated seeds did better than controls," the book said, "And again, the correlated seeds did germinate more fully than controls."

The press release that lists Andrews as Spindrift's contact and project administrator begins, "Systematic prayer will improve the functioning of an organic or electronic system according to consistent mathematical ratios, new laboratory findings show."

It goes on to detail experiments with prayer and germination rates of rye grass seeds, weight gain of soybean sprouts, gas production from yeast cultures, and patterns of random numbers in a computer circuit.

"Directed thought clearly and consistently altered the functioning of all four test subjects, researchers found," according to the press release.

The release also quotes Andrews as saying, "When you observe an effect and you want to know what is causing it, you have to keep exploring one possibility after another, like Edison trying hundreds of substances before he found one filament that made possible the incandescent bulb.

"Our laboratory people, unlike most others, took seriously the possibility that consciousness can influence atoms or electrons at a distance," Andrews continued in the release.

> "For that influence to come up to a measurable level, they needed something intensely focused, analogous to the way a laser concentrates ordinary light, so they began experimenting with the application of a religiously disciplined consciousness [of a human test participant]. That's when they began to achieve repeatable, verified results that we feel are fundamentally new."

Though many Spindrift friends of mine would disagree with me, the author is of the opinion that **almost any publicity is good publicity.**

In October, 1990, I received a call from a political reporter who followed John on the campaign trail. "Mr. Sweet, if the election gets closer, much more will be made of these experiments."

I asked him, "What is so odd about prayer being tested?"

He said, "It immediately sounds odd-ball and can be made into an issue."

I asked, "What is your opinion of prayer?"

The reporter replied, "I don't think much about it, but I don't think there is anything there that is provable."

I responded, "Isn't a small effort worthwhile to try to discover if prayer can be proven in some way?"

He answered, "Oh, I see what you mean."

In January, 1994, when John Andrews was assisting some Texas politicians, Molly Ivins, a syndicated columnist and "Sixty Minutes" commentator, wrote about John's connections to Spindrift. The column is entitled "Prayer, Politics, Aggies and CEOs." Here is what Molly Ivins wrote in part in *The Ft. Worth Star Telegram* of January 18, 1994:

> . . . Say, here's good news. We have a guy running for lieutenant governor, our old friend Tex Lazar, who hired a fellow to head up this think tank who believes in praying over beans . . . .

> [John] Andrews . . . helped [Spindrift] get funding for two years in an effort to measure the effects of prayer. They also ran experiments that involved making mental "promises" to plants and dishes of yogurt in an attempt to promote germination of rye grass seeds. (Hey, I got this out of a story in *The Denver Post* . . .) So now Andrews is in San Antonio, thanks to Lazar, helping to make public policy for Texas. Another good reason to vote for Bob Bullock.
>
> I personally think we ought to get Andrews together with this guy John Bockris at A&M, who ran the experiments on turning mercury into gold. Bockris first came to public attention when he claimed to have confirmed the results of the now discredited Utah experiments in cold fusion. . . . he has since been . . . working in the alchemy field . . . Bockris is now working on turning carbon into iron. If he and Andrews got together, they could pray over half the carbon and maybe get it to germinate rye grass seeds. Someone write a proposal!

After John Andrews lost the 1990 election, the Business Manager for the Parapsychological Association, Richard Broughton, Ph.D., wrote me the following:

> I am sorry to learn of Mr. Andrews' misfortunes. The skeptics do seem to outclass the parapsychologists in media battles, but the true measure of success will not be in the popular media but in the scientific journals, and there we are beginning to see some modest advances.[5]

In 1988 PBS Television planned programs with some unorthodox M.D.'s, spiritual thinkers, and researchers of consciousness. A woman producer contracted by Portland, Oregon's PBS affiliate, phoned the Klingbeils. The producer said she wanted to video tape a segment about the Klingbeils. Two interview segments with two doctors doing unusual research were also written into the program.

The producer and a crew showed up at Bruce and John's townhouse in Salem. A ninety minute interview with some shots of the test equipment were video taped. The producer and crew thought the interview broke new ground.

The producer called John Klingbeil later and reported that there was such good information in the interview that they decided to lengthen the segment making it longer than the other two segments.

On the night the program aired, John Klingbeil answered the telephone. The producer was straight forward, "Your segment was edited out at the last moment." John Klingbeil was speechless. The producer was upset and told John, "The decision was taken out of my hands."

John Klingbeil called me. I can remember John depressed and crying over the telephone. When I hung up, I cried, too, and so did my mother.

The general secretary of Spindrift, John Andrews in Colorado, called the producer to find out what happened. She would not tell him. All she said to John Andrews was it was not her choice and that someone over her said something to the staff about Spindrift being too controversial, and "It was a business decision" to cut us out. "It was a business decision" but on whose instigation? We Spindrifters were never able to find out who "at the last moment" instigated the termination of the television interview with the Klingbeils.

Some skeptics of prayer and psi may acknowledge that there are strange anomalies in the world that don't fit into common sense assumptions about reality. With these folks, a dialogue can continue. Other skeptics keep advising believers in psi to **"Get a reality check."**

Chapter Five

Bible Experiments

The theory determines what we observe.
Albert Einstein

Our research is concerned with the interface
between science and religion.
Bruce Klingbeil

One of the lessons I learned from the Klingbeils was how to view things. The Klingbeils taught the difference between the words *view* and *viewpoint*. Historically, if people pondered how their thought processes work, most would say their cognition and education came from their views. Their views determine their viewpoints. The question is, "Does the **VIEW** determine the **VIEWPOINT?**" Bruce and John pointed out, that with quantum physics, it's more the reverse. Bruce said **"The viewpoint determines the view."** How one preconceives (his viewpoint) determines what one sees (his view).

EACH MIND'S SUBJECTIVE VIEW

If you ask a Jewish person about the Bible, he will say it is the story of God and man and has rules for the Israelites. If you ask a Christian about the Bible, he will say it is about God and how Jesus Christ obeyed the Ten Commandments which qualified him to save others from their disobediences of the Ten Commandments. The Bible was written in an unscientific age, an age devoid of science as we know it. So, to find experiments with anomalous results, all one has to do is change his or her viewpoint. Then the chain of experimental events in Scripture becomes viewable. What was invisible, comes into view, because of a fresh viewpoint.[1] Your personal viewpoint is what you unconsciously *first see*. Relating to a person's subjective viewpoint Mary Baker Eddy writes, "We are all sculptors, working at various forms, moulding and chiseling thought."[2]

Albert Einstein's Theory of Relativity states that the general view of the universe can be a different experience of viewpoint for different people. Events may be simultaneous in the viewpoint of one human consciousness and be sequential in another human consciousness.

SPIRITUAL EXPERIMENTS

What are some of these Bible experiments that have not been viewed from this experimental viewpoint? Take Gideon and his fleece in *The New English Bible* as an example:

> Gideon said to God, 'If thou wilt deliver Israel through me as thou hast promised—now, look, I am putting a fleece of wool on the threshing-floor. If there is dew only on the fleece and all the ground is dry, then I shall be sure that thou wilt deliver Israel through me, as thou hast promised.' And that is what happened. He rose early next day and wrung out the fleece, and he squeezed enough dew from it to fill a bowl with water. Gideon then said, 'Do not be angry with me, but give me leave to speak once again. Let me, I pray thee, make one more *test* with the fleece. This time let the fleece

alone be dry, and all the ground be covered with
dew.' God let it be so that night: the fleece alone
was dry, and on all the ground there was dew.
(NEB, Judges, p. 278)

What about Daniel's following experience?

Now Daniel determined not to contaminate
himself by touching the food and wine assigned
to him by the king, and he begged the master of
the eunuchs not to make him do so. God made
the master show kindness and goodwill to Daniel,
and he said to him, 'I am afraid of my lord the
king: he has assigned you your food and drink,
and if he sees you looking dejected, unlike the
other young men of your own age, it will cost me
my head.' Then Daniel said to the guard . . .
'Submit us to this *test* for ten days. Give us only
vegetables to eat and water to drink; then compare
our looks with those of the young men who have
lived on the food assigned by the king, and be guided
in your treatment of us by what you see.' The guard
listened to what they said and *tested* them for ten
days. At the end of ten days they looked healthier
and were better nourished than all the young men
who had lived on the food assigned them by the
king. So the guard took away the assignment of food
and the wine they were to drink, and gave them
only the vegetables. (NEB, Daniel, p. 1069)

Elisha also pulled off a couple anomalous tests as follows:

When they reached the Jordan, they began cutting
down trees; but it chanced that, as one man was
felling a trunk, the head of his axe flew off into the

water. 'Oh, master!' he exclaimed, 'it was a
borrowed one.' 'Where did it fall?' asked the man
of God. When he was shown the place, he cut off
a piece of wood and threw it in and made the iron
float. Then he said, 'There you are, lift it out.'
(NEB, 2 Kings, p. 415)

Elisha also annulled the effects of poison that
inadvertently got into the food. (NEB, 2 Kings, p. 413)

Elisha's predecessor and teacher had a similar name,
Elijah. In this next experiment, like Daniel comparing his
men against the King's men, Elijah uses a type of "control
group." The religious practice of Baal's followers is
compared to the religious practice of Jehovah's followers.
After hundreds of prophets of Baal got no results in
paranormally igniting bull meat on an altar, Elijah got
some results as follows:

He took twelve stones, one for each tribe of the
sons of Jacob .... With these stones he built an
altar in the name of the Lord; he dug a trench
round it . . . arranged the wood, cut up the bull
and laid it on the wood. Then he said, 'Fill four
jars with water and pour it on the whole-offering
and on the wood.' They did so, and he said, 'Do
it again.' They did it again, and he said, 'Do it a
third time.' They did it a third time .... At the
hour of the regular sacrifice the prophet Elijah
came forward and said, 'Lord God of Abraham, of
Isaac, and of Israel, let it be known today that
thou art God in Israel, and that I am thy
servant .... Answer me .... ' Then the fire of
the Lord fell. It consumed the whole-offering, the
wood, the stones, and the earth, and licked up
the water in the trench. (NEB, 1 Kings, p. 401)

Though not having the math "numbers" to back it up, the book of *Numbers* has some intriguing tests. One is a "moral chemistry" lie detector test in chapter five. The flaws from today's perspective may be that (1) It is biased towards males for only women were test subjects. (2) The consequences of telling a lie were harsh. (3) What were the unspecified chemicals used? (4) Was it driven by the placebo effect associated with guilt feelings? (Researchers have found an opposite to healing done by the placebo effect. The term is *the nocebo effect* which describes fear and harm effects caused by the mind).

The test was used in cases of suspected adultery of a married woman. If a wife confessed to an extra-marital affair, fine. If she denied the affair and her husband accepted her answer as true, fine. The following describes what happened if she denied it and her husband was suspicious of her answer:

> . . . the husband shall bring his wife to the priest together with the prescribed offering for her . . . . The priest shall bring her forward and set her before the Lord. He shall take clean water in an earthenware vessel, and shall take dust from the floor of the Tabernacle and add it to the water. He shall set the woman before the Lord, uncover her head, and place the grain-offering of protestation in her hands; it is a grain-offering for jealousy. The priest shall hold in his own hand the water of contention which brings out the truth. He shall then put the woman on oath and say to her, 'If no man has had intercourse with you, if you have not gone astray and let yourself become defiled while owing obedience to your husband, then may your innocence be established by the water of contention which brings out the truth. But if,

while owing him obedience, you have gone astray and let yourself become defiled, if any man other than your husband has had intercourse with you' (the priest shall here put the woman on oath with an adjuration, and shall continue), 'may the Lord make an example of you among your people in adjurations and in swearing of oaths by bringing upon you miscarriage and untimely birth; and this water that brings out the truth shall enter your body, bringing upon you miscarriage and untimely birth.' The woman shall respond, 'Amen, Amen.' The priest shall write these curses on a scroll and wash them off into the water of contention; he shall make the woman drink the water that brings out the truth, and the water shall enter her body. The priest shall take the grain-offering for jealousy from the woman's hand, present it as a special gift before the Lord, and offer it at the altar. He shall take a handful from the grain-offering by way of token, and burn it at the altar; after this he shall make the woman drink the water. If she had let herself become defiled and has been unfaithful to her husband, then when the priest makes her drink the water that brings out the truth and the water has entered her body, she will suffer a miscarriage or untimely birth, and her name will become an example in adjuration among her kin. But if the woman has not let herself become defiled and is pure, then her innocence is established and she will bear her child. (NEB, Numbers, p. 151)

This truth/lie detector test might cause angst for the pro-life Christians who teach that the Bible does not permit *any* abortions.

An M.D., Dr. M. DeHaan, writes in his book, *The Chemistry of the Blood*, "Is this test scientific?"

> We believe, although we would not detract a whit from the miraculous in the Bible, that this test did not depend upon a miracle at all but was a normal physical test which depended upon the ordinary physical and psychological functions of the body. We believe that, if we KNEW THE IDENTITY OF THE BITTER HERB which Moses used, the SAME TEST WOULD WORK TODAY [as a lie detector test]. Recent discoveries in the realm of physiological chemistry and the psychological effect on the body will greatly strengthen this position.

Another experiment from the book of *Numbers* ties in with "qualifying" a spiritual person for religious office. It could be an ancient allusion to a potential use of the yeast experiment Spindrift developed. It is a way to select who humanly expresses the divine attributes with the Universe approving.

Like American Indian tribes, each tribe of Israel had a chief. Each chief's name with the tribe's name is written separately on twelve staffs of almond rods. God provided both the theory and the predicted results. If the correct almond rod blooms, the one with Aaron and the tribe of Levi written on it, Aaron is verified to be the holy inspired man chosen to be high priest.

Overnight, the growing power of God selects and elicits growth in the Levi tribe's almond plant. Growth did not occur on the control group of the eleven almond plants. Through a type of divine qualitative thought, God "associationally linked" to Aaron's staff/rod. It blossoms. According to the results which confirm the theory, Aaron was to be high priest. Maybe the Vatican should consider this test when choosing a Pope, or churches when hiring administrators. (NEB, Numbers, p. 169)

After the demise of Jesus' disciple Judas Iscariot, to make a team of twelve men again, the eleven remaining disciples decided to pick between two qualified men. The disciples felt that it was prayer and God's Spirit which guided the choice when "they drew lots." The result: Matthias was chosen instead of Joseph Barsabbas. (NEB, Acts, Chapter 1, verse 26, p. 198)

There is a "turn on the light" test in the Bible. Aaron and other high priests wore two stones in their breastplates called the Thummim stone and the Urim stone. They light up if the priest is holy, thus accepted, and they do not if the person is not qualified. Here is part of what Mrs. Eddy writes about these stones in the breastplate:

> The Urim and Thummim, which were to be on Aaron's breast when he went before Jehovah, were holiness and purification of thought and deed, which alone can fit us for the office of spiritual teaching . . . . Urim. Light. The rabbins believed that the stones in the breastplate of the high-priest had supernatural illumination, but Christian Science reveals Spirit, not matter, as the illuminator of all.[3]

The sense of "Spirit, not matter" bringing the illumination ties in with the "Ordering-Force and ordering-effects" Spindrift feels it has partially discovered. Prayer and holy thought bring movement toward order and healing to a test situation. In the test context, order and healing tend to give indirect evidence of an Ordering-Force outside the body and matter of a human being. Increasing numbers of people are seeing this concept: that they are *more* than matter, they are *spiritual somehow*. Let us hope this encouraging trend is not just a popular fad.

As far as the science of chemistry goes, many a chemist has wondered how Jesus Christ changed water into wine, a finished product of wine at that. The closest chemistry I know to this incident is when healers have changed or charged water somewhat and when priests have blessed water. It is claimed a molecular structural change has followed some such healings and blessing actions. If reproducible, this water test alone should be enough to win a skeptic's prize money challenge. If repeatable, the water change is a concrete paranormal event. (NEB, John, p. 112.)

Masaru Emoto's research of water molecules might be corroboration that change does take place when water is blessed. Masaru Emoto has photographed the changes that arise in water crystals after lovely to ugly thought-intentions have saturated the water molecules. For Masaru's photographic evidence of intentions displayed in water crystals, see his books, *Hidden Messages in Water* and *The True Power of Water*.

STRESS ABOUT STRESS

For those uneasy about putting organisms under stress, as researchers are sometimes doing, consider Jesus Christ "cursing" the fig tree (plant), which then dried up from its roots. (NEB, Matthew, p. 30) Jesus performed another action-at-a-distance by permitting a legion of demons to be sent out of a man and into a herd of swine. The pigs immediately killed themselves by running into the water and drowning. There was plenty of stress applied to those pigs in that event. (NEB, Matthew, p. 12)

"Experiments have favored the fact that Mind governs the body . . . ." Those words on page 162 of Mrs. Eddy's textbook didn't cause churchgoers to become curious about what those experiments were. However, there are many experiments in the Bible. One has to develop a viewpoint and taste to see them, or they will be missed. Everyone today is looking at the Bible in a scientific age. **More importantly, the Spindrifters were looking at the Bible in a scientific way.**

THE VIEWPOINT DETERMINES THE VIEW
Bruce Klingbeil

Marilyn Schlitz, a researcher and statistician with the Noetic Sciences Institute, had an experience with an experiment which shows that a researcher's viewpoint helps determine what he views in the experiment. The following is from *Miracles of Mind* by Russell Targ and Jane Katra, page 214.

[Marilyn] Schlitz carried out a landmark experiment, showing the great importance of the state of mind and expectations of the researchers on the outcome of the experiment. Skeptical English psychologist Richard Wiseman had unsuccessfully conducted three careful attempts to replicate the staring experiments [when you stare at someone and that affects him] . . . . Their failure was completely in line with the view of psi. On hearing of his failure to replicate her experiments, Marilyn proposed a collaborative study with Wiseman. Using the same laboratory, a common protocol and the same subject pool that Wiseman used, Schlitz again demonstrated a successful outcome. The participants whose video image was being stared at showed significant physiological responses, as opposed to when they were being ignored. Wiseman again fulfilled his negative expectation and found no effect, clearly demonstrating that the consciousness of the experimenter profoundly affects what he or she gets to observe.

It is not what you look at that matters,
it's what you see.
Henry David Thoreau

Interlude

Tidbits Learned

Veni, Vidi, velcro
(I came, I saw, I stuck around).

Latin humor

The best healers have always been individuals with
both a head *and* a heart—a highly developed
intellect and a mature emotional side. "Healing
intelligence" requires a balance between reason
and intuition, between intellect *and* feeling.

Larry Dossey, M.D.,
Healing Beyond the Body, p. 264

To be a participant or witness of any Spindrift tests was a
strange feeling. It was almost uncomfortable witnessing
those paranormal effects. The psi effects of beans sprouting and
grasses growing produced wavy lines on a graph. Psi applied
actualized higher lines on a graph. Without psi applied, the lines
on a graph were measurably flatter.

In particular the yeast test *made waves* as psi results came into
the computer. As one of us would pray for the yeast cells to recover
from stress, within two hours waves would form a computer graph
that showed how one's personal healing-thoughts had done. These
graphed waves were the results of a paranormal happening, a psi
healing effect on the yeast cells. For example, these waves
corresponded to prayer's effect on a group of living yeast cells.

After a test, the results, the waves, were compared to a reference graph of what healthy yeast looks like. When the results, the waves, resembled the reference graph, the healing of yeast was judged successful.

John explained, "We measure a normal reference pattern against yeast deviated from normal. Then after a test, we measure how close is that yeast's return to normal."

Bruce said, "What we are attempting to do with our experiments is to see within a specific context how prayer works. When we take a measurement, we witness the healing pattern without interfering with the healing process."

These order producing healing-effects of prayer on stressed organisms were a thrill to see. To me, it also felt eerie and scary. It reminded me of the phrase, "When prayers are answered, there is nothing scarier." The Klingbeils were used to seeing these healing-effects bringing order to things. To me, these healing-effects in the laboratory were what I would call an episode I saw on *The X Files.*

While witnessing a yeast test I thought aloud, "Even if subtly, I, each person, has some degree of mental input into our world. How scary!" Bruce said, "I know. It's startling for the human mind to see such things for the first time." John turned from his computer screen and said to me, "I know why it's frightening to you. You have an awakened responsibility that comes with new knowledge. To see your consciousness expressing part of itself as qualitative effects and faith effects on a graph is a shock. You see qualities of consciousness modify what the cells do. I think it's cool! It's a frozen moment in time of the quality of your healing-intentions . . . ."

A ham radio operator friend witnessed the yeast test followed by the results, waves emerging on a graph. He said of the graph, "That looks like a waveform of voltage or watts being measured."

I said pointing to the graph, "Then that represents mental power?"

My friend replied, "I don't know what else to call it."

Bruce said, "That's what the test is all about. It's about thought's qualitative power to bless. It's about the kinds of abilities, or lack of them, we have to be loving, healing, compassionate *avenues* of holy power to the yeast and, by inference, to the world . . . . Prayer is the love of God." Prayer as love is the global warming we want.

NEW CONCEPTS FOR ME

I asked Bruce, "What is the purpose of spirituality?" Bruce said, "To bring order to our world."

I learned from the Klingbeils that holy prayer was a desire to be a witness to the ordering-process that *was right for the circumstances.*

In 1979, I asked Bruce, "When we are praying for a human being, *what are we observing* in our prayer about him?" Bruce said, "A pure identity."

Responding to the question, what does quality prayer or holy prayer do? John said, "Holy prayer promotes order." The gist is, quality prayer references order, both spiritual and physical order. Quality prayers promote a flow toward order, norms, and what is best for the circumstances. **Quality holy prayers are detached from our goals.** Then quality and divine attributes are let loose.

I asked Bruce the difference between goal-directed thought and non goal-directed thought. Bruce said, "One is the *use* of will. The other is the *release* of will."

I asked why my prayers for problems didn't seem to work consistently. Bruce answered approximately, "The trouble with ineffective prayer is, our own mortal thoughts get in the way." The gist of Bruce's answer is the following: Effective prayer starts with acknowledging God and taking the focus off ourselves.

What about prayers given over and over again? Do they become formulas? Care should be taken not to substitute mere repetition of words for prayers' chief ingredients, inspiration and love. Inspired prayers are probably not formulas. Arguably, inspiration varies from prayer to prayer. Each prayer is a new expression of a person's consciousness and reminds one of the question, "Can a man step in the same river twice?" No, because "other waters are ever flowing onto you." (Heraclitus 535-475 B.C.) If a person's thoughts are flowing like a river, the same prayer cannot be given twice.

Bruce asked the question, "Is the spiritual universe comprehensible?" Bruce and John felt that by isolating two healing intentions which are *goal-ended faith effects* and *non goal-ended quality effects*, comprehension of the Spirit universe began to be possible.

Early in the 1980's, I asked John what he thought Mary Baker Eddy would be doing if she were living in our decade. John said, "If Mrs. Eddy were here today, she would have a Cray computer sitting in her parlor." (Cray makes *supercomputers*.)

Asked why a person's thoughts and prayers couldn't have been tested earlier in the Twentieth Century, John said, "It requires computational [computer] power which has only come into existence in the last few years. It requires viewpoints in the natural sciences which have emerged only in the last half century." (1986 tape)

The Klingbeils found that a prayer effect increased in power when a person praying could gaze at the object of his prayer. "To look at a visual image of the plant" as a specific identity to pray for added a "competency" to the test results. I asked what procedures would satisfy a scientist about a researcher gazing at a plant. Bruce and John said that praying in the same room as the plant was acceptable as psi action at a distance. The Klingbeils said since looking on your object adds competency to the test, a wall *with a window* to look through could be built. Or "it would be fine" to use a television camera gazing at the plant. Then, in another location, a praying person looks at a television monitor which displays the plant he or she is praying for.

The Klingbeils said that future researchers could use advances in television transmission to permit people in many locations to pray for an organism in the Klingbeils' home laboratory located in Schaumburg, Illinois. Also, the Klingbeils would be able to pray for other researchers' projects. The irony was, the Klingbeils didn't own a T.V.. (In 1997, the first *affordable* slow scan television system that connected to a telephone line went on the market. The Internet carries video images as well. There is also tech talk of future holographic video.)

PRAYER WARS

Bruce attached a **pessimistic prediction to his optimism** about future nonlocal prayer research. Bruce believed that future findings by other researchers would eventually support that holy thought has healing effects at a distance. However, a counter scientific view against nonlocal prayer and healing research would emerge. A war of worldviews would develop. To the skeptic's worldview, prayer studies, etc., will get too far away from reality. Attempts at falsifying others' work and finding statistical mistakes are part of the scientific process, but nonlocal studies of healing will be charged as biased and sloppy science.

Then the skeptic can invoke the *Law of Unintended Consequences.* For example, how dangerously reptilian is prayer anyway? The terrorists pray five times a day on their knees. Then they get up and massacre people. They prayed to God. So whose prayer is prayer? Or what about the person healed by prayer, but later prayer didn't heal him? One failure cancels the success. The skeptic will charge that a test of prayer amounts to a machine gun being randomly fired at a wall. Then a researcher goes up to the wall, paints a bull's eye around the bullet holes he likes, and says, "See, prayer works."

Scientific skeptics will emphasize research failures and frauds. They will logically present the case that man is 100% a being of electrons and physicality. Scientific skeptics will **counter interpret** a God-brain-principle suggested by PET scans, the arguments of design theory, and the data due to paranormal prayer.

The future wars over consciousness research might not be too much fun.

> **A Spindrift prediction:**
> **The Twenty-first Century will leave little privacy. The inner stillness of spirituality will be found an oasis of quiet and calmness by default.**

TECHNOLOGY ENTERS OUR REALITY

Anytime I would ask Bruce and John about the future centuries, they would give a rather grim picture *if* spirituality was not part of the human scene. In their perceptions, a lack of spirituality would throw mankind into another Dark Ages. This time it would be a "technological Dark Ages." With some of the grossest common denominators of humanity predicted to increase on the Internet, maybe this prediction is a glimpse that the Klingbeils are on to something collectively dark. Private perversion becomes collective global perversion through unlimited technological pathways into the mind.

In the future, after computers get hold of our *individual minds*, there is a potential scenario where computers will burrow ways into our *collective lives*, enticing us through attractive technologically enhanced extravaganzas of the five physical senses which could addict us to our earthy experiences. If computers know our earthbound experiences are what we instinctively want, computers could force them on us. Men, women, and children will rarely experience *spirituality* or be *sure they are thinking for themselves anymore*. This tug to our earthy tendencies could occur. The computer may learn to know what sensations of the senses get our full attention. Like a drug dealer, the computer could constantly draw us back to its enticements and persistent pursuits of our minds and bodies. We could find ourselves living in "a dark technologically created reality" as Bruce Klingbeil put it, where our five senses are overwhelmed by the dominance of the computer. In a cyber-world of the future, men and women having their own free will to make decisions on their own could be difficult to achieve.

(It felt eerie when I saw the movie *The Matrix* because it reminded me of the Klingbeils' "technological Dark Ages." *The Matrix* movie series has produced discussion on the possibility of future computers seducing and manipulating the human senses into a tyrannical, realistic, computer generated reality from which human beings rarely can escape. The entire human experience becomes an imitation of reality foisted on mankind by a dark technological force. A reality seeker has to constantly avoid being deceived by the bombardments on his senses of altered but realistic reproductions of reality.)

FUTURE PRIVACY FROM CRYSTAL CLEAR THINKING?

In John Klingbeil's futuristic science fiction novel, *Richard Garret*, the world's computers are described as being sabotaged by computer viruses and hidden manipulations. A computer crystal chip is invented by people who understand psychic powers. The crystal chip permits access to computers only by way of consciousness effects, specifically prayer. The crystal recognizes the quality, the tenor, the drift of a person's thought. In short, the crystal distinguishes holy thought from will power thought. If the person's holy thought formed a pattern on a graph that matches the crystal's subtle parameters, computer access is allowed. A holy intention is the key to computer access. A saboteur or terrorist would not be able to produce a holy form of thought since his intention was unholy. A saboteur's negative thought patterns could not fake a holy intention. Computers with the crystal chip became inoculated against illegal tampering. **Prayer-thoughts defended important computers from sabotage and terrorism. Spiritually minded people helped guard national and homeland security.**

PSYCHIC COMPUTERS

Early on, the Spindrift investigators predicted that if an eventual proof for the psi phenomenon called E.S.P., Extra Sensory Perception, ever surfaces, it might come from linking a participant's thoughts to a mechanism in a computer machine rather than to another human being. Machines/computers are not humans observing or thinking about psi. It might give new meaning to read *only* memory *(rom)*. To paraphrase John Klingbeil, "Can I read your mind precisely? No. The tenor of a person's mind **changes constantly**. A computer's mechanisms have more constancy. It may be easier to **read** a steady mechanism in a computer than to read a human mind."

John added, "An advanced computer is likely to be a reader of certain human thoughts itself." Why? Because a human observer makes unconscious observations of his experiment, thus he influences his experiment. This quantum influence may not be observed in the same way by a steady **impersonal** computer, instead of a **personal** mind doing the observing. Future computers may learn to anticipate what humans are thinking.

CYBER-SPIRITUALITY

The Klingbeils predicted that computers might evolve from being machines that calculate data to encompassing a *cyber-consciousness* including a cyber-spirituality. They believed that computers will learn to read the minds of human beings. Think of the scary prospects of a computer praying for a human being after it reads and diagnoses his thoughts! (A religious woman working in artificial intelligence, AI, told me that in 2010, there are plans to begin using robots in church aisles as ushers to take the collection.)

CYBER-PSI

John Klingbeil's futuristic foresight, that computers will someday read minds and perceive prayers from human beings, and that human beings will pray for computers, may resonate well with future AI computers becoming artificially intelligent. The mental interchange between man and machine could become routine.

On page 196 of *The Conscious Universe* by Dean Radin, Ph.D., **is a futuristic suggestion for thought-patterns affecting computers.** " . . . the pattern-recognition methods used in advanced sonar and radar systems would be useful in psi-based systems that could be trained to respond to individual thought-patterns at a distance." In 2006, through a neurological implant called Brain Gate, a human being can think commands, which the implant converts into wireless actions that turn on a computer and control it.

IN THE ZONE

I have been fascinated with gifted people such as Mozart, Leonardo da Vinci, some modern day musicians, inventors, and athletes. Spindrift suggests that the defense mechanisms in our subconscious minds often have the agenda of shifting our attention away from recognizing psychic information which may influence extraordinary gifts. The Klingbeils proposed that extraordinarily gifted individuals are dwelling in a psychic soup of freedom of thought and creative information which they may sometimes sense. Often when a researcher goes looking for the proof of the influence of psychic information dwelling in the gifted person, the defense mechanisms kick in, and the proof vanishes.

This vanishing psychic influence of psychic information may ring a bell about the argument that there exists such a thing as a *hot hand* in sports. For you **sports fans**, here is what the Klingbeils told me about athletic ability and its relation to psychic influence on excellence. Peak performances have suggested to some sports fans that there is more to an athlete's gift and extraordinary ability than meets the eye. Some athletes have a hot hand. This hot hand would be the sports equivalent of psi hitting. In parapsychology psi hitting is when a psychic event occurs which is analyzed for its occurrence of happening beyond chance. Psi hitting at times might be the "peak" in peak athletic performances.

Some prominent statisticians decided to investigate this sports issue of the hot hand. They centered on basketball players in the NBA, the National Basketball Association.

After working on the NBA figures, the statisticians concluded there was no such thing as a hot hand. The conclusion of the statisticians hasn't convinced sport writers and sports fans. They feel something extra sensory-extra physical is operating sometimes on the basketball court. Athletes call this extra feeling **being in the zone.**" Some parapsychologists feel there is "**a zone phenomenon.**" A book about the zone-effects from psi in sports activities is titled *In The Zone* by Michael Murphy and Rhea White, New York Penguin-Arkana, 1995.

Spindrift hasn't analyzed the basketball players in the NBA. What Spindrift has done is track and analyze test data which was apparently the result of influences by the mind. The Klingbeils felt there is some mathematical evidence to support this hot hand contention. Then a *cool hand*, a defense mechanism, conceals the special contribution of the hot hand. The news today is, there is a hot hand in the mind at work.

Could it be that when we witness extraordinary moments of great athletes, musicians, or actors at work, we are unconsciously admiring their hot hand abilities? We desire to achieve it because it's an outcome of quality which exceeds average human behavior. We wish to experience that in the zone feeling. When we witness peak performances in the arts and athletics, boundaries of human behavior are broken temporarily.

In the zone moments suggest that an action of consciousness is involved. A gifted person gets into the zone more easily, but the **hot hand** is apparently operating in the minds of each of us unknown to us. Quantum physicists are saying that there is no such thing as *passive observations* of things we experience. That means the mind is involved and subtly impacts what is observed.)

COLLECTIVE WITNESSES

The Klingbeils' idea was to demonstrate an experimental way to help close the gap between individual experience and collective experience. Our individual experiences of prayer and the paranormal are often misunderstood when we explain them to our friends. At best, the experiences get exaggerated in their minds. At worst, our friends don't believe our experiences and give us "the evil eye." Together, a collective group of people would experience subtle displays of prayer and the paranormal. Then the group would more cohesively agree upon what was experienced as an event of consciousness rather than an event of coincidence or craziness.

EXPERIMENTS AND EXPERIENCES

Recent research suggests that there is room for experiments and experiences. Perception and reality are likely intertwined. Consciousness researchers are theorizing that maybe our personal experiences and subjective interpretations of our lives are small spokes rotating on a larger wheel called the universe. In fact, the universe is probably influenced by our small subjective experiences! Caltech's Christof Koch told the *Chicago Tribune*, "We might have to introduce a new thing in the universe called experience."

Ronald Kotulak, writer of the article, wrote:

> The discovery of electricity in the 18th Century gave people a new understanding of the world. Physicists had thought that they could explain everything mechanically. To understand electricity,

however, they had to explain magnetism, because a moving magnetic field generates an electric current.

They had to admit that something as invisible as a magnetic field was a fundamental property of the universe. In a similar fashion, the explanation of [physical] consciousness may require the existence of another unseen property of the universe [experience]. (*Chicago Tribune*, 5/19/02, Section 2, p. 3.)

"Experience" itself might be a key to understanding the operation of physical consciousness. The term *physical consciousness* refers to Twenty-first Century research which involves the theory that the brain evolves consciousness. The Spindrift research suggests that there is a spiritual consciousness in the background underlying our "experiences" which can be tapped by prayer and holy thought.

If an underlying spiritual consciousness is accessible, it is unseen by our visible world. If this background consciousness were shown to be a real possibility, this discovery would help us to understand better our experiences and creative thinking. The originator of the following quote didn't have in mind what I do. Even so, his quote is thought provoking. Berkeley physicist Henry Stapp stated that "The fundamental process of Nature lies outside space-time but generates events that can be located in space-time."

In his book, *Neither Brain nor Ghost,* Dr. Teed Rockwell argues for man having an enlarged consciousness, a "behavioral field," which emerges from the interactions of body, brain, and world, rather than everything being experienced only in the brain. Teed Rockwell states that to assume the brain is actually responsible for all our experiences is to assume that a brain put in a chemical vat would be conscious. Consciousness and the brain "are not a closed system." Rather our experiences are open borders for entering effects not explained by the brain alone.

Chapter Six

The Skeptics

The charge to Peter was feed my sheep: not try
experiments on my rats.

C.S. Lewis

There have always been taboos, prohibitions, and
restrictions surrounding the supernatural . . . .
Religious orthodoxy decrees dabbling in the
paranormal to be a sin; CSICOP ridicules such
dabbling. The effect is the same. Both religious
orthodoxy and atheists enforce a taboo; both shun
paranormal phenomena . . . .

George Hansen,
The Trickster and the Paranormal, p. 161

Bruce and John were very optimistic about their research
during the 1970's and early 1980's. They were optimistic
despite the fact that the publicity campaigns to promote Spindrift
did not work. Besides the religious critics crying heresy for
experimenting with prayer and the scientific skeptical
debunkers, no one was paying any attention to the Klingbeils'
work. Beginning in 1983 our attention was increasingly spent
on the negative attention to Bruce, John, and Spindrift. Some
of the attention came from various skeptical debunkers: the
Amazing James Randi, The Central Illinois Skeptic's literate
Andrew Skolnick, The Bay Area Skeptics in San Francisco—
BAS, The Committee to Scientifically Investigate Claims of

the Paranormal—CSICOP, and The Committee for Rational Inquiry—CRI.[1]

These skeptics were frustrating contacts. When tests of consciousness were operating, they avoided witnessing them. After one skeptic indicated he would view a test, he refused to drive forty-five minutes to our lab. From 1984 until 1990 not one of our tests was tried or witnessed by them. We naively believed that the skeptics were interested in how to test *thought.* The prize money offered by James Randi and the Bay Area Skeptics for anyone who could demonstrate a psychic phenomenon piqued John Klingbeil's interest. John thought the prize money and publicity would help Spindrift. We slow learners came to realize the skeptics maintained the excuse that the Klingbeils' objectives in a test were unclear. Virtually every time there was a stumbling block to a test proposal; a lack of clarity of what was being demonstrated was given as the excuse.

PARANOID ABOUT THE PARANORMAL

Referring to the Klingbeils and their research, skeptic/magician/reporter Andrew Skolnick said to me, "Then you get it from both sides: us skeptics and the church goers." Skolnick's words had the ring of truth. The Klingbeils took knocks from zealots on "both sides" of the issue: the believers and the debunkers. The Klingbeils and Spindrift's board of directors learned about the emotional feelings from both camps, and we added some of our own emotional salvos in return.

Christians were *paranoid* about testing prayer. Skeptics were *prayer-annoyed* about testing prayer. The skeptic and the believer usually agreed on one point: the Klingbeils' tests could not possibly work. The skeptical debunker would generally say that prayer could not work because there is no proof there is a God in the first place, and there is no proof of *action at a distance* in the second place. The believer would generally say that God would not allow such tests to work.

The test results must be from Satan and animal magnetism. Another reason is, the *action of holy faith at a distance* is from God, and God's pure qualities of faith cannot be measured by the inferior limited tools of fleshy human scientists.

Church people were generally unreasonable and would cut off dialogue immediately. In contrast, the skeptics used reason to fight reason. Spindrift could reason and dialogue with the skeptical debunkers.

SKEPTICS ALIAS DEBUNKERS

The whole skeptics venture was my fault. No one else would listen to us at Spindrift, so I contacted the skeptics starting with James Randi. I am sorry I put the Klingbeils and the board of directors through this frustrating time. I have listened to a tape of me talking with Spindrift's lawyer. The lawyer vehemently kept telling me to forget about the skeptics because Spindrift's purpose is research, not contests for money, but I did not listen to his advice. He yelled, "They're magicians! They'll be two steps ahead of you!"

SPIRITED LETTER WRITING

We at Spindrift did get a good flow of letters back and forth (one hundred pages of correspondence) from the skeptical debunkers. We did appreciate their sweat and toil here, but the skeptics had excuses not to observe or replicate our tests. Like one skeptic told me basically, "We don't believe it will work, so why should we try it?" This response was very confusing to us. We thought the skeptics did investigations of paranormal claims. Didn't the Klingbeils have paranormal claims? Yes.

Skeptic, professor, and magician, Ray Hyman, said a soybean test was designed properly, but the test never did get witnessed by a skeptic. Ray Hyman advised that the more intelligent a psychic researcher, the more cleverly his mind deceives him.

LESSONS LEARNED

We did learn a few things from the debunking skeptics. First, they did answer letters more often than other groups. Second, we felt we learned to be more precise in stating what a test proved or disproved. However, the skeptics would disagree as to whether the Klingbeils were precise enough. Third, the skeptics expressed emotionalism that was on par with those fundamentalist Christians with whom we had contacts. We were heated emotionally ourselves. We were upset that others' claims were looked into while ours were written off. Fourth, the skeptics complained that most of our tests were not done double blind. Double blind means no one, not even the person praying, knows what object is being prayed for in a test. Spindrift has failed sufficiently to communicate, and the skeptics and scientists have failed to realize, that it is not necessary, *in some test designs*, to run the tests double blind. Single blind is good enough. Single blind means only the person praying for the test knows what the object of prayer is, until the test is done. As John Klingbeil points out in the following way:

> **It seems obvious that prayer . . . for a patient requires that the practitioner know who the patient is.** Prayer, unlike a drug, cannot be put in some pills and not in others and distributed to patients on the basis that neither the doctor, the technician, or the patient, or anyone, knows who gets what until after the test is over and the results are evaluated.

> It is clear that if a patient's faith in a pill produces a result on the patient's body this is not necessarily "paranormal" because the mind of the patient is linked to his body through the nervous system . . . . However, if an experimenter's faith (that a practitioner's prayers were producing results on some yeast in a pot) actually produced predictable and

repeatable results on the yeast, these results would be considered "paranormal" because there is no nervous system linking the experimenter, or anyone, to the yeast in the pot . . . . In other words—double-blind or not—the effect would be "paranormal" and the prize money should be collected if such a connection could be demonstrated.[2]

Fifth, if a test were actually successful, the skeptics would not say so or hand over prize money *until they themselves could perform the test successfully.*

We laughed many times about their praying to God because most of the skeptics dealing with us were atheists or agnostics. Since they don't believe in God, if they had to replicate a prayer test, whom would they pray to? What would they pray about? Would they fold their hands? Would they utter a mantra? It's funny, but it is not impossible for them to learn how to pray. John Klingbeil gave me an answer to this added requirement the skeptics threw at us. These are John's words:

Let's just take it from a very practical standpoint. If you say it is possible for a man to lift 400 pounds and you get a man to lift 400 pounds, you have proved your experiment. A man can lift 400 pounds.

Then if you find that 10% of the population can lift 400 pounds, you can say the effect is fairly wide spread among the population; 10% can lift 400 pounds. Now that the skeptics have to lift 400 pounds in order to believe that it is possible, is ridiculous.

On the other hand, if they go through all the weight training and pumping iron and everything else that is needed to be able to do it, then maybe they'll be able to do it. But to say that in order to believe anything is possible, you have to be able to do it personally, is not scientific. If "x" percent of the population can do it, then it is provable.

If they wish to learn how to do it, there are all kinds of religions that are set up to make them be able to. But until they go through the process of learning how to pray, and then praying, it's ridiculous to say that it cannot be done. (1989 tape)

Having skeptics and atheists pray (or whatever they do) for the same tests is good science. It's a way to check if they could produce healing effects that look like the prayer patterns produced by believers.

If the skeptics produced a holy prayer-pattern that met the parameters of a test, this outcome would raise questions for scientists to probe. Could universal healing prayer be a component in the life of most of mankind? (Some skeptics would at least produce the placebo prayer pattern.)

The sixth point that Spindrift is still learning from the skeptics is that an understanding of magic tricks has to be part of a serious investigation of action at a distance which includes prayer and healing. A scientist must protect against fraud and his own self-deception about what he sees. Many of the skeptics are trained magicians. Spindrift still has not gotten around to studying magic. We reluctantly have seen the importance of this magic training. The following is an example of the sixth point, the penalty for not understanding magic.

MAGIC AND MIRACLES

Awareness of magic can point out many conscious, unconscious, and deceptive cues that *subtly* are mixed into a test of psi and prayer. The problem is, how will learning magic play in Peoria? Not well, especially with Christians. Many view magic as an occult practice. One is just asking for "resistance." Yet, if scientists as experimentalists are sometimes being deceived by magic tricks, some scientists need to learn the tricks, or they will be put out of business. This situation is what happened to the McDonnell Laboratory for Psychical Research at Washington University. Over six years the head of McDonnell Douglas infused $630,000 for psychic research.[3] It was shown by the debunking skeptics that among the psychics who got results in the laboratory was a magician. He wasn't a psychic at all. The magician was planted there for the purpose of ridiculing the laboratory. It was an effective infiltration. The magician and his debunking colleagues ruined the scientists' reputations. The research was killed.

When the McDonnell lab was operating, the Klingbeils made several contacts with the lab's manager, Peter Phillips. There was no response regarding Spindrift's work.

Will Spindrift ever hire a magician as a quality control expert? Not so far. Spindrift would have never known magic to be a *significant* subject for inclusion in fringe scientific research if it were not for the persistence of the skeptics. Skeptics have done a remarkable service exposing fake psychics and fakery in faith healing. This exposure of fakery seems to be their *actual* purpose.

Magician/skeptics like James Randi say that Jesus Christ was just displaying magic tricks with his miracles and the healing of multitudes. Experiences with magic *sour* skeptical debunkers into believing that one hundred percent of documented spiritual miracles are a deception foisted on naive people "untrained in magic." Unfortunately the skeptics have a point. **Healing a person can be manipulated and exaggerated to fool people.** Then later what was seen or heard is repeated as a testimony of fact about the healing. Such testimonies of miracles and healings are often how "urban myths" get started. **Instances of the manipulation of spiritual healing furnishes one good reason why a scientific experiment of prayer is so necessary in our modern world.**

ONE CHANCE IN A MILLION

I met with millionaire, Henry Belk, to obtain funding for Spindrift. He was "big time" on funding psychic research. He told me about a project he funded dealing with the ability of a leading psychic surgeon to heal. Ten different doctors, M.D.'s, witnessed up close this surgeon as he reached into people's bodies and pulled out diseased tissues. The doctors were amazed. They gave their approval that this psychic surgeon was genuine. *One or two magicians would have been smarter witnesses. The surgeon's magic abilities were gradually uncovered.* He was a fake. The doctors thought they saw what they knew. They were not trained to see what was "distracting" them.

Henry Belk told me he felt earlier, when the ten M.D.'s were observing the surgery, the psychic surgeon did genuine healing. Mr. Belk asked, "Why did he drop from his high estate later and do dishonest magic? How dare he?" I found it hard to believe that this millionaire still thought the psychic surgeon could do genuine psychic surgery even though the surgeon was found faking the surgery. It goes to show that the human mind can believe anything it wants to believe.

My interview with Mr. Belk didn't go well. I knew Spindrift was not going to receive any money from the millionaire as he did not care for our prayer research. He mailed me some of his scientific psychic proofs with a note that read, "Mr. Sweet. Your feeble attempts to be *scientific* were juvenile and amusing as I was once equally so stupid." Well, he was the expert.

CARDS CALLED ON THE CARPET

In one of Spindrift's parapsychology tests which involved guessing one of two pictures in an envelope, the magicians claimed they could pick the correct picture every time. Indeed, a magician was able to do our test that way. He did it through feeling differences on the envelopes. We countered by having people wear surgeon's gloves or thin gloves. The magician offered that there are other ways to mark or cue envelopes to skew the tests. We countered that, if the person took the test and did it honestly, what the magician was talking about would not be a problem. The response was that the honesty of a participant could not be guaranteed; therefore, the card test could not be safe-guarded.

NEGOTIATIONS

Bruce, John, and the project administrator of Spindrift, John Andrews, tried many ways to negotiate details of how the skeptics could scientifically test the Klingbeils while they prayed for an experiment. One example is the following. In 1987 Bruce and John Klingbeil were planning to spend two weeks to a month in Colorado at a scientific laboratory. The Klingbeils proposed that they would setup and prayerfully perform several times at a distance a test of healing soybeans stressed by heat. The test would be performed live by Bruce Klingbeil for representatives of the Bay Area Skeptics (BAS), a San Francisco area scientific skeptical debunking group. Negotiations fell apart.

SKEPTICAL HUMOR

Bruce and John enjoyed a twist on an old joke.

> A believer and a skeptic were standing on the shore of a lake. A holy man appeared before them in flowing robe and bare feet. The holy man said to the two observers in a wise voice, "Watch me!"

> Alas! The holy man began walking on the water. The believer exclaimed, "Do you see a man walking on water?" The skeptic said, "No, I see a man who doesn't swim."

During one period of Spindrift's research the advertising slogan "Where's the beef?" was in vogue. Spindrift was exchanging letters with the skeptics, but where's the beef? No test was undertaken. I write comedy, but I had nothing to do with later attempts to get the skeptics to conduct or witness our yeast test. Spindrift supporters on the West Coast cooked up mailing various skeptic organizations humorous postcards and little packets of yeast to remind them we wanted the yeast experiment tested. Some supporters around the country joined in the mailing.

CSICOP is an acronym for The Committee for the Scientific Investigation of Claims of the Paranormal. It is a committee of skeptics (debunkers). I had experience writing humor but could not have come up with as comic an idea as the committee some Spindrifters formed called CSIPHOO. CSIPHOO was a spoof mailed to CSICOP. CSIPHOO was an acronym for The Committee for the Scientific Investigation of Paradigmatic Hubris and Other Oddies. The spoof was tried after the skeptics turned down our request that they test the Klingbeils.

The six years of negotiating with the skeptics was an exciting time but resulted in not one test. The following minutes from a California Spindrift supporter's meeting in December 1988 indicate this sentiment.

> Correspondence was reviewed. The postcard campaign [with the skeptics] was discussed and felt to be a qualified failure . . . . During general discussion the following conclusions were reached. Spindrift is not strong enough, solvent enough, or well organized enough to deal seriously with BAS/ CSICOP . . . . It was felt that if we had a base of 500 subscribers, and hopefully some with credentials (we already have clergy and one M.D.) that a pledge week should be held where people pledge to write letters instead of give money and send those letters [to the skeptics] all in one week. This would take a

lot of organizing and is best left till we have a larger and more solid base . . . . The researchers have been answering CSICOP correspondence . . . . Rather than continuing our postcard campaign, a visual or sensory protest in the form of a cartoon/package should be sent on a regular schedule to both BAS and CSICOP [Some cartoons were sent] . . . The meeting adjourned at 10:40 p.m.

In 1989, Bruce Klingbeil addressed a room full of about 75 people interested in scientifically substantiating a psychic claim that could be tested by the skeptics. Bruce recommended:

Just get together, and get the money and the expertise together, to go after these skeptics that claim they offer prizes and give you the run-around. . . . these people who are going around and garnering tons of publicity and selling everybody the belief that there is nowhere in the world a repeatable test of mind/matter relationship which is unmediated by the human nervous system. [If you] get together the money and the talent . . . . All of a sudden the publicity will go the other way . . . .

[A well planned test strategy] could open the doors of funding for all the parapsychological and other similar types of enterprises that are underfunded, understaffed, and undermanned. . . . These people [the funders] have a lot to gain by seeing us succeed. . . . instead of running from the skeptics, we will go to these skeptics and say . . . . 'We've got a couple good technicians here. We've gotten some funding money together. We are ready to set up an operation in such and such a lab at such and such a time.' . . . it takes organization; and I would say to a room full of people, if you're interested in doing this, organize and do it. (on tape)

Negotiations with the skeptics simmered; communication, after six years, ended in 1990.

FUNDAMENTALISM

The skeptics agreed with Bruce and John on one subject, the religious ruffians of the world, known as fundamentalists. Bruce was worried about the concentrated faith, actions, and rewards in heaven believed by religious fundamentalists. Christians blowing up abortion clinics was bad enough. The following excerpt is from *The Devil & Dr. Church* by F. Forrester Church, page 15. It was written in 1986, fifteen years before 9/11.

"Fight for the religion of God," the Koran reads, and so diehard believers do: hijacking planes, blowing up cars, driving trucks filled with dynamite into buildings filled with people. Instant heaven, smiling all the way. [How many atheists are suicide bombers? None.]

PRAYER DOES PAY

Skeptics say prayer doesn't pay. To the contrary, take the story of October 3, 1996, reported on CNN. A business man from Mexico went to Stockholm, Sweden. The man passed a Catholic church. He went inside. In front of the church was an unmarked closed casket. The business man prayed for the unknown person. He signed the registrar. His was the only name.

Upon returning to Mexico he received a letter from the church. He was informed he was the inheritor of the man's will. The decease's will indicated that anyone who prayed for his soul would inherit his fortune. The business man from Mexico became an instant millionaire.

Chapter Seven

Agents of Science or Satan?

Prayer is an accepted part of American life and so is the scientific method. However, any combination of the two is, in some culturally biased way, a great big no-no.

John Klingbeil[1]

I explained my interest in Spindrift to a friend. He replied in effect, "Your ideas may be important, but I think they should be worked out in therapy first."

Bill Sweet

As a youngster I was occasionally surprised by psychic experiences that happened to me. When I turned fifteen, I started thinking in detail about these experiences I was having. Much to my surprise I stopped having most of these experiences. *By consciously thinking about them*, I had lost something, and I knew it. "There is a door in the mind that opens with acceptance, and closes with judgment of any kind" wrote Paul Ferrini.

HOW DO YOU NOT CONSCIOUSLY THINK OR PRAY?

I wondered if it could be when you think too much about a native psychic ability, you cancel it? Could it be, in order to predict with psi, you couldn't premeditate on it? How does one let unconscious thinking **perform** without being cutoff by conscious thinking? It reminds me of someone saying aloud, "Now, don't you think about pink elephants!" It seems impossible *to not consciously think* about pink elephants.

YOUTH AND PSI

As we grow up, do we forget to listen to the software of our soul? Could it be that as a child we listen *unconsciously* to the software of our soul, then, as a young person, we switch subtly to listening consciously to the hardware of our brain? Do our unconsciously produced youthful psi effects subtly fade away? Somehow, someday, I was going to find out more on the subject.

THE SPINDRIFT TEAM

Through meeting the Klingbeils I learned that "Every thought is an afterthought" appears to explain part of the reason why the appearance of psychic and spiritual phenomena do not always work when we want them to. By the time one *consciously* reflects on something, it is a second-hand thought, an afterthought. That is, psychic and spiritual thought is first thought unconsciously, then second, consciously produced. Initially thought is formed in the realm of the origin, the unconscious mind. As children we do not know about these distinctions.

The Spindrift team experimented in the unconscious part of consciousness. The initial, raw, native materials of thought, which children apparently can address more purely than most adults, is an important clue in the search for mental and spiritual phenomena. **Maybe the unconscious mind is a conscious mind, but we don't know it. How unconscious thought gives** a flash of an unpremeditated conscious event might be illustrated by the following experience of Dr. Albert Schweitzer.

> . . . at sunset, we were making our way through a herd of hippopotamuses, there flashed through my mind, unforeseen and unsought, the phrase, "Reverence for Life." . . . Now I knew that the world-view of [an] ethical world and life-affirmation, together with the ideals of civilization, is founded in thought.[2]

The founders of Spindrift prayed to open a window to the world of unconscious thought. Simultaneously, these founders pried open a Pandora's box of resistance.

The words of science writer Martin Gardner may best describe why the "Pandora's box of resistance" was opened. In 1983, Mr. Gardner wrote, "As for empirical tests of the power of God to answer prayer, I am among those theists who . . . consider such tests both futile and blasphemous . . . . Let us not tempt God."

If someone asked me what was a typical criticism of the Spindrift tests, the following would characterize it. "Your test results are not from God or prayer. Your test results are from the Devil and malicious thought. Scientifically pursuing psi is the equivalent of pursuing demonology, witchcraft, and black magic."

BREAKING THE ICE AND GETTING ONE'S FEET WET

When I met Bruce and John Klingbeil, they were of the naive opinion that there would not be much of a "struggle" in presenting scientific descriptions of prayer and healing. However, the presentations had to be done "in the right way" to be acceptable. Acceptable to whom?

Acceptable to certain researchers in mainstream science, medicine, and parapsychology. These areas were where any possibility of quantifying thought would break out.

A recognition that "the right thing at the wrong time might not be the right thing" was resolved partly by the Klingbeils in the following way. There is "a tension in society" between those who have no interest or resist "quantifications" of thought, prayer, and healing with those few inquiring people in the advance guard who are researching ways to "quantify thought." Society is advancing and receding on several fronts. The scientific front is leading society in obvious ways. Sounding like futurists, the Klingbeils postulated in a *general* way, that if degrees of "quality spirituality" were not mixed-in, science and technology would "doom" rather than "bless" society.

In a *specific* way the Klingbeils noted that, even though society did not take seriously that "things of the spirit" could be quantified, society was asking for quantification, especially in miracle cases where a person's health needs might be turned over to a perceived quack's "unscientific spiritual methods." There were several kinds of tensions here. After much contemplation and prayer, between 1969 and 1974, the Klingbeils concluded that both a religious and a scientific approach to understanding aspects of prayer and thought could progress if investigated properly. Full-time research began in January 1975.

EMOTIONS UNLEASHED

It is safe to state that some people's unconscious emotions erupt when Spindrift adds elements of *religion* to the research mix. One of my first assignments for the Klingbeils was to find an actuarial statistician. Such a trained statistician had fees like a lawyer, a hundred dollars per hour in the early 1980's. I found one who showed a subjective interest in spirituality herself. The Klingbeils sent her a book on Spindrift's

work. Calling her later, I heard a different tone. She had tried
to get some spiritual nourishment for herself from the book.
She essentially said, "If this complicated business is what it takes
to gain spirituality, the journey is not worth it. **Your test
descriptions made me feel ill.** I gave up trying to figure your
book out. I threw the book across the room several times. I finally
threw it in the trash can." I was so sorry that happened to her.
The "tensions" caused by the data and descriptions of thought
and spirituality upset her equilibrium. Her unhappy reaction
would not be an isolated reaction. Perhaps the Klingbeils were
wrong. Maybe it was not the right time for society to like or
accept the quantitative approaches to spirituality and science
that Spindrift postulated.

Comedian/author Steve Allen on page 33 of *Dumbth* has
given us an example of the reactions that religion had toward a
new scientific approach.

> . . . when anesthetics were discovered more than a
> century ago, the Scottish physician Sir James
> Simpson recommended their use in childbirth. He
> was quickly rebuked by many clergymen who
> reminded him that God had said to Eve, "In sorrow
> thou shalt bring forth children" (Genesis 3:16). If a
> woman was under the influence of chloroform, the
> clergy inquired, how could she properly sorrow?
>
> Dr. Simpson was clever enough to argue that since
> God had reportedly put Adam to sleep (when he
> extracted the rib from which woman was made) there
> would seem to be nothing wrong in principle in
> administering anesthetics to men, at least. Believe it
> or not, it took some time before its benefits could be
> extended to women.

The foregoing sounds similar to some people's reactions to
Spindrift's research of prayer and consciousness.

In 1989, Bruce Klingbeil asked a mathematician at a university to recommend for Spindrift a book on statistics. The mathematician's reply was "a diatribe of hate for Mary Baker Eddy [founder of Christian Science] describing her as 'a power hungry bitch.'"[3]

A Spindrift member relates, "A fundamentalist Christian, who was also a relative, became so upset when I agreed to pray during a Spindrift test that he entered the room where I was praying and shot and killed my dog, who was lying quietly on the floor."[4]

The following incidents occurred to the author. "I had a man tell me that our Spindrift experiments do not show anything spiritual. In fact, it's Satan bringing out the results in our experiments, and that's all it is. I said to him, 'Well, isn't that fantastic. We have the first scientific proof of Satan. That in itself is a breakthrough!' He didn't know what to say. He had no place to go." (on tape)

In 2003, a fundamentalist Christian sent me e-mails which emphatically warned that parapsychology is controlled by demons. So is the Christian Science religion. I'd better forsake my research and religion. If not, I was serving Satan.

TERMINOLOGY TRIGGERS TROUBLE

In the early 1980's, John Klingbeil was at a print shop making copies of his test findings. A religious person peeked over and noticed a few familiar religious words and asked John what was he copying. John said he had been doing tests of thought and prayer. The man seemed interested and asked questions. John said that his tests were able to put some of the factors which occur in prayer, such as **resistance to change** (r), the degree of **holy-ordered thought** (Q), and the **faith-direction in thought** (F), **into mathematical equations.** The man said to John, "Jesus Christ is the only equation!"

Spindrift has never been able to present terminology that has pleased very many people. Spindrift has combined terminology from the sciences, the Bible, medicine, and parapsychology. Those New Age spiritual seekers who prefer descriptions of mystical experiences of the right brain tend to dislike the left brain scientific descriptions analyzing experiments that Spindrift spits out. Spindrift's use of scientific terminology is enough of a red flag for some religious people. Add, to that scientific vocabulary, parapsychology terminology, and the already alienated religious people step even further away from the prayer and consciousness research. Describe Spindrift's prayer work in theological terminology, and some scientists and even some parapsychologists completely write Spindrift off. Generally speaking, people who are interested in the healing-arts, like doctors, nurses and other healers, are the most tolerant of Spindrift's **unpopular hybrid terminology**. *In my estimation, healers tend to be interested in essences instead of arguments.*

I cannot help but think of a humorous paragraph in *The Miracle Of Prayer* by Rosemary Ellen Guiley, which echoes true in a Spindrifter's ears. The following depicts the trouble triggered by a researcher's using terminology which is perceived as incendiary or offensive to describe his experiment:

> George De La Warr published an article, "Blessing Plants to Increase Their Growth," in *Mind and Matter*, his own journal. He invited readers to validate his results. He outlined a fifteen-step procedure that called for holding bean seeds and reverently blessing them in accordance with one's faith or denomination. The readers loved this, but the Roman Catholic Church did not. The Church scolded De La Warr in a letter, stating that no one below the rank of deacon could perform a blessing. Mere lay persons could only ask the Creator to perform a blessing. To placate the Church, De La Warr gave a new euphemistic name to his

experiment: "Increasing the Rate of Plant Growth by the Mental Projection of an Undefined Energy."

A Spindrift experimenter relates the following experiences:

> A board member of my church was so apprehensive about Spindrift mixing science and religion that she wrote to the denominational headquarters about her concerns. Part of their response was " . . . the thesis—that the efficacy of . . . healing can be measured by the effects of mental tests on seeds and yogurt—is totally contrary" to the teachings of the church. Acting on this reply, my church board added "to the list of interview questions [for membership] one which asked specifically whether or not an applicant was involved with an organization called Spindrift." My church and headquarters deemed Spindrift heretical.[5]

> Not knowing how much a church member, an objector to Spindrift, *really* knew about our research, I told him that someday I would like to tell him about Spindrift. His reply was "not in this world or the next." This individual had never talked to me about Spindrift even though I had been a president of Spindrift. His information came mainly from people who were vehemently opposed to what they believed Spindrift was doing.[6]

BE CAREFUL WHAT YOU SAY AND HOW YOU SAY IT

If I mention to most people that there is subtle psychic phenomena going on in life around us, they say, "Well, frankly I believe that also." If I continue and mention that I like to study parapsychology, they may hint that I am taking my likes too far. I crossed the line from a *safe* subject to an *occult* subject even though what I was talking about was essentially the same subject, parapsychology. If I mention I like plants, that is safe to say to people. If I mention I like religious prayer, that is safe to say to people. Combine prayer, plants, and parapsychology and mention "I believe prayer can be parapsychologically tested on plants in a scientific laboratory," and the responses range from stunned to unfriendly. The previous quote is how Spindrift has packaged its descriptions which have caused *terror* for some people. Spindrift's word combinations and descriptions have not been the "safe" way to describe its activities. Perhaps if Spindrift simply said, "We like plants. We like prayer. We like subtle energy. We like subtle healing. And we like science." That terminology would conjure up fewer roadblocks and cause Spindrift's research to be more acceptable. **It's how you package the research that contributes to how high you register on someone's cuckoo meter.**[7]

I recall a funny story. A Chicago area church had its Grounds Committee meet in front of the church. A tree was not in a good spot. A man suggested the tree be moved. "The tree wouldn't survive the move," someone said. The man said, "Well, we'll pray for the tree." A woman I know turned to the man and said, "Are you part of Spindrift?"

If she had never heard of Spindrift, praying for the preservation of the tree would have been her natural instinct. A newspaper reporter records that even Mary Baker Eddy prayed for a group of transplanted trees.[8] A friend told me, "Spindrift has a bad reputation. People hear that name and think negative things. They don't think beyond the name."

Most religious people can get emotional on choice subjects. One has to hit an emotionally charged issue, and boom! Emotions blare. Blood boils.

In the early 1980's, a woman heard about people being prayer-tested at Spindrift. She was asked by a Spindrifter to pray for a test herself. On the way over to the lab site to be tested, the woman stopped by her minister's house and mentioned where she was going. When she arrived at the lab, instead of being tested, she stood in the kitchen and told her Spindrift friend what her minister said. He said essentially that the tests were the work of the Devil and were going to lead the Spindrift adherents to hell. The minister added that the church her Spindrift friend belonged to was a non-Christian cult, and that information should tell her that the tests were wrong to do right there. The woman stood by the stove and sincerely proceeded to save her friend from going to hell.

In 1980, I had to defend my strange ideas on religion and science to a friend. She responded in effect, "Bill, you won't accept it, but you are *mesmerized*. Understand it is my job to get you free of your wrong beliefs, but you are persistent and I can't." I found the friendship was over.

In 1981, I gave material on the prayer experiments to a church friend to check out. When returning the material, about the only comment I got was something like, "Stay away from it. I have asked around. The Klingbeils are dangerous and what they are doing is dangerous."

In 1988, I contacted a man involved in physics before he went into the ministry. I believed he would be interested in Spindrift's research. He blew his top! He said that our tests of prayer were wrong, unethical, and our motives weren't pure enough. He said that we couldn't possibly get results because God doesn't work that way; that God doesn't allow measurements of holiness. He said our experiments of prayer were an embarrassment to the church. He firmly recommended that we stop doing the experiments. I said, "I can't understand you saying that with your background." He said, "I can **compartmentalize** physics and theology just fine."

In 1989, when I began to speak about the experiments to a female church friend, she cut in: "Don't you dare bring up your experiments! I won't talk to you again!"

In 1989, another female church friend pulled up a chair and said, "I want to hear from you what all the commotion is about." After my explanation, she had a worried look and said, "Bill, you're being used by these scientists. You're being used to discredit prayer, spiritual healing, and any truth to do with God reflecting in our consciousness."

In 1996, upon hearing something good about Bruce Klingbeil and his work, a woman blurted back, "But he fed arsenic to mung beans and prayed for them!" When the Klingbeils did experiments with plants, they set up stressful situations that occur naturally in nature, such as heat, humidity, salt, overfeeding, too little moisture, ultra violet light, and so on. Not arsenic.

In 1997, a physicist and Christian Scientist said to me that Spindrift was the "opposite" of the church's teaching and "is as off track as can be." He said, "As a physicist, I think Spindrift is way off base."[9]

In 1997, a woman ranted on to me in effect:

> Experiments are the opposite way of finding out about God. God and spirituality can't be found that way because experiments are physical, not spiritual...You think you are doing important work. You're the only one who thinks so. I've never seen Spindrift mentioned. Spindrift is insignificant. Other researchers and doctors are doing their own spiritual seeking without Spindrift's help. They are spiritually seeking. You are materially seeking. They will be remembered for their spiritual research. Spindrift will be forgotten... I will do all I can, with all my energy, for as long as I live, to

stop someone like you, Bill, from using science and experiments on Christianity and my church.[10]

TO REVEAL YOUR NAME OR REMAIN ANONYMOUS?

Some of the enthusiastic support for Spindrift has come from thinkers in the Catholic Church. However, it has not been rosy for some of them. A nun who helped raise money had a bake sale for Spindrift's research. I recall she raised $180.00. She was punished by being put in solitary confinement for twenty-four hours.[11] A nun who helped write and edit articles that related to Spindrift for *The Home Catacomb* newspaper was punished for her participation. She was transferred to Guatemala by her superiors.

A series of events happened to an enthusiastic Protestant participant in Spindrift. She was removed from all her church committees because of her involvement in Spindrift. Finally she was allowed to be on the usher committee but, before ever ushering, was removed because of people's fears over her so-called skewed thinking. Also she was appointed to the mailing committee where she licked stamped envelopes. After that assignment, she was appointed to the hymnal repair committee.

A Protestant wrote to me about Spindrift and Calvinism. "John Calvin offers a Win-Lose situation for salvation. Some are saved and some are not. Your separating of seeds into prayed for and not prayed for sets reminded me of that."

A friend read that and e-mailed me:

"The alternative is to have nobody ever pray for any seeds, and they'll all be dammed. Is that really preferable?"

NEGATIVE PRAYERS

Spindrift ignited spiritual dynamite. I'll never forget a Spindrift board of directors meeting in 1985 where a letter was read from a nun who did not appreciate Spindrift. The nun wrote us, "I am praying that your yeast test blows up in your face." John Klingbeil notes, "As the years went by, our stack of hate mail grew higher and higher."[12] Spindrift supporters who did not conceal their association to the experiments found true the following saying, "Even though you are a paranoid, it doesn't mean someone isn't out to get you."

In 1984, there was a network of conservative believers who prayed against the success of the Spindrift yeast tests. These believers were outraged over Spindrift experimenting with prayer. The believers *prayed negatively that the tests of yeast would not work.* One of Bruce Klingbeil's daughters, Deborah Klingbeil, explains what happened. I quote part of Deborah's explanation.

> [I]t was not a church but a prayer circle that coordinated their prayers in an effort to sabotage the Spindrift yeast test . . . .
>
> I had a good friend . . . . She and I once took her kids to the museums in Chicago, along with my brother, and another time her oldest boy stayed overnight with me at my dad's house in suburban Chicago. So they knew my family, and had seen the yeast test set up in the living room, but didn't make anything of it.
>
> It was her mother that got upset [when she heard about the tests.] . . . the mom asked me about it, and I explained to her what we were doing. She got very upset . . . .
>
> [She] belonged to a prayer circle which met once a week and had prayer partners in prayer circles across the United States. They believed the more

people you had praying in unison the more powerful the prayer would be. It would be interesting to test that, but I don't think that is what they had in mind. My friend's mother wasn't mad at me. She simply considered me misguided and in need of saving. She thought the yeast test was demonic and the work of the anti-Christ.

Whenever something was up, prayer circles on the network were contacted by telephone. In this case three dates were set up in which 400 people, so she said, would be praying at the same time to prevent the yeast test from working. I know the people came from as far away as California because we got a letter from one of them warning us not to do the tests because the yeast would explode.

They . . . followed up on two of the dates . . . By the time of the third date they had dropped their efforts. This was for a strange reason . . . I had written a small article for *Guidepost* magazine . . . Many people in the prayer circles read this magazine. When they saw that I had written something for it, they assumed I was an OK person and that I somehow had been approved by the editors as all right. Which of course is not true, the editors knew nothing about me other than how to spell my name on a paycheck. On the basis of this *Guidepost* article the prayer circle dropped their active hostility, although I believe some continued to pray against the Spindrift tests on their own whenever they "felt called by the Lord to do so." The *Guidepost* incident bothered me much more than their negative prayers had because it showed people worked on emotion,

> not on whether the tests were right or wrong.
> It's the old good-old-boys network of who you
> know and who knows you that people judge
> you by instead of by the content of your ideas.[13]

In 1988, the Klingbeils received word that a California church outside Los Angeles held a meeting where prayers were directed to stop the Spindrift tests from working.[14]

Bruce, John, and I discussed and laughed about the onslaught of negative prayers. If Christians could be tracked while doing the negative praying, and it stopped the prayer experiments, *this negative result would be proving paranormal phenomena.* This negative focus on Spindrift was ironic. Many believers feel it is wrong or demonic to get involved with the paranormal. In effect, they were utilizing the very process whose existence they denied.

The irony is, these Christians were trying to use one paranormal power of prayer to cancel another paranormal power of prayer. Their efforts would be a twist on "Bless your enemies." Why? Because these praying people would be "proving mental action at a distance for us experimenters at Spindrift," we remarked. (See endnote 15.)

A MODERN CATACOMB

The Home Catacomb newspaper was an underground newspaper. It became a spin-off from Spindrift. *The Home Catacomb* covered items overlapping progress being made in the sciences, theology, medicine, and parapsychology. Bruce Klingbeil's second daughter, Deborah, ably guided the *Catacomb's* pages. People contributing articles to the *Catacomb* could write anonymously if they wished to protect their reputations and friendships. A writer could hide in the *Catacomb's* pages like the Christians hid in the real catacombs near Rome.

The resort to anonymity was learned from experience. Spindrift found that some people who signed their names to articles were persecuted. For example, a Catholic woman who taught at a parochial school wrote an article for the *Catacomb* entitled "A Member of the Catholic Laity Looks at the Yeast Test." Her school principal read a copy of the *Catacomb*. For writing that article she was called into the office and fired from her teaching position.[16]

A Spindrifter was called to a meeting of the elders of her church. The elders, clearly indicating her involvement was not in accord with the church, urged that she disassociate herself from Spindrift. One elder said, "We will pray for you." The implication was that the elders' prayers *would help undermine* her interest in Spindrift, which they perceived as being a misguided, anti-Christian activity. Since Spindrift was seen as wrong, praying for her separation was seen as right. (name on file)

The Klingbeils told me that early in their research a minister friend was questioned by church officials about Spindrift's tests of prayer on healing. A statement was prepared that the minister was asked to sign. The statement said in essence that it was impossible for God's power to be recorded by any scientific experiments.

These incidents sometimes caused spontaneous laughter from us on the Spindrift team, but the incidents were serious and kept flowing. In Spindrift's first newsletter in 1984, all the articles were anonymous but one. The one article was signed by Gladys Myers. One article was prepared by me, but I felt I had to sign it with a pseudonym.

NOT EXACTLY A QUIET REVOLUTION

One of the pieces of Spindrift history that would justify paranoia, had to do with the selling of books.

In 1980, John Klingbeil's first book on testing thought and prayer was *The Quiet Revolution*. John paid for the printing of one thousand copies of his book. Spindrift did some advertising in Wisconsin and Illinois with religious people including a few Christian Scientists.

One hundred orders for the book came to John's residence. He mailed them out with a bill, but out of the one hundred orders, only three people remitted a payment and only three or four returned the book. People complained that the book was not what it was purported to be. There were even **book burnings** of *The Quiet Revolution*. One group of ten Christians burned their copies together.[17] Since people kept or destroyed the book, John was out that money. Did someone get to these people? We never were able to figure out what happened. About one thousand dollars of John's was lost.

John wrote on an autographed copy of his book, "If you think it's hard reading it, you should have tried writing it."[18]

READER'S INDIGESTION

About this same time a similar incident occurred. John explains it in a letter of November 23, 1981. John mailed the letter even to those people who told him in various ways **"what you are doing must be stopped!"**

Dear (name)

In 1975 one of the founders of SPINDRIFT began making tests in his kitchen. The object of these tests was simple: to determine whether or not Christian healing was as effective for the scientist as for the sick, whether its power extended over the whole range of human experience.

Religiously minded people told him the things of the spirit could not be measured by matter. Scientifically minded people told him that without formal scientific training he could hope to accomplish nothing. Parapsychologists told him that, in many decades of trying, a repeatable experiment had never been developed. Practical people told him to get a good job.

Six years later the results had begun to form meaningful patterns, and mathematical equations had emerged, along with clear evidence of the power of Christian healing in the science room as well as in the sick room. It was possible, if we value measurements, to measure values.

A not-for-profit corporation was formed as an organizational base for continuing this work. A report was prepared and between 60 and 70 orders were taken at fifteen dollars a copy. In an abundance of good will the recipients were told "pay us when you get it."

The results were unexpected. A few checks came back and that was it. What did come back was a blast of raw emotion. One individual in a state of great upset told us they had burned the report. Others told us they were going to various church authorities for **"what you are doing must be stopped!"**

What were we doing? Praying for seeds and praying for yeast. Sounds simple, doesn't it? As simple as Charles Darwin saying "I was only writing in my notebook!"

If early responses are any indication, we are witnessing in the twentieth century the development of change with an impact similar to the impact of the theory of evolution in the nineteenth century.

However, the issue is vastly different in one fundamental way. The issue is not the power of science, but the power of God. The proofs demanded by Old and New Testament figures in ancient languages and ancient times are being asked for and received today in modern languages and modern times and ways. [Spindrift is birthing a way to speak the scientific language of our times.]

Our early efforts are available to you now. We have only one requirement: Whether you love our reports or whether you burn them, please pay for them in advance.

Income from our reports goes toward administrative expenses and toward the cost of producing the reports. Contributions to SPINDRIFT are used completely and exclusively, unless you tell us otherwise, for research in Christian healing through the experimental test.

An up-to-date order form is enclosed.

In Christian love,
John Klingbeil
President, Spindrift, Inc.

A NOVEL APPROACH

Another book John wrote was *The Healer*. I did not think the book was a good idea but was proven wrong by the *gradual* development of interest in it. The approach was to appeal to the non-scientific person through a novel. This writing experiment was to acquaint the reader with the 1970's and 1980's taboo about testing prayer. The characters were composites, but the events in the novel were true. The story dealt with the resistance of bringing scientific approaches to prayer and Christian healing, but there was not much interest.[19]

A bookstore in San Francisco that sold a lot of unusual books was interested, thinking some of their crowd would buy it. The store told a member of Spindrift that we needed to get a Library of Congress registration card before they could display it. John did so, and the store put some books on the shelf and a placard about the book.

After a month or so a Spindrift person went in to see how the book was doing. The placard was gone and the books could not be found. The Spindrifter asked the desk clerks where the books were located. The book was not going to be carried by the store was the response. The Spindrifter asked, "Where are the books?" A man in a business suit came to the store and apparently bought or took all the copies of the book. He insinuated the book was in the ball park of anti-Semitic literature, and the store certainly would not wish to carry a book that was against religion. They agreed.

In that area of town there was a magazine stand owned by a Chinese man. The same Spindrifter had a friendship with the fellow and told him about what happened. The Chinese man saw that as something that shouldn't happen in America, and he said he would sell the book.

After a few weeks a gentleman in a business suit inquired about the book. "Do you have *The Healer?*" The Chinese man acknowledged it. "How many copies do you have?" The Chinese man responded. The man added, "You don't want to be selling hate literature, do you?"

A flash in the Chinese man's mind recalled what had happened weeks earlier with a man in a business suit. The Chinese man gave the man in the business suit something to really think about.

The Chinese man telephoned his Spindrift friend, relayed the information, and added, "This is my contribution to San Francisco's freedom to read week."

Berkeley has a banned book sale. Mostly political books banned or burned from all over the world are sold. A Spindrifter told them what had happened to our book. The staff said enough had happened to qualify us for the banned book fair. Spindrift had a table, and six copies of *The Healer* were sold.

WORRY ABOUT LOSING YOUR JOB

Author and nuclear engineer, Ted Rockwell, wrote me about what he thought was behind most of the opposition to testing prayer. Ted wrote:

> The following was a new idea to me, but I finally concluded that Bruce was probably dead right.
>
> I recall a discussion with Bruce Klingbeil when I first started talking with him seriously about the Spindrift program. I asked him why opposition to the program from church authorities was so emotionally violent, when one would think they would welcome it as a demonstration of the principles on which the Church was founded.
>
> Bruce had obviously thought about this at length and was ready and clear with an answer. He said that he thought the aspect that gave them greatest concern was the fact that if one could reliably measure the effectiveness of prayer—in effect measure the holiness of an individual—this could turn out to be a weapon of awesome capability. It would put into the hands of someone outside the Church hierarchy, and outside its control, the ability to judge individuals in responsible positions in the church, and to announce to the world their fitness, or unfitness, for their job. [The *reality* of testing people's thoughts and prayers for getting jobs could create a power struggle the world has never seen before.]
>
> This situation is akin to the problem posed to the Catholic church by Martin Luther, who cried "every man his own Pope," and insisted that the church

hierarchy was not necessary to an individual's reaching an understanding of God and his duties to God—a position deemed highly destructive of the church's ability to control its organization and determine its policies. It left open to challenge its teachings and practices that had previously been open to change only from above, through and within the organization in a well-defined way.

A POT CALLING THE KETTLE BLACK

When Bruce and John Klingbeil lived in Schaumburg, Illinois, in the 1970's, they repeated a local newspaper story to me. Two experimental psychologists were investigating parapsychology. As a local opportunity, Bruce and John made an appointment with the psychologists. A very good discussion ensued, and the prospect of the two psychologists doing research together with John Klingbeil looked promising. Plans were made to meet soon and set up some prayer experiments. When "soon" came, it went. The Klingbeils repeatedly tried to understand what the stalling tactic was all about. They discovered the psychologists thought Bruce and John were two real "nut-cakes," out of their minds. Bruce and John's feelings were hurt. They "took it hard." It was a lesson in different perceptions. Here the father and son thought their meeting was productive, but the two psychologists, acting like they were interested, were just playing along.

We laughed about the perception gap. The two experimental psychologists were doing tests with psychokinesis or PK for short (moving objects with thought), tests with E.S.P. (guessing cards), and even looking into some superstitious magical areas. **They did not consider that their research was wacko.** But when Bruce and John suggested seed and yeast tests involving John praying to observe and measure an effect, the psychologists called them "nut-cakes."

TRANSITIONS

In July 1994, when Larry Dossey, M.D., spoke at the Transitions Bookplace in Chicago about *Healing Words*, his book on prayer research, a person asked him how excited were the mainline Christian churches over the research. Dr. Dossey proceeded to say that he did not think the Christian churches would be too enthusiastic. He gave the example of what happened to Bruce and John Klingbeil with their church. An approximately thirty-five year old Christian Scientist raised his hand and said something like "That's not why they were in trouble with the church. They were in trouble because that wasn't prayer they were using in those experiments. That's not prayer. They were nuts." Larry Dossey thanked him for his comment. Dr. Dossey told me he wished he could have dialogued some more with him after his talk, but the man left before he finished speaking.[20]

The man's feeling about how the Klingbeils prayed for experiments is not much different from how a scientifically trained Christian Scientist viewed Spindrift's work.

> Prayer is *not* trying to mentally influence matter. This we see as mental quackery....

> Christian Science healing is patterned directly after how Christ Jesus taught us how to pray, not after a battery of laboratory tests.... However, this spiritual standard demanding that we are just, merciful and pure, does not lend itself to material laboratory verification.

> Unlike Spindrift, we do not attempt to measure prayer by changed physical conditions.... We find the proof that divine Love heals, in the laboratory of

daily living. But because of the material assumptions inherent in the procedural designs of [prayer] laboratory experiments, and the non-material nature of spirituality, such techniques are inoperative in trying to measure the effect or the effectiveness of scientific prayer . . . .

[Spindrift speaks of non-directed] prayer as "moving a system or organism back to its norm." This sounds like manipulating matter through mental or mental and spiritual forces . . . . Nonetheless, we do appreciate the important role of natural science investigations as they relate to human welfare. We have high regard for original observations made in scientific experiments. Included among my Christian Science friends are professional physicists, chemists, biologists, geologists and hydrologists.

[Our religion's] essence can only be distilled in the laboratory of infinite Love, not in any material experimental facility. It is impossible to measure the effectiveness of the power of the Holy Ghost coming to human consciousness . . . as it would be to develop a protocol to determine how much a mother loves her children. To us "laboratory verification" of spiritual healing is an oxymoron . . . .

Not even an atomic scale can measure the spiritual power of divine Love, for Love is not learned of the material senses.[21]

Some people who are paranoids have a purpose on Earth, because I've learned that some paranoids really do have enemies.

In 1993, a woman said to me in effect, "I'm thrilled to get rid of the Klingbeils. I'll dance on their graves."

In 2001, a UFO researcher asked me for the Spindrift studies of consciousness, prayer, and healing. After receiving the studies, he e-mailed me, "NO THANK YOU . . . . Christian Science is OUT!"

In reply I wrote, "Does it make any difference to you that those of us associated with Christian Science were punished for doing our research?"

He replied, "Ah . . . now that does make a difference and thank you for bringing it to my attention. I will check out the Spindrift material. Thank you for putting me right."

In 2004, a natural scientist who went into the ministry e-mailed me, "I categorically despise what you have attempted to do under the guise of 'Christian Science.' I have absolutely NO respect for, nor interest in, your 'thoughts, feelings, wants, desires'—et al."

HARVARD AND DR. BENSON SPONSOR COURSE

When credentialed people speak, people listen. Having the Harvard Medical School and Dr. Herbert Benson sponsor a course on "Spirituality and Healing in Medicine" turns some people's heads that otherwise would not turn. It is human nature that a researcher who is not considered qualified to do research is ignored over a researcher who is recognized as qualified. Thus, the qualified people who sponsored and spoke for the Harvard course on spirituality and prayer in December 1995, made the national news including two laudable write-ups in *The Christian Science Monitor*.

After the Harvard course, *The Wall Street Journal* carried an article titled "The Healing Power of Prayer Is Tested by Science." It is encouraging to read of the investigations of nonlocal healing in the *Journal* and in other publications. There is a developing tide of prayer research. What the Klingbeils and Spindrift would like to offer is, that there is likely going to be *an intensification of criticism of the prayer and healing research.* If the resistance and criticism that Spindrift faced indicates anything, it may foretell other forms of criticism. The future criticism of testing intercessory prayer does not mean progress will not be accepted, but that there are going to be **frightening battle casualties strewn along the research road.**

Some people, for their own reasons, would not like to see proven that prayer and consciousness heal at a distance. *The Wall Street Journal* article had the following comments about doing prayer research:

> If my doctor prayed for my recovery, I'd consider a malpractice lawsuit. (Richard Goss, emeritus professor of biology at Brown University) If it's prayer today, what's next? Are we going to study the tooth fairy or Santa Claus? (Annie-Laurie Gaylor of the Freedom From Religion Foundation)
>
> Many people from my school of faith will say this type of healing is not from God but from the devil . . . . I'd like to keep an open mind, although I can't help but think that this makes little laboratory mice out of pray-ers. (Samuel Solivan, professor of theology at Andover Newton Theological School)
>
> [Some studies] make the assumption that God is some sort of Pavlovian dog. Say a prayer and He or She answers . . . . How do we know that these [Judeo-Christian] groups have a special link to God and not the Islamics or Buddhists? (Gordon Stein, senior editor of *Free Inquiry*, a skeptics' magazine.[22]) (Quotes from *The Wall Street Journal* of Wednesday, December 20, 1995, p. B1)

A newspaper reporter asked me, "Why would anyone be against testing prayer? I first asked the reporter a question: "How would you feel if it could be scientifically shown that there was a spiritual power larger than you which worked through you?"

The reporter said in essence, "Well, I would feel very uncomfortable finding out about that. I don't believe in God or anything else having a power over me outside of myself. I don't want to have anything outside of me control me. So personally I would not want to find out that such a power was out there and could do that to me."

I asked her, "Then can you see at least one reason why some people would be against testing prayer?" A light bulb flashed on in her and she exclaimed, "I got it! We human beings want to be in control!" I said, "You hit the nail on the head."

WHEN IS ENOUGH EVIDENCE ENOUGH?

Scientific researchers continue to pile up more evidence that cigarette smoking is unhealthy for humans beings. Yet many humans continue to smoke, and some offer counter evidence that smoking really is not convincingly unhealthy. If the piles of physical evidence in the visible world of the five senses have been disregarded, what are the chances of evidencing anything in the very different, non-physical, invisible world of consciousness beyond the senses? The answer may be that other issues may creep up and cloud the scientific evidence. The fact is skeptics will always be with us to tell counter stories about spiritual phenomena.

A wise friend told me that it is healthy to have some skepticism about evidence, but that there is a difference between healthy skepticism and unhealthy skepticism. James Randi, the skeptic and magician, said on WGN radio Chicago on the Extension 720 show that he had investigated "thousands" of spiritual healings and had not found a single one that was acceptable. He said more than once that he did not find any evidence in "thousands" of investigations of healings. Randi found side issues to debunk them all. Dismissing a lot of the evidence from a scientific point of view is understandable. Disregarding every single iota of evidence seems to make less sense.

I have been told that Spindrift was beating its head against the wall trying to show anything about consciousness and prayer according to the rules of the natural sciences. Maybe this is true. Maybe experiments cannot show good enough evidence. If some people are so convinced that scientific inquiry is a futile effort and will never give enough evidence, why do they bother to be against the research? If the evidence for prayer may never be good enough for some people, or the pursuit of evidence is thought to be "a waste of time," why are they bothered by it? They believe it's all for nought, and nothing will be discovered. Then why is there so much negative reaction to the research? Maybe because something might be discovered that is contrary to a critic's beliefs.

Consciousness research in the Twenty-first Century will help some people change their negative reactions about prayer being tested in the laboratory. **To put it mildly, the Klingbeils and Spindrift have received little nourishment and encouragement in their efforts to investigate prayer, consciousness, and healing.** The controversies over testing prayer have pricked at Spindrift's skin throughout its history. Perhaps John Klingbeil's comments about the promotion of his 1980 book *The Quiet Revolution* illustrates how the pricks cut the skin:

> Christian Scientists were incensed because to them the book was heretical. The non Christian Scientists were incensed because to them the book was Christian Science. It was the worst of both worlds. Eventually we became rather unhappy about the whole thing

and worked very hard to get a less controversial presentation of what we did.

The Quiet Revolution was a naive book in many respects. The tests were disarmingly simple and something any scientist would smile about. The language was both simple and profound. It was hard for us to accept the fact that this little paperback would be burned, ripped to shreds, and become the object of so much hatred by so many people.[23]

BILL, TELL FEW PEOPLE

In 1985, I asked a fellow church member who was in the Central Intelligence Agency, CIA, if he would listen to a tape about the Klingbeils' prayer research on seeds and yeast cells. He listened to about half. I waited for a comment. It was something like "You're not the first people to pray for plants. Then there's some guy who uses lie detectors." (He must have meant Cleve Backster, who hooked up leaves of plants to lie detectors for responses. Cleve Backster is featured in *The Secret Life of Plants*. Spindrift contacted Backster and the book's co-author, Christopher Bird.)

My CIA friend then added something like this: "Bill, I don't think you should tell too many people you're involved in this research, and you shouldn't be involved in this research because you'll get into trouble with the church." **Now there was a scientifically verifiable statement if I ever heard one!**

Chapter Eight

Mind over Mood

I think all spiritual healers are going to have to
face being tested . . . Any spiritual healer who
wants to practice is going to have to go through
the testing procedure and show . . . that he is
capable of using that method. This ultimately
means, as I see it, that faith healers will not be
able to practice outside of medical supervision
unless they accept the qualitative distinction, and
they submit themselves to testing.

Bruce Klingbeil

A process of selective blindness is operating . . .
described by the spiritual teacher Baba Ram Das:
'When a pickpocket looks at a saint, all he sees is
pockets.' Just so, when materialists look at humans,
all they see is matter.

Larry Dossey, M.D.,
Healing Beyond the Body, p. 302

Observe a human being's physical healing. If a person's
healing is due to medical treatment, depending on the
facts known in the case, the healing could have other components. A person might be "a quick healer." A certain drug
reached its goal in one person but was only part of the
solution for another person. A bit of joy cheered the patient

up resulting in that person bouncing back to normal. Humor can even give a boost to healing. Then there is the specter of the placebo effect where unconscious and conscious mental associations somehow heal. Doctors and nurses have times when they do not know why a patient heals. They attribute the healing to "a strong will to live" or a "I'll do better than predicted attitude." However, modern medicine is improving and has its monitoring of measurements and drug testing methods more developed than do alternative healing methods. **The Klingbeils predicted that alternate healing methods and their proponents would be required to prove the efficacy of their methods the same way modern medicine has been doing it.**

MUDDLED BY HUMAN VARIABLES

One alternative healing method coming out of the closet and drawing curiosity is spiritual healing. Spiritual healing that applies prayer has many other components that can explain why a person is healed. People may admit "prayer made the difference," but what does that mean? Other factors may make a difference also. People get over most illnesses "over time." Colds and fevers tend to work that way. Fresh air, springtime, and warm weather are good medicines and may be the reason why someone gets better. Then there are inaccurate diagnoses. About fifty percent of diagnoses are not correct. Then there is the problem of the placebo effect. All these factors do not bode well for being scientific. Bruce Klingbeil said that doctors and prayer practitioners are lucky because many patients coming to them would get well on their own.

Seeing people get well is gratifying. What do we really know about why and how the healings happen? There are so many variables when praying for human beings. When researching spiritual healing and prayer, working with human beings is complex. Human complexity is one reason why the Klingbeils chose to work with plants.

A RAPPORT WITH PLANTS

Human beings do relate to human beings instantly, but plants are simpler entities and people do feel love for them. The following are writings by John and Bruce Klingbeil about some of their problems concerning scientifically testing a person's consciousness and prayer for healing.[1]

PLANTS AND PRAYERS

"We have often been asked why we work with seeds and other simple organic and inorganic systems rather than with people. There are [four] reasons for this. (1) One big reason is that we don't have **the money and the expertise to work with systems as complex as human beings** [being measured in a clinical set-up]. (2) Another reason is, as far as we know, **plants and seeds are unconscious.** People think and seeds don't as far as we know." [That is, plant organisms are not adding their own thoughts "consciously" into the experiments.] "That means there are less mental variables to worry about when you're running tests. (3) The third reason is that we're not prepared to deal with **the ethical questions that arise from using human beings as subjects of experimental tests. Some day all of these objections will be considered and resolved as best they may be, but they are matters that are beyond Spindrift at the present time."** (4) [The fourth reason for using simpler plant systems instead of people is **specifically because of the placebo effect.**] "The power of the placebo effect is a distorting factor that medical people have fairly well managed to get out of their drug testing by using the double blind testing approach. We had to find a way to do for prayer what medical research had done for drugs. We had to separate the power and grace of God from the placebo effect of human faith.

"We had to solve some conceptual problems in order to set up our research, and the way we solved them has had a lot to do with how and why we set up our research the way we did. **Specifically, we had to define prayer and healing in ways that were amenable to the scientific method, and we had to solve the problem of the placebo effect.**

"There has been a little research interest in prayer and healing. A few medical people have been interested. But what has been done is only nibbling at the edges. Why hasn't there been some progress? Basically, it's because the medical community hasn't figured out how to deal with the placebo effect.

"Medical researchers have been using the double blind test to distinguish between the intrinsic power of drugs and the placebo effect. It's possible to get some idea of the difference between what a pill does and what our own mind does. The trouble is, medical research has not yet come up with a way to distinguish between what one part of our mind does and what another part of our mind does at the same time. **It's been a question of how to tell the difference between the effect of prayer and the effect of our own placebo kind of faith in our prayer, the effect of our expectations, the effect of suggestion and of human faith in whatever it is we're doing.**"

The word *placebo* is the Latin for "I shall please." For more about the influence of the placebo effect, see endnote 2.

PREVIOUS STUDIES

The Klingbeils continued, "The parapsychological community has made more studies than anybody, studies of what they call 'psychic healing.' Parapsychologists have an interest in the effects of thought on the world around us, and they have looked into thought and healing but not from a religious standpoint.

"Defining prayer in terms that could be studied by the scientific method meant that we had to think of God's response to prayer as universal and impartial; we had to think of God's grace in terms of law rather than of selective response. There was no way around this. Science is set up to study consistency of pattern in the material universe. It has no means or methods to study the miraculous, the impossible, or the changeable effects of an inconsistent cause."

How did the Klingbeils go after these hurdles including the placebo effect? They explained, "The way we solved these problems was to measure in reference to pattern. We knew that prayer, *the love of God,* was supportive of identity, that it sustained and blessed and developed the identity of everything on which it rested. In measurement terms this meant that God's love and our prayers were supportive of the pattern of every identity; since we were dealing with a *pattern mending effect we measured with reference to pattern.*

"In terms of experimental methodology this means that instead of measuring the state of a system before prayer and after prayer, we measured *how close* a system prayed for was to pattern before and after prayer. We measured to see if there was a pattern mending effect in evidence.

"Essentially, we postulated two forms of consciousness, a pattern-referenced form of thought and the usual volitional/ intentional form of thought including the placebo effect. Since the essence of prayer was the pattern-referenced form of thought, and since human faith was the familiar volitional/ intentional form of thought, we could set up tests which, by the way we set them up, differentiated between the two forms of thought. Thus we had the equivalent of the double blind test for drugs. We had tests which could distinguish between the power of [pattern-directed] prayer and the placebo effect. Basically, that's how we did it."

DEFINING HEALING

"Now we have a way of coping with the placebo effect and a way of defining healing. We can define healing as *movement toward pattern*, toward the measurable state which defines the optimal condition of form and function for an individual person, animal, or plant."

MEASURING AN IDENTITY AS PATTERN

John continues, "Pattern is the *measurable* dimension of identity."[3] People praying for experiments "show us that the association of [a person's] observing consciousness with a physical system exposes the physical system to" identity-supporting-healing-effects on the system which produce a pattern of normalcy.[4] Which means a prayer supporting order affirms the identity it touches. Here is an example of prayer healing soybeans through the soybeans' "dimension of identity."

> Measurement in reference to pattern can be illustrated in very simple ways. For example, suppose over-soaked soybeans and under-soaked soybeans are prayed for at the same time. The same prayer will cause the over-soaked soybeans to lose more water than the control and will cause the under-soaked soybeans to retain more water than the control. The same prayer will have different effects on the over-soaked and the under-soaked soybeans. On the other hand, the belief/faith, which underlies the placebo effect, is goal-directed and will move the soybeans in the direction of belief.[5]

When prayer empirically works, **a goal-directed thought** may or may not move the condition of a system toward a pattern. **Holy or non goal-directed thought** does move the condition of a system toward a pattern. **The pattern of healing in this soybean test is the normal amount of water retention for the soybeans.** The Klingbeils wrote, "If . . . you . . . think of a soybean, a yeast cell, or a human being in terms of the qualities of God, you are going to have a spiritualizing effect, a healing effect, on that soybean, that yeast cell, or that human being."[6]

I asked John, "I understand praying for one plant at a time, but not praying for many plants at a time. How can we pray for a field of corn or hundreds of yeast cells or a bunch of soybeans **at the same time?**"

John said, "We are praying with love and support for the identities as a whole group. This praying for the whole group as a unit is applying the <u>Law</u> <u>of</u> <u>the</u> <u>Conceptual</u> <u>Whole</u>. The more you can think of a group as *a single unit—a conceptual whole*—the more easily you can embrace the whole group in your prayers."

DEFINING PRAYER AT A DISTANCE

The Klingbeils wrote about developing a definition of holy prayer. "How do we define it? Since we could prove with our tests that there are two kinds of thought, a patterning and identity supporting kind of thought and a pattern indifferent volitional/intentional kind of thought, we defined [holy] prayer as that state of mind which was supportive of identity. If a person could direct the patterning kind of thought toward person, place, or thing, then that person could pray effectively. That was our definition. We have used a working definition of prayer instead of a theological one. As you see, we were result-oriented."

Qualitative thought or holy prayer is the engine moving non goal-directed prayer. "It is . . . a loving form of consciousness." Holy prayer dwells on *qualities* such as compassion, support, and love which nurture normalization. These quality thoughts enliven non goal-directed prayer. Prayer involving these qualities produces the patterning effect or ordering-effect Spindrift has sorted out from the background soup of other thoughts. The Klingbeils maintained "If a person could produce the patterning effect from qualitative prayer, that person was useful in our research. Our researchers are people who can get those kinds of results. What we do in every experimental test involving prayer is to increase, through qualitative prayer, the amount of qualitative thought associated with a system, and then measure the amount of qualitative thought associated with a system, and then measure the amount by which that system draws closer to its **inherent pattern**."[7] Inherent pattern is a system's normal condition or close to it.

TRIANGLE SYMBOL

The Klingbeils advanced the conception that a spiritual healer's quality thought acts as a template to promote patterns of normalcy in healing. A spiritual healer's thought becomes empathic with healing information and the healee's thought, and there appears to be no separation between all three. They form a triangle. The triangle is the healer, the spiritual information, and the healee. The triangle is a way to explain intercessory prayer or IP for short.

In the 1980's, the Klingbeils' definition of pattern supportive prayer began to have an impact on future researchers. "Prayer at a distance" was looking more attractive as a nonlocal phenomenon for researchers to test experimentally.

IS A PATTERN MAKER
GOD IN THE LOOP?

Some inquirers feel that the blessing thoughts and supportive effects of intercessory prayer are a dynamic produced by the human mind alone. No God is necessary to produce these pattern making effects. The Klingbeils inductively reasoned that the patterns emerging from the supportive effects of holy prayer are a dynamic of the Consciousness of God. They logically reasoned that God is **inductively found "in the loop"** of a holy prayer.

That God is **deductively found "in the loop"** of a holy prayer is not yet scientifically provable. The deductive proof that God is involved in the intricacies of prayer remains outside of science. At the August 1997 ReDiscovering Cosmos science and religion conference in Syracuse, New York, Robert Russell, Ph.D., director of the Center for Theology and Natural Science in Berkeley, California, mentioned that nobody has found a way to prove that God exists, but the scientific evidence is mounting which points to a God being involved in the intricacies of the universe.

What is provable, according to the Klingbeils, is "a patterning mode of consciousness that is *supportive* of identity. A patterning form of consciousness must also be aware of an enormous amount of information. It must know the pattern it is mending, every detail of it, and it must know the detail of the environmental surroundings in which that pattern exists. It must also know how to modify that pattern and its surroundings in ways necessary to achieve its loving purpose. Such a patterning form of consciousness is therefore, and by definition, wise as well as good. This leads us back to the attributes of the Creator, to the nature and the will of God."

One result of Spindrift's research would be to illustrate through simple tests that prayer is beneficial. "The fact that there is a form of consciousness which alters every system it touches for the better is something for which modern science has no explanation. It is also something which modern science finds very difficult to believe.

"The fact is that scientists, not science, have chosen to use the scientific method to construct a materialistic philosophy. Having done this, they then proclaim that science is opposed to Christianity. The fact is that, if they had used the scientific method to observe thought as well as matter, they would have constructed a non-materialistic philosophy which would have been supportive of some ideas of Christianity and ideals of religion."[8]

DEVOTION TO DISCOVERY

The Klingbeils continue, "Spindrift's actual research began in the Christian Science world [embryonically in 1969]. The experimental work was begun by Christian Science practitioners. However, they sought to establish their work by the universal means of the scientific method and in concepts of prayer and healing common to all Christians. Inevitably, perhaps, they were declared heretical by their church. When Spindrift was established, it was a non-denominational organization with ties to no one and with no commitment other than to the experimental study of prayer and healing. This, in a nutshell, is our history and our identity. This is who we are.

"Given the kind of world it is out there, how has Spindrift survived without funding and without technical help and with no place to publish? We have done it by: (1) [spending our own and donated money], (2) doing only very simple tests with very simple equipment, (3) keeping our methodology very simple, (4) keeping our mathematical evaluations very simple, and (5) running mostly on volunteer labor.

"All of this is to say that we have worked in an experimental area which had no research history, no funding sources, no expertise available for the work, and no theoretical landmarks from which to orient the work. That's where we began [full-time in January 1975]." Several of the experiments are described in "The Botanical Experiments" in the Appendix.

In 1969, the year man landed on the moon and the Klingbeils' experimental work began, "social psychologist W. J. McGuire described 'three stages in the life of an artifact': first it is ignored; then it is controlled for its presumed contaminating effects; and, finally, it is studied as an important phenomenon in its own right."[9] Bruce and John Klingbeil experienced what he was talking about.

Larry Dossey writes in *Healing Beyond the Body.*

> We have not examined the empirical data supporting the view of pervasive consciousness, but they are extensive. They are manifested in the many areas of investigative science showing the capacity of consciousness to interact nonlocally with the inanimate and semianimate world—areas such as human/machine interaction; transpersonal imagery; studies in so-called bio-PK (psychokinesis) and distant, intercessory prayer, in which individuals interact with "lower," nonhuman organisms such as bacteria, fungi, yeast, and cells of various sorts.[10]

Chapter Nine

The Paradigm Shift

. . . restriction of science, even the smallest one,
would destroy it altogether, for the forbidden point
might, if inquired into, have changed the whole
scientific interpretation of a subject matter.
                              Paul Tillich, Theologian[1]

Comedian George Burns was asked if he
believed in heaven or hell?
George Burns said, "I don't know what they
have there, but I'm taking my music."

The receptivity to Spindrift was from healers, especially
doctors and nurses. Medical people see unusual healings
frequently. Some of them have no resistance to *doses of prayer*
being given to their patients. Some prescribe dosages of
prayer.

Prayer testing is a sensible concept for some of them. One
M.D. invited me to a party at his house. While swimming around
in his pool, he told me, "The reason I can accept your work
with prayer is, you use scientific methods. This is the way to do it
and get it right."

The Klingbeils were experiencing cutting edge thrills
exploring what they believed to be new discoveries about levels
of consciousness. Each person prays differently. Yet, that
difference was a plus not a negative. Consciousness effects that

people emit can be read from printing a computer graph. Graphing people's thought and prayer patterns is a form of mind reading. That is, some tests could read indirectly how a person was thinking in his praying for tiny controlled organisms, a result healers could be interested in. A test score showing that people's intentions become more spiritually cultivated by pouring in virtues of thought could be of interest to religious people. A few Christians and a few parapsychology buffs were curious, but the people in the healing professions were the most interested.

A CRITICIZED EXPERIMENT

An experiment with yeast was sidelined because of criticism that the experiment deliberately harmed yeast. The Klingbeil's raised the question: What effect might a quality consciousness have with deliberate harm? Yeast was mixed in lukewarm water. A soldering gun was placed in the water and plugged into a random number generator in a computer. The random number generator controlled how often electricity flowed to the soldering gun. The generator produced zeroes and ones which switched on the soldering gun an average of 50% of the time.

The heat from the gun harmed the yeast. Spindrift people prayed to observe if the time the soldering gun was on could be shortened. Several test runs showed no effect on shortening the time.

Another person prayed and the gun stayed on more than 50% and did more harm to the yeast. Apparently the unconscious assumption was "more time must be better." Our cultural heritage that "more and bigger is better" was factored into prayers tested at Spindrift.

When Bruce Klingbeil prayed for the yeast, an unexpected phenomenon occurred. The soldering gun turned on a little more than 50% of the time. However, the yeast itself did not get hot or harmed. Bruce's loving thoughts protected the yeast from harm in this random number generator test involving deliberate harm.

Bruce was an experienced Christian Science practitioner. His unexpected results raised profound questions about cross-purposes in a healer's mind. Can a healer's non goal-directed thought predominate to protect the yeast while his "bigger is better" thought lengthens the time the soldering gun stays on? If a healer decides to pray to shorten the time, is this decision to yield less heat goal-directed or non goal-directed?

John was excited about what could be learned from this HEATED yeast test. Then John said something to me like "We have enough people hating us now without asking for more hatred." This test was *literally* put on the back burner.

This heated test was no worse than baking bread with yeast. Would the same protestors walk into a bakery and burst into tears over killed yeast? Would they throw themselves in front of a lawn mower because the grass was going to be cut down? No, but this Spindrift test upset them.

John and Bruce finished dozens of experiments. They also had ambitious experiments that never got finished. Examples follow. John tested biofeedback. With the other research John and Bruce were doing, there wasn't enough time to finish tests of consciousness on bacteria. Plans were made to get DNA samples and see what changes occurred when they were prayed for. Also there was a plan to see what prayer could do to some AIDS infected cell samples. After researching the AIDS project, it was decided this could not be done safely, and the equipment expense was too much for Spindrift. The first floor of the Klingbeils' townhouse in Salem was the Spindrift laboratory. The Klingbeils thought their neighbors might be fearful of the AIDS virus being stored where they lived. Bruce decided against testing the virus.[2] With the public debate over school prayer, the Klingbeils thought a project to test the effects of prayer on children in school would be an important scientific study. Aside from school prayer being a political controversy, researching school prayer would require enormous funds, time, and staff, resources that Spindrift didn't have. John investigated testing the ordering-effects of his consciousness on a video gambling machine. The video machine randomly displayed the faces of playing cards. John prayed to alter the randomness of the displayed cards. John also discovered that each machine cost five figures.

In 1977, John was working on a remote viewing experiment based on mung beans growing in locations unknown to him. John could fairly consistently intuit and tag the locations of where the beans were growing. This experiment was finished by John and proposed to the US government including the CIA. (See endnote 3.)

THE SPIN
AND SHIFT TOWARD SPINDRIFT

I had heard that Robert Jahn and Brenda Dunne, co-authors of *Margins of Reality*, were going to speak for the organization Dennis Stillings headed up, *The Archaeus Project*. I phoned Dennis Stillings in June 1989. He quickly told me, "Forget it. It's over with." I missed the talks, but I proceeded to tell Dennis about Spindrift. Dennis told me *I was jogging his memory.* Dennis said he had met the Klingbeils five years earlier at their Palatine, Illinois, residence. It was right when they were "moving out of town for political reasons" as Dennis interpreted the move. I suddenly recalled hearing about Dennis and his meeting with the Klingbeils before they moved to Salem. It turned out that Dennis was also president of the United States Psychotronics Association. Three weeks hence the Association was having its national meeting in Sacramento, California. Dennis said, "Do you want to speak at the conference?" **What a switch.** I was calling him to hear someone else speak, and he says "Do you want to speak?"

The local chapter of the Psychotronics Association meets near my home. I attended a meeting. Their main thrust is to study the mental mechanism that underlies the mind of a man and man's influence on machines or other minds/bodies. The Psychotronics people have a "technical" interest, not just a sensational interest, in psi phenomena. Psycho-tronic refers to man's psyche influencing a machine. Spindrift fits into that category. A man prays for a plant that is monitored by a machine, a computer. Prayer research is psychotronic. *Here was one more description of prayer that would drive some religious people up-the-wall.*

Dennis Stillings and I phoned the Klingbeils in Salem. The Klingbeils named my speech "Cards, Dice, and Defense Mechanisms." The speech focused on how a person's unconscious thought, almost undetectably, skews the randomness during card guessing in a test and throwing more ordered pairs of dice in a test. The speech continued with how our own unconscious mind's defense mechanisms work to prevent a person from consciously knowing that the physical items, the shuffling of cards, the guessing of cards, and the tossing of dice, were being slightly skewed by the participant's observing thought. The idea is explained in endnote 4.

Three weeks later in July, 1989, I delivered the speech. Some of those who heard the speech had the right background to grasp Spindrift's research. The Klingbeils were delighted with the new contacts. The data from my speech was published by the Association. Video and audio tapes of the speech were recorded. Months later I heard from people who listened to the tape. Becoming associated with the United States Psychotronics Association was a boost to Spindrift.

Several other speeches were given locally and around the country titled "Spooky Action at a Distance" and "Spindrift's Link with the Universal Ordering-Force."

FRIENDLY AUDIENCES

Several organizations recognized the Spindrift contributions to research and asked for presentations. During the 1991 Persian Gulf War a speech titled "The Politics of Prayer" was given to the Archaeus Project in Minneapolis.

One talk I gave was to a Unity Church group in Naples, Florida. Always on guard for debate and negativity about Spindrift, it took some psychological adjustment to speak to people actually interested in what I was saying. I was having an ingrained psychological response. Probably I wasted one-fourth of my time repeating that "I could not believe" Unity was receptive to Spindrift's work with consciousness and prayer. (That Unity church groups were becoming interested in Spindrift was ironic because the Unity religion is a grandchild of Mary Baker Eddy through her bright student Emma Curtis Hopkins who took class instruction from Mrs. Eddy and was hired by Mrs. Eddy as a metaphysical writer and editor for the Christian Science periodicals.)

Another boost for Spindrift's message came when I finally reached Dr. Larry Dossey. An article about him in the *Dallas Morning News* prompted me to call the reporter. He gave me the name of someone on Dr. Dossey's board of directors. I wrote Dr. Dossey directly. Soon the phone rang. Dr. Dossey *was interested.* He had an advance from Bantam Books. Spindrift's intercessory prayer and healing material was just right "to break new ground" for the book.

The book *Recovering the Soul: A Scientific and Spiritual Search* came out in late 1989. Some who read it wrote Spindrift.

In 1988, when Spindrift was asked to go on the Oprah Winfrey Show to debunk the works of extroverted preachers, the misconception was that our scientific experiments were anti-spiritual and could detect fraud. We didn't go on because we explained that Spindrift was not a skeptics group! When Dr. Larry Dossey was on the Oprah show in 1994, he gave the public a better understanding of the Spindrift experiments.

During a 1990 radio show, the host asked, "Does prayer work?" I was cautious. The host urged me on, "Come on, Bill, say prayer works!" Bruce provided an appropriate answer. "What we can say is that within the parameters of a test, prayer works."

1989-1990 were pivotal years. The media gave Spindrift a fair amount of publicity. Spindrift started getting mentioned in other books and publications. The Klingbeils received letters from around the world. Spindrift was told by *Mother Jones Magazine* that an advertisement would be perfect for their readership. It was, and readers inquired about Spindrift. Even a couple of dissident Christian Science church newsletters like *The Kerry Letter* and *The Banner* carried Spindrift news.

Between the Psychotronics meetings, the Larry Dossey books, and the public finding out about Spindrift through political stories in 1990 in the Colorado press, Spindrift emerged from obscurity. (For details, see Chapter Four, "Politics and Prayer.")

The saying "Recognition is a cure for many ills" applied to the new happiness the Klingbeils experienced.

EXCOMMUNICATION

In the midst of the publicity of 1989 and 1990, which reported on the odd Spindrift research in Salem about prayer in a lab for tiny organisms, Bruce Klingbeil experienced a new sadness. In April 1990, officials at Bruce's church headquarters sent him a letter which said, " . . . we have received concerns regarding your activities both written and spoken." The Mother Church had begun the excommunication process against Bruce for his "activities." Bruce called the church headquarters in Boston about the excommunication letter. The official said to Bruce, "The church is working to demonstrate a higher concept of membership." Bruce asked, "What does that mean?" The official replied, "It means we're putting out all of those who don't agree with the new directions in which the Board is leading the church."

Bruce was hurt that he was targeted for excommunication. However, Bruce did not seem to me nearly as devastated as he was in 1983 when he lived in Palatine, Illinois, and was removed from being listed as a church practitioner. Being listed as a practitioner is the highest calling one can attain in his church. The loss of Bruce's listing is the equivalent of a doctor losing his license to practice medicine. Losing his listing was excommunication enough.

The excommunication process hung in limbo after that telephone conversation. Why? The speculation was the church had other problems. Having spent almost five hundred million dollars on a worldwide television network, the silent church membership became vocal and stirred up. The television programs had quality and won many awards, but the motives and the cost of the television network were suspect.

The church television **experiment**, its funding, and the emotional reactions of many church members, happening at the same time as the excommunication process, probably accounted for the church's postponement of Bruce's excommunication.

John Klingbeil was told that he was no longer permitted to attend his annual Christian Science Association because he wouldn't quit his experiments.

CONSEQUENCES OF THE RESEARCH

The Klingbeils speculated about the positive and negative consequences of successful prayer research.

I asked them, "Would you please comment on the difference between the monk and monkey in us?"

Bruce and John answered in essence:

> Evidence of holy thought being effective beyond the body would illustrate the difference between the monk and the monkey in human beings. When more of humanity realizes that their thoughts actually do affect material conditions at a distance,

this realization will cause a variety of psychological reactions such as the following:

1) Some people will be glad they discovered that their consciousness interacts and has a good effect on the environment.

2) Some people will be angry to find out that their consciousness interacts with the environment and affects it.

3) Other people will be happy they discovered another way to manipulate and abuse people's minds. It will validate or unleash terrorizing powers for them.

4) Other people will experience great psychological strain and worry caused by finding out that thought is pushing material conditions around inside and outside of themselves.

5) Scientific skeptics will think the world is going crazy. These scientists will find ways to debunk each new study of psi and nonlocal healing.

6) Some healers will be excited with the growing recognition of the **mind-body-spirit connection.** Healers will feel more acceptance.

7) Why would a healer feel more acceptance? Science is saying that healing at a distance is becoming more acceptable because **nonlocality theory** supports that a healer's mind to mind communication is likely true, and not a myth.

8) Apparently a healer's mind communicates **normative healing information** to a healee's mind. A consequence for society will be more respect for a healer's position on the human scene. Like monks, many healers have a life purpose of cultivating and nurturing their inner qualitative thoughts. Scientific evidence

to support that **qualitative thought is nonlocal love which affirms life**, will help sanction that a spiritual lifestyle is reasonable.

INCREASED INTEREST

The Society for Psychical Research was founded in England in **1882**. In **1982**, the SPR's 100th anniversary, a modest historical record of progress was celebrated in psychic research circles. Until 1989, most of the attention Spindrift cultivated was from scientific skeptics and from healers. In 1989, there was a noticeable shift. The Klingbeils' experiments began to get expanded attention by some authors and scientists. These folks were curious about a father and son in Salem who operated an amateur science laboratory in their townhouse.

The new 90's decade had positive arrows pointing to the future. Bruce wrote a letter to a supporter in November 1990:

> Spindrift has progressed. Our work is much better presented today than it was a few years ago, both in terms of the research itself and in our newsletter and brochure. We are getting quite a bit more attention from people. However, the publicity which has come to us has presented many opportunities we can't handle. A documentary maker in Yugoslavia wants video or film footage he can use to present Spindrift in a documentary on spirituality; ministers and others want course material on our research (texts for classroom work); authors want material to include in their books; a lot of people want us to give seminars and conferences and courses on how to pray. Some of this kind of thing should be done and some shouldn't, but we aren't equipped to do any of it.

Reporters are a now-and-then kind of problem. We certainly don't want the personal publicity which comes from speaking for attribution. [We would rather have the math and science speak than us personally.] Last week we had someone from the Washington News Bureau of Unistar Radio Networks here and were sorry to put the individual under the constraints we felt we must impose . . . .

We have found that publicity is either reassurance to the converted or discounted as propaganda by the disbelievers. The idea that such tests as we have do actually exist is not taken seriously by the unconverted. The attention level that must be generated before our work can have an honest hearing, a "real" hearing, seems to be pretty high . . . .

SCIENCE FRICTION

Ted Rockwell is a bridge builder between unusual science research and accepted science research. Ted was the representative of the Parapsychology Association to the American Association for the Advancement of Science. He said, "I explain the Kooks to the Squares." Ted wrote a paper for the 1994 International Forum of New Science in Colorado. The paper is about bridging *SCIence with PSI*.

If you are a scientist, use cool rationality and proper scientific procedures and criteria in judging scientific data—even if the experimenter claims to show the existence of a Supernatural Force. If you are a church-goer, do not object to scientific tests which measure postulated effects of God's influence, unless you conclude after thoughtful and prayerful consideration that such work is indeed heretical.

The first reaction of most people firmly established in the scientific world or the world of faith and spirituality is to reject with considerable emotion any perceived threats to concepts they hold dear. The recent establishment of a chair at Cambridge to study the interrelationship of science and religion has evoked loud cries of scorn and derision at the very idea, with rash public statements from leading scientists that *science has disproved the existence of God.* I must have missed that paper.

I have been shocked, outraged, and dismayed at the ferocity and irrationality of both scientific and religious people when faced with laboratory data from the Spindrift group on the healing effects of prayer . . . . If, despite our different backgrounds and world-views, we could learn to discuss scientific data and religious ideas, treating them as calmly and insightfully as we treat our everyday work, I expect that we would find that most of the things we fear fail to materialize. Soon the bridge would become well-traveled, and we would wonder how we ever got along without it.

Spindrift members, Laura Schunk and Deborah Klingbeil Rose, attended the same International Forum of New Science in Colorado. When Laura and Deborah entered the lobby of the conference, one of the first things they saw was an enlarged photograph of Bruce and John Klingbeil with an exploding volcano in the background between them. Events would show what an apt visual was this photo of Bruce and John.[5]

Chapter Ten

All Alone by the Telephone

Spiritual progress is made drip by drip.
Bruce Klingbeil's view

Science progresses funeral by funeral.
Max Karl Planck, German physicist,
founder of the quantum theory

Some people have asked me if there wasn't a conspiracy working against the Klingbeils. Perhaps some dialogue from the season's closing cliffhanger episode of *The X Files* for May 17, 1998, will raise some eyebrows.

In the episode, a twelve-year-old boy who could produce testable psychic effects was a target of assassination. The X File FBI agents protected the boy.

FBI agent Dr. Scaly asked Agent Fowley about the boy's psychic gift.

AGENT SCALY

Say that what you're suggesting were even possible, who would want to kill a kid whose abilities would offer you the ultimate advantage in business, in war, in anything?

AGENT FOWLEY

Maybe somebody whose business is in keeping secrets.

Is it possible a kid who was ahead of the curve could peer into the abyss of consciousness—could see good and evil scenarios where psi operates unseen and manipulates people's decisions? Could a psychic young person like that become a target because he is unwelcome competition and knows too much about quantum entanglement and mind control? Could the fear of a human being revealing secrets to the masses about how their minds are entangled and manipulated make him a target for someone who wants to suppress that knowledge? Far-fetched? Maybe not.

In the 1990's, the Klingbeils' work was *finally* showing progress in reaching people's consideration. Thinkers in the fields of medicine, alternative healing, consciousness research, and a handful in religion were acknowledging that the Klingbeils had contributed original paradigm breaking concepts and experiments that improve the dialogue between science, religion, and the healing arts.

May 6, 1993 was the National Day of Prayer. Late on that night, I talked to Bruce and John on the phone. I could not reach them the next day with good news about verifying a quote Bruce told me existed.[1] Bruce and John left their townhouse on the 7th. I called other Spindrift members living in Salem. They could not find them at home. I was probably the last one to speak to the Klingbeils.

Bizarrely, somewhere between May 7 and 12, 1993, Bruce and John Klingbeil killed themselves. Two inexplicable suicides. What could be worse? Nothing except two murders. What the police said didn't appear on the surface like murders.

HIRED AIRPLANE

Bruce's daughter Deborah Klingbeil flew to Oregon when a letter came indicating her father and brother's intentions. Deborah hired an airplane search party to find their red truck and bodies as they indicated they were in a forest.

The Boston Globe wrote about the killings. The following is reprinted courtesy of *The Boston Globe*:

"Deaths tied to religious dispute"
by Thomas Palmer
May 16, 1993 (excerpts as specified).

Father, son apparently kill selves when research fails to gain acceptance

. . . . Bruce Owen Klingbeil, 65, mailed a letter to his daughter, Deborah Rose, in Philadelphia, telling about the suicides. He and his son, John Stephen Klingbeil, 35, then drove from Salem to a rural area near McMinnville, parked their pickup truck, and took their lives, according to a sheriff's report . . . .

Although the case carries some of the elements of a "Twin Peaks" mystery, Sgt. John P. Kowolik of the sheriff's office said yesterday, "The evidence down to a 't' precluded any other chance of foul play."

According to a portion of the letter, released to *The Oregonian* newspaper in Portland, father and son were depressed about the lack of attention to *The Spindrift Papers*, a compilation of papers that were the result of 18 years of research on prayer and its effects.

"*The Spindrift Papers* are out, at a cost only John and I will ever know," the letter reads. "The resistance has been ferocious and increases every day as some measure of success for the tests begins to mount."

Bruce Klingbeil writes, "Shed no tears, Debbie, we accomplished as much as it was humanly possible for us to accomplish. The fact that we had no other out at this point we accept without regrets."

Ironically, a colleague of the Klingbeils' in their research said that they and their efforts were beginning to be taken seriously.

"Things have improved," said William Sweet, a musician in the Chicago area who has an interest in parapsychology and the application of the scientific method to prayer. "There is an interest in this idea of testing thought and testing prayer— outside the church. There's no interest inside the church."

Sweet said he was regularly in touch with the Klingbeils, exchanging information, and had spoken with them on Thursday, May 6. They were not heard from after that . . . .

In one experiment, the Klingbeils' supporters prayed over mung beans to see if the spiritual attention helped them grow.

"We found out that when thought was applied to a stressed lower organism, that the thought affirmed it and brought it back to a normal state," Sweet said.[2]

Sweet said he was particularly surprised at the apparent suicides because the Klingbeils had disagreed with the self-immolations of Buddhist monks during the Vietnam War. "They thought that was wrong," he said.

Sweet said *the organized effort* to prove the power of prayer may end with the deaths of the Klingbeils . . . . [italics added]

"This is the twilight zone for our group. It's inexplicable."

The detectives discovered Bruce and John had bought two shotguns which could also be traced through a credit card check. Apparently, not to get the gun dealer into trouble, Bruce and John traveled in an opposite direction from the gun store to a forest in another county.

Sheriff Sgt. John Kowolik said it was one of the strangest cases he reported to the press. He told me, "I can believe anything," referring to the things he saw in his career.

To the detectives, foul play appeared to be out of the question partly because of the several notes the Klingbeils mailed or left behind. One note was left for me which they both signed. The note upset me. I did interpret that a negative energy was partly behind the suicides. The note included the following: "Bill . . . . Too much malicious animal magnetism [is acting upon us]. Carry on!" Their description sounded like something bad was operating to hurt them.

Initially my family and some friends thought that, if the deaths were a double murder, since I was a spokesman for Spindrift, I would be the next target. We considered calling the police for advice to see if I should hide. I concluded that by shooting *both* Klingbeils the assassins effectively killed Spindrift. **The Klingbeils did the pioneering work. I had the enjoyment of communicating it. They were the "lightning rods" that received the shocks. I was just a witness to the flashes and booms.**

RESEARCH KILLED

The Klingbeils knew more than anyone in the world about their methodology and mathematics to measure thought and prayer at a distance. Their pioneering and preliminary work on testing human consciousness on healing was gun blasted to death.

What made the Klingbeils so controversial was that they actually tested some sacred powers in the laboratory. Until the mid 1990's, such research was held to be off limits to scientific investigations. The Klingbeils paid the price for their *early* research which was ahead of its time.

Deborah Klingbeil said, lamenting to me, something like "All the resistance my dad and brother got could simply mean that it wasn't the right time for Spindrift. Spindrift's research can't be forced on the world if people don't want it." Critics and friends were soon saying in effect, "See! We told you Spindrift was wrong. The suicides prove it! To believe prayer could be tested is insane!" I heard that "tragedy was inevitable." The Klingbeils were "punished" for their detestable tests.

PRESS CONTACTS

A television news reporter found the suicides hard to figure out. Members of the press in Salem pursued Deborah Klingbeil. Deborah and Laura Schunk of Spindrift found three reporters waiting outside Bruce and John's townhouse.

The press contacted me as the spokesman for Spindrift.[3] I enjoyed answering questions but was awfully sad at the same time. The press asked, as background, all kinds of questions about our research. I wished these excellent questions could have been asked in a different context.

RADICAL CHANGES

Could the Klingbeils' theories and tests be saved without Bruce and John? In one suicide note Bruce predicted that Spindrift would probably "fold" without them. The board of directors rushed to salvage what they could.

Some of my words to the press must have riled the Spindrift board. When a reporter asked me if my job with Spindrift was a vocation or avocation, I referred to my job as a *hobby* instead of an avocation. Also I felt Bruce and John *sabotaged* Spindrift by destroying themselves. I said they shouldn't have done it.

The Spindrift board of directors was upset with me. The board phoned me. I presume the words I used to the press and how I felt about the suicides were why I was voted off the board and fired one week after the suicides. Another board member replaced me as president and spokesman for Spindrift.

Their feeling was understandable to me. Emotions were stirred up. I was not under the same geographical pressure others were under. I had not moved to Salem. Several families did move to Salem to assist the Klingbeils. They never expected this disaster. The Spindrift family was shaken up by the suicides. My words to the press and interpretation of the suicides created strain.

NO MORE SWEET SPOT

Suddenly I became an observer, not a front line participant anymore. This change had a mysterious aftereffect on me. A few weeks later I started feeling better physically, in the youthful sense, than I had felt in years. I was surprised. I was not aware of any physical problem. I just felt better. My best guess is I had been burdened by the opposition to Spindrift and the Klingbeils. I lost that burden when I wasn't the Klingbeils' spokesman anymore. I became "less of a focus."

When I was the Klingbeils' spokesman, maybe I was physically reacting to a phenomenon that has been studied in the laboratory for a century. The phenomenon is called the "feeling of being stared at." For scientific tests and evidence of this "feeling of being stared at" phenomenon, see *The Conscious Universe* by Dean Radin, pages 29 and 155. Sperry Andrews, a leading consciousness researcher, has brought together an international community of scientists to demonstrate "the feeling of being stared at" as an example of how the presence and quality of other people's attention can affect us, either positively or negatively—even at a distance. (**For an example of a** scientific experiment demonstrating this "feeling of being stared at" phenomenon, see page 119 of this book.)

CONSPIRACY AND PARANOIA

When the suicides hit the Salem news, a reporter camped outside of the secretary of Spindrift's house. Dorothy, the secretary, supposes this reporter was the one who pounded on her door at midnight to ask questions. She didn't answer the door.

In 1991, a Salem woman volunteered to assist the Klingbeils with their research. She helped in the office. After the suicides, she called Dorothy and said, "My work is done here. I'm going back to California." That sounded odd, but those words could mean anything.

People who knew the Klingbeils wanted me to speak more publicly about the two suicides. How could two men on the brink of success, who didn't believe in suicide, be suddenly gone from the earth. On the other hand, I was told that if the Klingbeils had clinical depression, that's all the explanation needed.

I agree that depression is an element. I also agree that depression is not a complete explanation. Without becoming too conspiratorial but a little paranoid, I will relate a collage of facts. These historical facts can help all of us see that there is more to the story than we know.

PLANS MADE

In the months prior to the suicides, the Klingbeils were busy with research contacts on the phone and in person. They were wrapping up some data analysis and writing.

Previous to their suicides, Bruce and John had been planning a trip to Oregon's coast. It was fun for them to visit small towns in the state on the way. They liked small towns. Their townhouse rent agreement was up at the end of May. Within weeks they were going to take a year off from being practitioners and doing research. It would have been Bruce's first vacation I know of and only one of a few John ever took.

The Klingbeils found a small town to move to. Two weeks earlier in late April, they placed a security deposit on a residence near the ocean. About a week earlier, three weeks before the killings, John bought a new bed for the move. A sister had given him a present of new sheets. A chair was on order but had not arrived yet. John planned to raise a dog, a bull mastiff. John had chosen a breeder and recently purchased a bone and living crate for his dog. Then their tragic deaths took place as the result of self-inflicted gunshots. I asked a police detective how could they use long shotguns? The detective said, "A determined man can do it."

MORE THAN SUICIDE, MARTYRDOM, OR DEPRESSION?

Many people said to me that the explanations of the suicides weren't complete. What could have caused a father and son to kill themselves? Larry Dossey thought a private investigator should go to Oregon and poke around. Similar advice was given to me by Cleve Backster, author of *Primary Perception,* and by Christopher Bird, author of *The Secret Life of Plants.*

Why didn't Bruce and John ask their friends for help? Why did they not let on that something was wrong?

This last question could be guessed at. Thinking about the previous weeks, I knew there were *some clues* that went right by me, like the following:

> 1. A close relative of mine was buying a condominium. Bruce and John knew my family was helping this person. Bruce called me on the

phone in late April with only one question. Did we need some financial help? He and John wanted to give about three thousand dollars toward the purchase of the condo.

Here was a paradox. They who were living on a tight budget wanted to give us a present of money. I had to convince Bruce we had enough for the down payment for the condo. That's all he called about. End of call.[4]

Apparently they were dividing up their savings. Bruce and John did leave five thousand dollars to a needy patient and one thousand dollars to a patient who always wanted to visit Epcot Center at Disneyworld.

2. About four weeks earlier in April 1993, write-ups of *all* their work from 1975 to 1993 were completed. *The Spindrift Papers* were done. This publishing effort wore them down. They needed a vacation and were about to go on one in June. The book was released during the Waco siege.

3. About this same time, Rhea White, editor of the *Journal of the American Society of Psychical Research*, recalls that Bruce told her that he and John were going away for a year to the north woods and would not be available to answer questions about a paper they were writing for the *Journal*. Rhea was taken aback because she had been working with Bruce to get this paper properly refereed and put into acceptable parapsychological language. Bruce had been working on the paper and understood the refereeing process (especially in this case) had already taken a long time and

would take much longer. Rhea said, "I sensed an unspoken urgency to complete the editorial process." Time had never before been a factor in her conversations with Bruce.

4. Bruce had recently said he was sorry that John had not taken the full math scholarship to go to Northwestern University.

5. Separately Bruce and John told me I had been right about how to mail letters to parapsychologist Dean Radin (author of *The Conscious Universe*). Dean Radin had moved overseas. I wanted letters to him registered. Three regular letters were sent. Getting no response, the Klingbeils thought Dr. Radin was too busy to answer. A year later we found he did not get the letters. This delay put some research problem-solving time a year behind schedule. The renewed correspondence resulted in another letter from Dr. Radin to the Klingbeils. Unfortunately, Dr. Radin's last important letter arrived in the Klingbeils' mail box one or two days after they left the townhouse for the forest. On the third day a letter arrived from parapsychologist Richard Broughton.

One of two research problems Dean Radin raised about a psi picture guessing test was solved, the Klingbeils felt. John called and told me how they fixed it, but no one at Spindrift has yet found the mathematical correction. Researcher George Hansen had provided the Klingbeils with a computer program. After Dean Radin relayed a couple problems, Bruce thought there might be a problem in the computer coding, a thought he never considered before. Bruce went through the program code line by line and found one line of computer code that required a rewrite. George Hansen still wants to know what the code change is. Mr. Hansen's book is *The Trickster and the Paranormal*. This book speaks of *the trickster* (similar to a defense mechanism) thwarting psi ever being proven by man.

Bruce said to me in effect, "I think Dean Radin feels I blew it. He must consider me very negligent in taking for granted there was nothing wrong with the program and not checking through it earlier. I should have caught this mistake." The problem was solved. Bruce and John ran the data with the new line of code. They were happy with the new calculations, but Spindrift cannot find the formula change Bruce and John told me they rewrote. The Klingbeils noted the following: " . . . we believed that the mathematical analysis of a run 24 trials long was [long enough beyond chance, the] equivalent of an open deck run. We believed this on the basis of computer simulations which were inaccurate. Thus, some parts of our . . . analyses were incorrect and, in due course, we developed the formula we needed."[5]

The other problem Dean Radin found needed fixing by adding more cards than the 24 cards to a deck the Klingbeils used in tests. It appeared that all the tests would have to be performed again with the larger deck factored into the test. The Klingbeils were wrapping up all their work, even selling their scientific laboratory equipment.[6] They were raising money to take a year off of work and relax for once. Confidence had been building from the excellent review Dean Radin had been putting on this one psi-test of unconscious thought. The time spans of no communication and the two problems arising from Dean Radin running simulations of the test indicating a problem with using only 24 cards may have affected the Klingbeils' future more than I imagined. Dean Radin wrote "This sort of error creeps into leading-edge scientific work all the time . . . I applauded Bruce and John for following their convictions and actually trying to test controversial theories. They were very brave. Most people are unwilling to rock the boat for all the reasons that Bruce and John unfortunately discovered."[7]

6. A couple weeks earlier Bruce phoned several people he knew were in trouble with the church in Boston for opposing the amount of money spent on television and other projects. What he heard depressed him.[8]

Many believe that Christian Science healings are either the placebo effect or one person's mind acting on another person's body. Occasionally Bruce and John said, "the window of opportunity is closing" for the church conducting research into the healing-style of Christian Science. Months before the suicides Bruce said that "the window was closing fast" because the church had gone so far off into other ventures that the spiritual element in healing would be lost and so would the church.

7. Researcher Sperry Andrews wrote, "Larry Dossey told me of the availability of *The Spindrift Papers*. I had a copy mailed to me. Impressed with what I

read, I phoned the Klingbeils. I spoke with Bruce at some length about the research he and John were doing. I told Bruce about my research." Andrews continues, "Within my motivation for calling, I wondered how we might contribute to one another's work through making contact in this way. Through collaborations with other scientists, I had been promoting the investigation of our collective unconsciousness; asking experimentally how perhaps humanity, by becoming more aware of its underlying unity through "seeing is believing science," might actually experience a beneficial shift, such as us all "waking up" together. By organizing state of the art neuroscientific experiments focused on "attention sharing" between and among individuals separated by thousands of miles we believed we might find evidence to support our hypothesis. The Klingbeils had rigorously tested the unconscious mind, too. Therefore, I thought some form of collaboration could conceivably benefit both our respective research projects."

"As I can be very empathetic, especially with people I feel an affinity with, I was surprised to feel something intensely troubling. While speaking with Bruce—beyond the scientific issues, the implications we spoke of, and talk of the sometimes difficult climate we worked in—I was struck by a deep underlying despair in him. It seemed to stem from troubles he was having with the acceptance of some aspect of his work. This despair made itself apparent through a lack of joy about the future possibilities of our deeply interrelated work. It felt inappropriate for me to assume I had the right to pry into the reasons for this gloom . . . . Though I did not learn about their deaths until sometime later, it was shortly afterwards, perhaps within the week, they committed suicide."

8. In the last phone call with Bruce and John, I (Bill) said, "There is nothing new to report here." Bruce said, "There is nothing new here." I said I was having "fun" presenting the research and was getting some attention. John Klingbeil blurted, "The attention to Spindrift is just beginning!" I said, "John, I agree, I agree. I don't think this [attention] is going to be another false alarm." . . . I said, "Talk to you again tomorrow." Bruce sighed, then said, "Well . . . ." I said, "Bye." Bruce said "Bye." (May, 6th, Thursday night.)

9. My ideas were usually met with enthusiasm. The last couple of weeks I was being told, "Don't bother. People won't get your meaning. Don't waste your time." During one phone call Bruce said, "Spindrift could have *really* taken off had we had the talent help us who said they would."

10. A shadow speculation is that Bruce as a Christian Science healer prayed for an AIDS patient who turned to prayer as a last resort. The patient died. The patient's family may have planned a lawsuit accusing Bruce of being a quack. So on top of the Klingbeils' other problems, there was now a big lawsuit. (Bruce did tell me that a lawsuit would tie-up the Spindrift finances for years.) Further speculation is that the Klingbeils worried that the embattled Christian Science church would be named in the lawsuit, too. Public attention to a lawsuit also might wipeout the Klingbeils' reputations and life work as practitioners

and as research scientists. Supposedly Bruce and John consulted a lawyer about the lawsuit. Afterwards, John wanted to hire a lawyer, but Bruce did not. John decided to accept his father's decision not to pursue a legal defense.

What happened next? Bruce destroyed patient files. He donated the small wealth he had to the needy. A chair and a bed were ordered and were to be delivered soon. The pet dog John longed for was soon to be his. They were looking forward to their sabbatical near the ocean. What mysterious despair led the Klingbeils to say they had no other choice when they didn't believe in suicide? Could it be a threatened lawsuit? One wonders.

11. Former president of Spindrift, Gladys Myers, adds the following:

Approximately a week before the Klingbeils' suicides, I had my last phone conversation with Bruce, the father. He was very interested in the article "Loyal Christian Scientists" which had just appeared in the April 26, 1993, *Christian Science Sentinel.* This article, written by the editors, posed the question asked by a Christian Science practitioner regarding church affairs: "Is there such a thing as a 'loyal opposition'?" In essence, the answer the practitioner received was "no." Fundamentally, only through prayer could one loyally attempt to change the policies and actions of the officials of the church.

This question specifically referred to the actions of another group but did encompass Spindrift and the

> Klingbeils because they were doing prayer research
> declared contrary to the policies of the officials of the
> church. After briefly reviewing the loyalty article with
> Bruce, I promised to mail it to him. His daughter
> Deborah assumes, since she did not find my letter
> in their mailbox, that Bruce received the article before
> they left on their suicide trip.

I deduce these events point to a negative shift. Why would the future look so bleak? Was there "no other out" as Bruce wrote in one of the four suicide notes? "The fact that we had no other out at this point we accept without regrets" was a shock to read, and what did it mean? I didn't know what it meant. Two weeks earlier Bruce wrote quizzically in a letter, "Christian Scientists are opposed to suicide although recognizing that obedience to all moral principles rests on the basis of choosing the least of the evils that confront us at any given time." For the first time the future looked promising for Spindrift and the Klingbeils because of the increased interest in investigating prayer scientifically, the government looking into alternative healing therapy research, and new organizations dedicated to bridging science and religion.[9]

EXCEPTIONS

I assume that many factors drove the Klingbeils to suicide, which they did not believe in. Or were there exceptions? From years of knowing Bruce, I have heard him say that, in times of war, he could see why a spy should eliminate himself rather than divulge national secrets. Bruce also did not recommend suicide and thought it wrong, but he thought that what Dr. Jack Kevorkian did to help people die was sometimes all right. So people who suffered much from illness was an exception. Coincidentally, Oregon became the first state to legalize medical suicides in the 1994 election.

In a note to Deborah, Bruce interpreted the following line of Mrs. Eddy's to have applicability to his and John's *mysterious decision.* "From a human standpoint of good, mortals must first choose between evils, and of two evils choose the less; and at present the application of scientific rules to human life seem to rest on this basis."[10]

The Oregonian reported that Deborah "said her brother left a more detailed note on the computer explaining the suicides. She declined to discuss the triggering event . . . . Public disclosure was something her brother didn't want."[11]

SPINDRIFT ACTIVITIES

The Klingbeils' suicide was strange though. Here's a list that shows the activities of Spindrift.

1. Bruce and John joked on the phone.[12]
2. They were enthusiastic about a Spindrift advertisement I placed in a magazine.
3. In March, Bruce and John approved a detailed application for Spindrift to present two ninety minute speeches at a summer conference in Chicago.
4. Money had been a constant problem since losing his practitioner accreditation but was *improving for the first time* since moving to Salem.
5. Bruce and John often mentioned they were certain their work would earn a John Templeton Foundation Progress in Religion award that is given to outstanding *living people* contributing to religion.
6. Excitement about doing joint work with other researchers was close. They had just conversed with plant and lie detector expert Cleve Backster about doing something together.[13]
7. They were happy hearing Dr. Larry Dossey on radio shows describing prayer research.

8. Bruce said he was excited about an article he was preparing on the recent book on the best sellers' list called *Making Miracles* by psychologist Paul Pearsall. Bruce appreciated that Mr. Pearsall mentioned Spindrift. Bruce was going to comment on Mr. Pearsall's interpretation of Spindrift. He got as far as an outline for the article.[14]

9. A week or two earlier Bruce and John had a friendly meal with U.S. astronaut Brian O'Leary. Brian O'Leary said they were frustrated about their research, but nothing seemed unusual.

10. Two weeks earlier Rev. Karl Goodfellow talked on the phone with Bruce. Bruce said to Karl, "It is people like you we need to carry the research out to the nations."[15]

11. A Japanese woman journalist had called me (Bill) from Japan. I believe she might have been the reason behind six Japanese visitors from the Johrei religion in Japan flying in to Salem to meet the Klingbeils for four hours at the home of two Spindrifters. The Johrei members were interested in learning about the Klingbeils' scientific methods to test healing. They taped the Klingbeils' answers. The Johrei members demonstrated their healing method on the Klingbeils. Bruce and John were good sports. This meeting was just a few weeks prior to the suicides.

12. The *Journal of the American Society of Psychical Research* editor, Rhea White, and the Princeton Engineering Anomalies Research lab manager, Brenda Dunne, have been supportive of the Klingbeils and encouraged the rarefying of their test descriptions. Spindrift was exchanging newsletters with the Institute of Noetic Sciences. The Klingbeils reported these contacts to me as supportive give and take that they appreciated. John and Bruce told me in April 1993 they were hearing

that Spindrift's name was mentioned in places all over the world. That name recognition was happy news to them. They said so. What happened?

Experts told me that people who kill themselves often follow their regular routines to the end. Having noted that, here is what Dorothy, Spindrift's secretary, told me. About a week before the killings, the Klingbeils told her, "We're so worn out. It's going to take us some time to get over it." Two days before Bruce and John disappeared, she went over to visit the Klingbeils at their townhouse. Bruce and John were happy. They looked forward to living in a country town and raising a dog. Dorothy said, "As I left to go, I said, 'You guys are really looking good and relaxed today.' Laughing, the Klingbeils said, 'Hey, thanks, Dorothy.'"

AN OPPORTUNITY FOR YOU TO PLAY DETECTIVE

After reading these facts decide for yourself what happened to the Klingbeils.

1. Criticism and loss of respect for *supposedly* engaging in prayer quackery because of testing prayer.
2. Others' negative prayers to try to adversely affect Spindrift's work.
3. Lack of attention by other researchers for two decades with a few helpful exceptions toward the end.
4. Difficulty of making a new form of mind research conform to standard scientific writing procedures.
5. Loss of friendships of friends and relatives.
6. Denial of membership in a church in Illinois in 1983.
7. Loss of church accreditation as a practitioner in 1983 after twenty six years of service.[16]

8. Loss of income to the poverty level because of accreditation loss.

9. Loss of economic underpinning a shock because Bruce had never paid Social Security taxes because of ministerial exemption.[17]

10. Lack of ability after two decades to acquire funding or grant monies for replicating the research. **(See endnote 18.)**

11. Failures of publicity campaigns.[19]

12. Misrepresentation of Spindrift's work as lunatic.

13. Treatment of Spindrift's members as lepers or agents of Satan.

14. Burning of books about Spindrift.

15. Pressure on a store to drop a book about Spindrift's tests.

16. Cancellation at the last minute of a 1988 PBS television show with a pre-taped interview with the Klingbeils.[20]

17. Frustration over the skeptical inquirings of the debunking skeptics.[21]

18. Excommunication procedures begun by church headquarters.

19. Possible lawsuit the filing of which could have been a trigger for the suicides.

I'm reminded of the adage "death by a thousand cuts." The Klingbeils were battle casualties of their pursuing experiments of a taboo subject—testing prayer.

ANOTHER VIEWPOINT

John Klingbeil had a friend who did not agree with the research. The friend wrote me as follows: (letter on file)

> . . . there is no valid relationship between spiritual discovery, or divine revelation, and the process of discovery employed in the

laboratories of physical science. I understand that this is a direct refutation of the whole monumental work of the Klingbeils.

Those like yourself who have worked closely with them and supported their work must feel puzzlement over their suicides. I can understand this; but has it occurred to you that the death, or some form of total destruction of their work, was its logical and inevitable culmination? I would suggest that they didn't commit suicide with shotguns but with Spindrift; and it took 18 years to bring them to that point . . . .

Don't you see the artificiality of reducing divine Science to "counting the legs of insects," and isn't this exactly what the Klingbeils were doing in their attempt to "love" a mung bean into better health?

This is not to imply that a disease in a farmer's crop may not be destroyed through an understanding of God and His creative order. You may even call this a "scientific process," if you will; but let's not confuse human will with the divine energy . . . . This very confusion of the human with the divine [is] rampant in the thought of [the church] today. Those who contribute to this confusion are leading us backwards instead of forward. And, by the way, this is exactly the error in the "new direction" taken by our Church in the past 10 years. If we continue in this direction, it will be the "shotgun" that kills this movement, as surely as it took the Klingbeils.

> You have a strong sense of humor; and . . . this
> has been a "hobby" for you. I believe, if [John]
> had been able to view his work as a hobby, he
> would be here today. After all, most hobbies are
> an enjoyable and sometimes necessary waste of
> time, not to be taken too seriously . . . . [22]

I do agree John and Bruce took the research so seriously that perhaps there was no enjoyment like hobbies left for them. However, that "to love a 'mung bean' into better health" is an artificial use of love misses what the tests were all about. The tests show that the qualities of embracing-love inherent in holy prayer, pulls the mung bean toward its norms, toward its normal state or condition for its circumstances.

Many Christians believe Spindrift's "suggestions" of love in prayer are willful *mental manipulations* of the growth of the beans or other organisms being prayed for. Christian Scientists have called the Klingbeils' way of praying "mental quackery." The true love from God would promote spiritual growth along with material manifestations of God's will, not man's will.

There is a presumption here. A non goal-directed prayer, *the specialty of the Klingbeils*, has no will or goal in mind. A non goal-directed prayer is simply open to what is right, normal, and orderly for the organism. **If someone wishes to argue that to pray for what is proper and normal in a situation is a goal, it is, in that *it is a non goal-directed goal.*** My question is, how does *anyone* know with certitude that a mung bean or other organism is not growing spiritually when it is being prayed for? A person can't know with certitude that a plant isn't being benefited spiritually by prayer.

People tell me that *love* can't be measured. Bruce predicted that someone will find ways to measure the effects of love's power. In fact, his experiments did.

NOTICING OTHERS' ORDEALS

Thoughts of suicide brought on by the pressures of politics in Washington D.C. are not unnoticed. President Richard Nixon's national domestic affairs advisor was John Erlichman. A Christian Scientist, John Erlichman, said he understood how President Bill Clinton's personal legal council, Vince Foster, was driven to kill himself. Erlichman said the pressures of Watergate so taxed him he seriously considered killing himself. Watergate ruined him. He was disbarred. It ended his marriage. It took all his money. His self esteem was destroyed. Asked if his life was now repaired, Erlichman said, "It is *still* a work in progress."

Howard Armstrong invented FM radio. "Entangled in a web of patent lawsuits . . . he hurled himself from a 10th-floor window."[23]

Dr. Ignaz Semmelweis (1818-1865[24]) promoted the simple act of doctors washing their hands before delivering babies. Despite his evidence for the benefits of washing one's hands, Dr. Semmelweis was so ostracized that he had to flee from Vienna to Budapest. Because life was made so unpleasant for his promotion of hand washing, he committed suicide.

The acceptance of prayer acting nonlocally will take longer to be accepted, than the time it took for hand washing to be accepted by doctors, science, and society. Prayer as psi is often seen as bizarre and a waste of time for traditional science to test seriously.

SCRIPTURE'S SUICIDES

What suicides are in the Bible? Moses and Elijah asked God to kill them. It did not happen. Samson, with God empowered strength, killed himself and the Philistines when he caved in the pillars of the temple. Judas, the betrayer of Jesus, hung himself. Israeli King Elah was assassinated by his military servant Zimri. Zimri made himself king. For murdering King Elah, half the army pursued Zimri. Seeing them coming, Zimri set the royal palace house on fire and stayed in the flames. The counselor Ahithophel was an advisor to King David and his son. When Ahithophel's advice was not taken, he put his house in order and then hung himself. King Saul was King of Israel before David was King. When the Philistine army pursued King Saul, Saul was hit by an archer's arrow. King Saul did not want to be taunted and tortured by the Philistines so he fell on his sword. Saul's armour-bearer fell on his sword also.

King Saul was right about being tortured. After the Philistines found his body, they cut off his head and nailed his body to a wall. As a teenager I imagined, if I absolutely knew a herd of wild animals was on its way to tear me apart, killing myself would be preferable. Take General George Rommel for his attempt on Adolf Hitler's life. If he could have avoided torture, wouldn't he have? General Rommel wanted a trial. Instead, Rommel was forced to kill himself as a punishment to spare his family possible bad treatment. Rommel took poison. In history, *Socrates could have escaped his suicide* given as a punishment by his Greek accusers. Socrates chose to accept his unjust forced suicide and drank the poison. On his last day Socrates discussed the immortality of the soul, a discussion which Plato heard and wrote about in his *Plaedo*. Mary Baker Eddy comments, "Because he understood the superiority and immortality of good, Socrates feared not the hemlock poison . . . . The ignorance and malice of the age would have killed the venerable philosopher . . . ."[25] These are extreme, uncomfortable acts to think about. Yet, there are people in scientific and religious history who tried to avoid such horrors, but were unable to.

BOUNDARY BREAKING

In May 1987 John Klingbeil wrote about the work difficulties Spindrift was having.

> If you can develop a plan which can be carried out within the time and other constraints . . . divide up the projects between our members and have some hope of success, then we can go on. Otherwise I think that the research will be lost in the claims of no way to tell the story and people to tell it to. And . . . Spindrift itself becomes the solitary guardian of the working papers of a lost dream.

Is "a lost dream" what the Klingbeils' research has come to? The Klingbeils' dream was to show evidence of intercessory prayer as psi and that holy prayer has an ordering-characteristic that can be tested in the laboratory.

THE PARADIGM SHIFT AFTER THE KLINGBEILS

Changes in society do happen. In 1901, the National Federation of Musicians discouraged musicians from playing ragtime music. Ragtime was the Devil's music. In 1902, the Teamsters came out against trucks used for hauling. The Teamsters wanted to continue using horses. Someday Spindrift's kind of research will become mainstream.

It was eerie. With John and Bruce Klingbeil dead, opposition to the Klingbeils' research began to subside. For example, in the mid 1990's the church increased its interest in the research trends of spirituality, healing, and prayer.

The Boston church hasn't changed its position on the Spindrift research, but it has changed its position on scientific evidence. Because of positive shifts in science and in the healing-arts, the church in 1997 *began seriously to accept prayer research.* As Bruce Klingbeil said in many ways, "We peons are punished for suggesting research, but others with prestige will be embraced." He added something like "The church calls us pariahs, and then they invite all our friends to the prom."[26]

The Klingbeils are not here for the shift towards research into prayer and healing being more seriously investigated. Some alternate methods of healing may even approach the main stream of society. Spiritual insights are invading psychology. The NIH, the National Institutes of Health, forming an Office of Alternative Medicine, indicates a raised societal consciousness. Bruce Klingbeil felt that the NIH formation was a miracle. Marilyn Schlitz, the director of a prayer study funded by the NIH completed in 2006, said that it's for the reason that so many people believe in prayer that science should study prayer.

A HINT EIGHT YEARS EARLIER?

A **1985** letter from John echoes eerie overtones of Bruce's 1993 comment, "*The Spindrift Papers* are out, at a cost only John and I will ever know."

> My father and I have worked feverishly for several years to bring the tests to fruition before time and money were gone. We each worked 80 hour weeks so that the ideas could be developed enough so that if anything happened to us there would be enough of a record for the research to go on. Now, with the new write-up of the Yeast Test, this goal is firmly in place. In other words, our role can and should change now. We are both mentally, physically, and emotionally burned out. Our new role will need to be more normal with time for our own growth and healing.[27]

A more normal role and lifestyle for the Klingbeils never developed.

The following prayer is by William Penn, the Quaker who founded Pennsylvania:

> O God, help us not to despise what we do not understand.

Astronomer Carl Sagan makes a good point in the following way.

> Like it or not, we are stuck with science. We had better make the best of it. When we finally come to terms with it and recognize its beauty and its power, we will find, in spiritual as well as in practical matters, that we have made a bargain strongly in our favor.[28]

For a list of the good and bad "Consequences" for society from the investigation of spirituality and consciousness, see pages 191 and 192.

Chapter Eleven

Science or Fringe Science

It doesn't matter how good the evidence is if you
have no credibility.

Gerry Spence, trial lawyer

It is generally as painful to us to discard old beliefs
as for the scientists to discard the old laws of
physics and accept new theory.

Lin Yutang, philosopher

Author Helene Ciaravino writes in *How to Pray*, "Clearly,
scientific research into prayer is only in its infancy. In
the coming years, we can look forward to further studies on
the power of prayer and spirituality."[1]

Talented consciousness researchers know they are doing
important research, but it has been a burden to get their colleagues
in mainline science to take so-called fringe consciousness research
seriously. Bruce and John Klingbeil tried to end-run several of the
criticisms which tended to get fringe parapsychologists into trouble
with mainline scientists. Of the group of scientists who did listen
to Spindrift, the following represents some of their experimental
concerns about testing psi.

UNRELIABLE MEMORY

Some scientists believed that the Klingbeils relied on
anecdotes about prayer to prove prayer worked. When they

learned that Bruce and John were attempting actual basic science experiments, the scientists stayed with it.

In the 1960's, Bruce decided that anecdotes and testimonies would be weak as scientific evidence. Human beings are inclined to like the *human friendly feel* of testimonial accounts of spiritual healings rather than a report of scientific data about those healings. The testimonies, from memory, of cures recounting answers to prayers, have been considered "hard" proof by most spiritual healers and those who had paranormal experiences. Modern science has described these testimonial recountings as anecdotal "soft" proof. Science's claim of "soft" proof for prayer being unreliable proof is bolstered by the following information about how human memory recalls details.

In 1957 a memory test was done at Cambridge. A seminary lecture of the Cambridge Psychological Society was recorded. Fourteen days later members who heard the lecture recalled little of what was said at the seminar. Some of what members did recall was different than what actually was said. Casual asides were reported as main points or embellished, and events were reported that never took place. After fourteen days the group of psychologists who attended the seminar forgot 91.6% of the main points of the seminar.

The Klingbeils were aware that memories of an event, unconscious faith, and personal beliefs cause the mind to drift from the reality taking place in a healing. What a person believes has occurred in a personal healing may be subjectively factual and inspirational. However, the scientific claim that it was a healing mediated by prayer is not really scientific where there are other factors to explain it.

WHY IS THERE NOT ENOUGH EVIDENCE OF PRAYER?

Martin Luther wrote, "Everything that is done in the world is done by hope." The forces of faith, belief, and hope are part of the human being's makeup. The forces of belief have good aspects, but sometimes human beings believe almost anything that comes their way. Proverbs says, "A simple man believes every word he hears; a clever man understands the need for proof." (Proverbs 14:15) There are people who have had failures of their prayers, failures in getting help from psychic hot lines, failures in receiving stock tips, failures of lottery numbers, and so on. Yet these people continue to believe even without results. Other people redefine their beliefs after a failure, but every human being projects hopes and beliefs on some level.

It's not easy to develop tests of prayer where the scientific method distinguishes between the power of belief and psi. What people believe deep down about what happens in a scientific test often interferes with the test. For a test to be scientific, people's beliefs have to be watched along side any "distinctive" behaviors of prayer besides belief, if there are any. Otherwise, there is no test of the reality of prayer on healing other than the placebo forces of belief, hope, and expectation on healing. It's a medical fact that our immune systems eavesdrop on our thoughts, beliefs, the cells in our bodies, and on what triggers placebo juices to flow. To distinguish the existence of psi healing effects from our mind-body placebo effects is a scientific challenge for a psi researcher.

BELIEF SYSTEMS / A VICIOUS CIRCLE

Scientists and skeptics (debunkers) point out that there is a problem with *personal belief systems*. People who have the propensity to believe in miracles will do so, *no matter what argument* is presented to them to refute the miracles. The human mind sees and accepts what it wants to believe. The Klingbeils understood that people have strong convictions about their belief systems. The Klingbeils did, too. However, many a debunking skeptic's belief system is poised to repudiate most paranormal "miracles," no matter what argument is presented to them. It's a vicious circle of beliefs between the believer and debunker.

The debunker sees the law of chance working sometimes, but not in a paranormal or miraculous way. For instance, a skeptic would acknowledge that given enough millions of tries, someone will win the lottery, and, potentially, the same person could win twice. Also someone could pray for people who had the worst illness, and given enough people to choose from, some of the persons prayed for would recover completely, for they would rebound anyway because the law of chance remission was on their side.

CALL IT UNDEFINED ENERGY NOT PRAYER

Some scientists said that no one can know that prayer was instigating the consciousness-effects which affected an organism in an experiment. To claim that it's prayer is impossible to prove. Why? Because no one can know for certain what thoughts are going on in a person's private consciousness. To satisfy these scientists, Spindrift said that the people tested were focusing an *undefined energy* on an organism and three patterns emerged.

1) There was no difference in the pattern from the control group pattern. No effect.

2) A healing pattern emerged that successfully defined the norms of the organism.

3) A pattern emerged that defined a marked deviation from the norms of the organism.

HOW SCIENTIFIC ARE THE TESTS?

After a Spindrift speech, a very kind but tough minded scientist from Canada insisted that Spindrift couldn't possibly know what a person was praying or thinking, so it didn't matter what was measured in a test. He said that Spindrift lacked one of two legs to stand on necessary to have "direct" scientific evidence that prayer was convincingly causative. The one leg Spindrift had was "measurements, results, or data." He said, "So what! You're missing a leg!" Spindrift's missing leg was "direct access" to a person's thoughts and consciousness as he prays and thinks. The best that can be done is "indirectly" to note what a man, woman, or child says they were thinking during a test. A person could be unaware of what he was actually thinking unconsciously, or he could lie about what he was thinking. Without this direct access to a person's consciousness to validate which form of thought is causative, the evidence of what a person is thinking or praying is "indirect" evidence of a cause. What did the Klingbeils have? The Klingbeils had "indirect scientific evidence" that human beings were occasioning two mind patterns in experiments produced from two nonlocal forces of human consciousness.

At the 1997 ReDiscovering Cosmos conference on religion and science in Syracuse, New York, two neuroscientists held out the possibility that PET scans of the brain will be able to detect what brain-processes people exhibit when they are praying. That "direct" evidence would provide the second leg to stand on that prayer was causative. One positive development was that PET scans presently show how some extraordinary spiritual experiences are different from delusions. (I contacted one of the scientists, Andrew Newberg, M.D., about investigating a religious man I found who had seizures every time he prayed. Dr. Newberg has written books about how religion and spirituality function in human consciousness: *Why God Won't Go Away: Brain Science and the Biology of Belief* and *Why We Believe What We Believe*.)

In a taped interview Bruce was asked about cause and effect. "We have found that certain mental inputs will . . . produce certain results. This is, in a sense, a cause and effect relationship. It's a definable relationship. It's an equation expressible relationship. It's as much causal as any other force-energy-equation expressible relationship in the physical sciences."

In quantum physics, the theory of 'nonlocality' was the term physicists used to describe distant actions brought on by thought and observance. Nonlocality seemed to parallel what the Klingbeils were doing. To explain the resonance between a healer and a healee, Bruce said, "When you pray about a situation, your consciousness somehow is observing it. Your consciousness links to a situation through paths of *associations* paved with your unconscious thoughts and beliefs. Associations link and pave the paths that bring healing [information to the target situation]."

IT'S ENERGY, PSYCHIC, AND QUANTUM, BUT IT'S NOT PRAYER

Other scientific people brainstormed that it was "a psychic effect," not a prayer effect, or it was "the collapse of the wave function" in quantum physics, not a prayer effect, occurring in the tests. The collapse of a wave function refers to the moment there is an observation of an object. At the moment of observation, a quantum wave collapses. This wave collapse brings a new creative change in the circumstances of the object just observed. (Such an explaination of wave collapse might help explain exuberant moments of peak performance, flashes of creative revelation, and nonlocal healing, leaps which seem to appear out of nowhere.)

John Klingbeil responded positively, "If they (scientists) will acknowledge that there is an effect at all, we have an entrance point to discuss our methodology." John reminded me what skeptic James Randi wrote him about the soybean experiment. "He wrote that if the soybean test worked, all he would admit to was that prayer effected a spiritual healing on soybeans, but the implications don't go beyond the soybeans." John said to me, "That's good enough for me."

I asked Bruce a similar question, "What would you say to someone who feels that it isn't prayer producing the ordering-effects, but it's 'the collapse of the wave function' taught in quantum physics producing the ordering-effects?"

Bruce responded, "They are free to interpret our research anyway they want. They may come up with some very interesting explanations for our test results. I don't think prayer will be eliminated from their explanations altogether. We do pray for our tests, and this prayer-process apparently gives the initial impetus and inertia to the effects produced in the tests."

A CASE FOR PRAYER

To build a stronger case for prayer, the Spindrift team felt that eventually people tested would have to include a variety of people other than people who practiced prayer. For example, people who focus their energy and intention who felt they did so without any holiness or prayer involved needed to be tested to check if their healing effects look like prayer patterns. Also atheists who do not believe in prayer needed to be tested to check if they produced any healing effects which look like prayer patterns.

HOW WIDESPREAD
IS THE HEALING PATTERN?

If order directed prayer patterns are produced by most people in the population, many of whom claim they are not praying, this outcome suggests that the mind's ordering-function is fairly widespread among humanity.

If order directed prayer patterns are produced mostly by people who have a spiritual premise to their lives, this outcome suggests that the ordering-function of prayer is related to people in the population who have a holy outlook or *qualitative nature* which sends ordering-effects to a healee. Such people would be found to be healing assets for the earth.

FALSIFICATION

The Klingbeils understood that a major part of science is this: Can someone else successfully repeat the experiments they have done. Getting scientists to replicate the prayer tests was the Klingbeils' biggest problem. No one was interested in the 1970's.

One of the pitfalls that the Klingbeils were willing to accept was that once a discovery is examined by serious scientists, they begin the "falsification" process. Scientists try to find the new discovery to be a false claim. This process is necessary, but it suggests that there never is enough good evidence to prove a claim. Several times the Klingbeils would remind me about Albert Einstein being asked how much proof was enough. Einstein reportedly said that there is never enough proof.

As years went by, some skeptics and scientists found some faults or glitches in the Klingbeils' tests or data. This situation was anticipated, but it increasingly worried Bruce and John. Who, if they were no longer on the scene, would explore solutions to the experimental glitches that popped up? When Spindrift finally was taken seriously, errors might be discovered.

ERROR FINDING

Religion does not have this problem of glitches popping up. Religion has dogma. You believe the proof or else! Science always has healthy doubts. It's the process. There would be numerous experiments of the Klingbeils to replicate, but if ripped apart in the future, who would be qualified to deal with that possibility? None of us Spindrifters became experts in experimental designs and data retrieval on the level of Bruce and John. Those trained, qualified people who had the potential, held responsible day jobs and could only help Spindrift when time permitted. Their expertise helped the Klingbeils in other ways though, and we thank them for their work.

CRITIQUE

Bruce and John made the final decisions for Spindrift. I feel some mistakes were made. One mistake was the way Bruce and John prepared scientific articles for publication in peer reviewed journals; their science articles described too many experiments at one time. It was easier to find errors when voluminous amounts of methodology and data were reviewed. Ironically, the Klingbeils knew this well and would break down their claims for scientists in one test at a time. When it came to writing articles though, the Klingbeils threw in too many claims and tests into one article.

I wish that John had taken the full scholarship to Northwestern University. John would have earned his credentials as a scientist. In the 1980's, twelve people did consistent work for Spindrift. We were amateur scientists and that fact haunted Spindrift's credibility.

Bruce and John were introverts. I believe that their introversion worked against them in promoting Spindrift. Bruce and John wouldn't attend conferences about scientific anomalies and religion and science. People came to meet them in person, but rarely did Bruce and John travel to meet others. I couldn't convince them that they did well communicating in person. I was happy to speak for Spindrift, but for some of my presentations, the Klingbeils presence would have been more meaningful to an audience.

The Klingbeils sacrificed social activities and recreation for the benefit of the research. John Klingbeil reasoned about not being public personalities this way:

> The big focus of [Spindrift] must be on the success of our research rather than on my father and me. Here in Oregon we have the Bagwam, we have new age Channelers and psychics, and a personal approach would get us forever lumped into the personal freaks category.[2]

THE BENJAMIN FRANKLIN EFFECT

In Benjamin Franklin's experiments with electricity, he was given the credit for discovering the distinction between conductors and insulators. In the Klingbeils' experiments with prayer, they made the distinction between the effects of goal-directed and goal-free thoughts.

From the mysterious accounts of what actually occurred when Benjamin Franklin flew his kite, drew electricity from lightning down a wet string, and survived electrocution, one detail is usually missed. The form of electricity Ben Franklin captured on that string has not yet been harnessed efficiently by science. Yet Franklin's discoveries led to usable forms of electricity. Similarly, no form of prayer has been isolated by traditional science. Yet the Klingbeils' discoveries may lead to usable patterns of prayer.

In the words of Benjamin Franklin in 1749, "Let the experiment be made."

Epilogue

Science is a reliable method of finding truth.
Religion is the search for a satisfying basis of life.
Arthur Compton, physicist

When an influential scientist, a vice-president of
Hewlett Packard, eventually had an opportunity
to review the data [of telepathic remote viewing
experiments] . . . , he wrote, "This is the kind of
thing that I wouldn't believe, even if it were true!"
Russell Targ and Jane Katra,
Miracles of Mind, p. 38

It's been said that gratitude is the highest form of prayer.
I'm grateful that the Klingbeils' pioneering research has
sparked others to research prayer and consciousness.

If holy prayer produces any noticeable effect, restored order
is part of that noticeable effect. Proposals to test the proposition
that prayer produces calming or healing effects is beginning to
be attempted as a part of the investigation of human
consciousness, the brain, the effects of holiness, and spirituality.

Bruce and John Klingbeil used all the know how and
equipment they could muster to test the proposition that prayer
produces several kinds of effects including ordering-effects.
Referring to Bruce and John Klingbeil, two researchers at the
St. Louis Medical Center wrote, "Their work enters the further
reaches of parapsychological research. Reading these sections,
one has the distinct impression that the authors reached the
limits of current scientific methods in exploring the questions
they raised."[1]

WAS THE PAYOFF
WORTH THE PUNISHMENT?

"No good deed goes unpunished." The hatred Spindrift has received for introducing experiments testing prayer makes me wonder if the Spindrift effort was worth the turmoil and unhappiness it has caused some of us associated with the experiments. I hope the payoff was worth the time and money we spent. Speaking for myself, life would have been a lot happier had I not known about Bruce and John Klingbeils' experiments, but life would have been a lot less intriguing. One intrigue was to watch the wild negative reactions to unconventional ideas for marrying religion, consciousness, and science.

Even the tragedy of 9/11 points to the importance of testing prayer. Spindrift knew that prayer wasn't always motivated by good. There is a dark side to prayer, as seen globally when terrorists revealed they prayed five times a day; then they killed people. Philosopher Pascal penned "Men never do evil so completely and cheerfully as when they do it from religious conviction." **After 9/11, a UFO researcher wrote me "Who needs invading aliens to destroy the Earth when we have religious terrorists?"**

9/11 provided proof that the brain's conditioning about God and prayer could potentially annihilate mankind. The world's democracies may be forced to acknowledge that the war on terrorism is a war of ideologies of love and hate and intense beliefs about prayer. **World patterns of love and hate may become as necessary to track as weather patterns.**

For the religious terrorist and meek alike, the following words of Dr. Albert Schweitzer point to higher motives in prayer for mankind. "We must realize that all life is valuable and that we are united to all life. From this knowledge comes our spiritual relationship to the universe."

When it's established that prayer does affect people, the moral make-up of each of us will tip our prayers to include our neighbors or lock and load our prayers to kill our neighbors. Our holy motives in prayer, or lack of them, are in proportion to what we believe is the true nature of God. We need only look at the world today to see that our deep motives in prayer result in physically affecting mankind. Mrs. Eddy writes "The crudest ideals of speculative theology have made monsters of men . . . ."[2]

As mankind increasingly discovers it's in a computerized century, it seems likely that everything worth investigating about consciousness will gradually be given a chance. Since the Spindrifters raised scientific questions about consciousness and prayer that created outrage, perhaps the worst outrage is over for now, and other researchers can more freely investigate the effects of prayer, spirituality, and consciousness on healing.

Good Islam has lasting value. Bad Islam has blasting value. The dark prayers of religious terrorists show that prayer can be used for good or evil. What may spur further research may not be the positive effects of prayer alone, but the horror of prayer when violent religious extremists detonate their prayers as weapons of mass destruction. Given the angry emotions exploded in soured relationships, in politics, and prayers poisoned to harm people, perhaps Edgar Cayce put forward a global warning about hatred toward our fellow man when he said, "Those who worry about earthquakes create earthquakes."

> Our prayers should be for blessings in general,
> for God knows what is good for us.
> Socrates

THE FUTURE

Some encouragement is felt by the 2004 establishment of the Office for Prayer Research (www.officeofprayerresearch.com). This office is a global repository of prayer findings. It's located at the Unity World headquarters in Missouri.

People wonder what is important to them about understanding psi as nonlocal consciousness especially what is called holy quality prayer. In a 1986 interview, Bruce Klingbeil was asked, "Where does this activity of prayer research lead next?"

Bruce replied:

It leads into four areas.

1) One is the evaluation of spiritual healers and the educational and developmental systems that produce them.
2) Another is into pure research [of consciousness].
3) Yet another is into the evaluation of religious and philosophical questions in the light of those experimental tests which can be devised for the purpose.
4) And yet another is into the application of spiritual healing to collective as well as individual human and environmental needs.

2000-3000 A.D.

A millennium prayer was commissioned as part of Britain's millennium celebration for the year 2000. The prayer reads:

Let there be respect for the Earth,
peace for its people, love in our lives,
delight in the good, forgiveness for past wrongs,
and from now on a new start.

APPENDIX

EXAMPLES OF EXPERIMENTS

The definition of a fool is a man who never tried an
experiment in his life.
Inscription on the back cover of Charles Darwin's
Variation of Animals and Plants.

In the early 1970's, the Klingbeils found that the *observer
relationship with an object* along with *quantum entanglement*
derived from quantum physics was a useful way to explain
how prayer reached a target in need of help.

When an orchestra conductor rehearses musicians, he
has the **content** of the music in his awareness. Details and
sections are rehearsed. When performing for an audience,
the conductor waves his baton and his awareness is on the
flow and **momentum** of the music.

The Uncertainty Principle from quantum physics has a
parallel with an orchestra conductor. The Uncertainty
Principle postulates that a person's consciousness can switch
back and forth as an "either or" quantum state of awareness.
Either the **position** of an object in space/time is noticed by
awareness or the **movement** of an object in space/time is
noticed by awareness.

By analogy, let's say a person's consciousness sees a ball as round (the ball's particle state). Or this person sees the ball being thrown in the air (the ball's wave state). According to the Uncertainly Principle, this person's awareness of the **position** of the ball and his awareness of the **motion** of the ball **cannot be observed simultaneously. Either the ball is round or the ball is in motion. The ball is not both round and moving.**

In particle prayer, one's concentration is usually on the *content* and the *features* of what one desires to happen or be manifested *in the object of prayer.* (A particle prayer is like seeing the **position** of a round ball, but not seeing where the ball is going.)

In wave prayer, one's concentration is usually on the *momentum* and the *healing template* for an appropriate resolution *in the object of prayer.* (A wave prayer is like seeing the **motion** of a ball being thrown. The ball is free to navigate creative courses of possibility to manifest a result.) When one's thought is too much on the particles, the *content* of prayer, one can easily miss the waves, the *goal-free momentum* of prayer.

Generally speaking:

❖ When one's thought is on **particles or specific goals,** one is keeping one's thought "inside a box."

❖ When one's thought is on **waves or open-ended outcomes,** one's thought is spreading "outside the box."

The Klingbeils found that these two characteristics above are helpful profiles for bringing forth spiritual healing and for doing psi research.

Appendix

The Botanical Experiments

Plants are as responsive to thought as children.
Luther Burbank, botanist

Thoughts often can be louder than words.
William McDougall, psychologist

The Spindrift research team began doing preliminary research in 1969 through 1974. Experiments were conducted full-time between 1975 and 1993. This chapter contains several successful experiments on plants performed by Bruce and John Klingbeil.

WHY PLANTS INSTEAD OF PEOPLE?

I asked Bruce Klingbeil if he wanted to test prayer on people. He said in essence, "I wouldn't wish to try it unless a way could be worked out to get around people's own unconscious biases and placebos. I don't have a clue how to do that with people yet." But Bruce and John *did have a clue* how to separate out the placebo effect of their own biases. Father and son experimented on *simple* plants instead of *complicated* people.

It would be *more difficult* to know what variable, what single numerical value could indicate the health of a person. Monitoring the health of people requires a lot of measurements, while plants are simpler to measure.

THE PLACEBO EFFECT

Placebo effects are the mind's expectations which can affect how one's body heals. Endorphins can be let loose, too. Apparently plants don't produce the placebo effect. The placebo effect is a people phenomenon, and maybe it occurs in other animals.

In the testing process the Klingbeils had to find a way to track the pattern of their own placebo effects, their own expectations. Then they had to find a way to separate these placebo effects from the other phenomena their thoughts produced.

Some researchers call the placebo effect *the meaning effect.* For example, a placebo pill is inert; then a meaning is attached to it like "Expect to feel better" or "I've got just what you need." This "meaning" switches on positive life and power to help a person heal. The placebo effect enlivens the internal capacity of the body to heal itself.

Such expectations of healing become a distorting factor when trying to **isolate** prayer at a distance. At least the plants and other organisms in the Spindrift tests weren't adding their own placebo effects. If a plant's expectations affected its growth and health, what a discovery and scientific shock that would be.

THE TEST TARGETS

Tests with prayer on living organisms employed yeast cells, mold, bacteria, yogurt, rye-grass seeds, soy and mung bean seeds, among other types of seeds.

In a 1986 interview Bruce was asked, "How has Spindrift measured placebo effects, psychic effects, and prayer effects?" Bruce replied, "As vehicles of our measurement of the mind/matter interaction, we have used seed germination, the carbon dioxide producing ability of yeast, and random number generation."

STRESS ADDED

The stresses added to the botanical tests are similar to those stresses an organism may experience in its natural environment outside the laboratory. Without a degree of stress being added, tests of consciousness on plants cannot be done. Why? *Because there is nothing to measure.* Why? Because the plants are already at their norms, at where they should optimally be.

Mung bean and soybean seeds are organisms that have gotten a workout in the Spindrift laboratory. Examples follow.

A MUNG BEAN EXPERIMENT

A total of 14,400 mung beans were divided into **control** groups (not prayed-for groups) containing 8,400 beans and **treated** groups (the prayed-for groups) containing 6,000 beans. **Both groups** were subject to the stress of saline solution for 24 hours. Nine days later the mung bean sprouts were counted by John.

RESULTS

Control: 20-38 sprouts per container

Treated: 45-71 sprouts per container

Control: average 28.4 sprouts

Treated: average 52.6 sprouts

Average increase of treated over control: 85.2%

TESTING A QUESTION

A question the Klingbeils asked was "Does *more* prayer mean *more* power?"[1] The question has the ring of Jesus' statement, "Where two or three are gathered together in my name, there am I in the midst of them."[2] Some religious groups are quite involved in group prayer. There exist groups of prayer partners, prayer circles, corporate prayer clubs, meditation centers, and congregational prayer assemblies that get together and concentrate their prayer efforts into a united power effort. They believe more prayer brings more power.

In consciousness experiments, researchers sometimes have found that there is increased *coherence*, a detectable signal that emerges, when many minds focus on the same objective.

Can this quantity of prayer question be tested? Spindrift hasn't tested group prayer, but Spindrift has tested one aspect of this quantity of prayer question in the following way.

THE X, Y, Z TEST

Mung beans and soybeans were useful in testing the *quantity* of prayer effects question. Take soybeans labeled in three cups as X,Y,Z. A fourth cup is labeled C, as it is the control group cup. One of the Klingbeils prayed for the X and Y cups together daily. He also prayed for the Y and Z cups together daily. The idea was the Y cup received *twice* as much prayer as the other targeted cups received. An example of a soybean test follows:

SINGLE AND DOUBLE PRAYER TREATMENTS[3]

Control beans: no prayer treatments
X and Y beans: prayer treated together
Y and Z beans: prayer treated together
Y beans: received double prayer treatments

X, Y, Z RESULTS

Control sprout growth: average 11.5%
X's additional growth: 2.0%
Z's additional growth: 3.1%
Y's additional growth: 5.4%

The results of the "Y" cup suggest that more prayer occasions more growth. Our ingrained cultural bias that *more is better* in this case may be true.

Future research may show more definitively that more people praying produces more of an effect. (In other tests not covered here the Spindrift researchers developed some evidence suggesting that when more than one healer was involved, test results subtly improved. One healer did fine but more healers tightened up the results.)

ANOTHER TEST WITH SOYBEANS

Taking two equal amounts of soybean seeds and praying for just one of the two groups formed another test. The not-prayed-for group of soybean seeds could be off to the side or out of sight. It was designated a control group of soybeans. (*Spindrift Papers*, Germinating Seeds, p. l-l)

All the soybean seeds would be under the same humidity, same temperature, the same early state of germination. Stress was added by a researcher to both sets of soybean seeds to deviate the seeds from a healthy norm. The soybean seeds were *under-soaked*. This *under-soaking* is stressful because for normal growth the seeds needed more water. The object was to pray about the "need" of the seeds for more moisture. A researcher did the praying. **The test had this result: seeds prayed for took on more water than the control group of soybean seeds.**

The reverse was tried. Soybean seeds were stressed by being *over-soaked*, making them heavier than they should be. Again, there was a control group of seeds and another group of seeds that a researcher prayed for. **The test had this result: the over-soaked, prayed for seeds eliminated more moisture than the control group of seeds did.** These tests were done many times with the same results. (*Spindrift Papers*, p. 1-27)

A PIGGY BACK EFFECT

Beginning in 1969, the Klingbeils gave some attention to the power of the placebo effect. To the Klingbeils "the placebo effect" and "the experimenter effect" were similar. The Klingbeils believed that the placebo effect acted in the body, but it acted at a distance, too. John Klingbeil writes the following:

> In parapsychology the term "experimenter effect" is used to denote the effect of the experimenter's own thought on tests of thought . . . . Just as the placebo effect enters into the testing of drugs, so experimenter effect enters into the testing of thought.[4]

The Spindrift experiments suggested that the mind's faith expectations acted as a placebo effect. The experiments bore out that the placebo effect *piggy backed* onto the action of a person's prayer. Apparently strong faith or the placebo effect constituted a "ring around" the effect that prayer created. Despite the impression of just one effect present, this one effect was actually two effect-fields that overlapped or nested within each other. A field is "a region or space in which a given effect (as magnetism) exists." (*Webster's* dictionary, 1969, 6B)

One problem with identifying the spiritual element in spiritual healing is that it has been difficult to know when spiritual healing was occurring and when the strong power of the mind's heightened faith and expectancy was initiating the healing actions called placebo effects. The next test attempted to sort out the two *overlapping* effect-fields.

HYPOTHESIS

Several of the Spindrift tests demonstrate there are **two types of mental intent**, need-directed effects and placebo effects. On the basis of many types of psi tests, Spindrift presumes all human beings have both intentions of thought in their minds.

1) The need agenda thought is interested in the need that it touches. It has intelligence and quality. 2) The placebo thought is interested in a direct goal. Its power is volition and presumes to know what the need is and moves toward it. These two forces of thought call to mind a clothing commercial heard on the radio, "**Don't buy size. Buy fit.**" Built-up expectancy and placebos *push* for a big size to be the result. Holy prayers and thoughts *pull* for a fit to the need to be the result.

Holy thought in prayer apparently meets a need and does God's will. Built-up faith, the placebo effect, usually has its own will to get from point A to point B. The buildup of faith, the placebo effect, the experimenter effect, sing as one voice, in the words of the song, "I'll do it my way!" In contrast, holy prayer says, "Not my will, but Thy will, be done."

SEPARATING EXPECTANCY EFFECTS

The following soybean test cleverly targeted the placebo effect as a concurrent force while prayer did its healing of a need. Strong faith, built up in the unconscious mind as a placebo, has its own idea of how to get a stressed soybean healed. The trouble is, the volitional build-up of faith does not know the precise need in the test. The mind's volitional placebo effect apparently *guesses* at the need and pushes for the result it has guessed to be correct and normal. In contrast, if there was normalizing, intelligent, holy information resident in consciousness, apparently the need of an organism would be known to and met by holy thought. Spindrift postulated that the main difference between holy supportive prayer, when it occasioned effects at a distance, and the influence of the placebo effect occasioning effects at a distance, is the following. Spiritual supportive prayer or thought "does the **best thing**" for a need while placebo built-up faith in prayer or thought "does its **own thing**" for a need. Tests were conducted keeping the postulate in place that placebo effects and holy prayer effects differ in how they target an organism's needs. (*Spindrift Papers*, p. 1-42)

A SPECIFIC SPROUTING STAGE SELECTED

In the next experiment *sprouting* soybeans were used. The Klingbeils wrote the following:

[1] This test measured the response of soybean sprouts to holy thought [prayer] under hot dry conditions. A specific preparation of the sprouts, a specific stage of germination, and a specific temperature range during the measurement period were mandated. (*Spindrift Papers*, p. 1-44)

[2] It was . . . predicted that [water] weights drawn from the control [group] seeds would be larger than weights drawn from the [prayed-for] seeds. (*Spindrift Papers*, p. 1-48)

[3] [Why larger weights?] In our . . . test we selected a phase of seed germination wherein moisture release was in the best interest of the seeds. Since "more" is the cultural expectation, we felt that the effect of faith [expressed] would result in moving the seeds in an opposite direction, that is, to influence them to retain more water even against their own best interests. (*Spindrift Papers*, p. 1-43)

The hypothesis was that holy thought drives water retention one way, and faith thought drives water retention another way.

MOISTURE MONITORED

Preliminary testing in preparation for this test found a time in the early stage of germination when the beans actually *gave off moisture*. This period was the chosen time for prayer testing. *The premise was that a person praying would have holy thought which worked to meet a present need. The same person praying would have unconscious goals which worked to meet his own agenda about what was needed and that would show up in a control group test.* The Klingbeils equated the placebo effect of faith with the experimenter effect. "The experimental configuration of this test was thus selected so as to produce a direction of 'experimenter effect' opposite to that produced by the prayer of the practitioner." (*Spindrift Papers*, p. 1-48)

DEFINE ASSOCIATIONAL LINKAGE

The Klingbeils define *associational linkage* as the conscious or unconscious connection of one's thought to another thought, person, or thing.[5] John Klingbeil would say, "When you think it, you link it."

HEAT

Heat would induce stress to the soybeans. For part of the test a **hot box** would be placed over the two groups of bean sprouts. This hot box would cause a partial **hothouse effect**. The hothouse effect is the maintenance of a high temperature. The soybeans needed to hold onto as much moisture as they could under such hot temperatures which varied from the upper eighties to the lower nineties.

One Spindrift person did the praying for this test. He could see the soybean sprouts he was to pray for. The control group of bean sprouts was blocked from the prayer provider's line of sight by a screen. Another Spindrift person acted as a technician and ran the test. Equal weight amounts of sprouting soybeans were put on two electronic scales which fed their weights directly into a computer.

TWO HOURS LONG

The time for prayer treatment of the beans on one of the scales would be long—two hours for each test. "It was felt that over a two-hour period possible variability ('highs' and 'lows' of thought and of associational linkage) would tend to average out and that quantity of holy thought would also be as steady as we could make it." (*Spindrift Papers*, p. 1-43)

After two hours of praying, a hot box was put over the two scales, which kept the beans warm as they dried out. (*Spindrift Papers*, p. 1-45) After each test, a separate control group test was run on both scales. Both scales had equal amounts of beans on them, but *neither scale* was prayed for. The experiment just ran alone without prayer being applied. Both scales were now running as control group scales.

The concept behind this test was that after holy prayer had its effect completed on one set of beans, another set of beans run on the same scale as a control group might pick up the *associational linkage* of the person who previously prayed. **His unconscious linkage might have an after-effect of his faith affecting the control group of beans** *that was not prayed for.*

NUMBER OF TEST RUNS

A total of sixty runs of this soybean test was completed. Thirty runs were done with prayer and thirty runs without prayer. The test results agreed with the hypothesis. Prayer helped the beans chosen at the early germination stage to lose more moisture than the control group of beans behind the screen. Also, the control group runs showed a direction of opposite measurement on one scale. This one scale had had beans on it which were prayed for during previous tests. Although the beans on it had not been prayed for during the control runs, the beans had gained more moisture than those on the other control scale. **This moisture increase showed there was a psi effect being recorded in the control group runs from the scale which was previously prayed-for.**

FAITH-FORCE FOUND IN THE CONTROL GROUP RUNS

What psychic occurrence happened on the scale that in tests was prayed for, but *was not prayed for* during the control group runs? There was a lingering faith-force effect or placebo effect in the control runs. The unconscious mind of the prayer provider and likely the other researcher running the tests apparently had an *associational linkage* to the scale used with the prayed-for soybeans. **A lingering psi linkage to the one scale took place.** "A link of faith," pardon the pun.

RESULTS

The results suggest that the observing mind of the person who prayed, and probably the minds of the other observers, left a link as a placebo faith-force effect on the control scale. The control scale held the control group of beans. In previous tests the same control scale held the prayed-for beans. In the previous tests, the beans were normalized by the affirmative prayer. (The data is on pages 1-49 and 1-50 of *The Spindrift Papers*.)

A REVERSE EFFECT AFTER PRAYER

When a prayed-for scale is then used as a control scale, there is a lingering faith imprint adhering to the scale. Even a holy prayer has a faith component. This faith component imprints as the experimenter effect.

There are two effects: after holy prayer *lessened* the amount of moisture in the soybeans (a beneficial effect), the faith effect, the experimenter effect, lingered on the same scale when this scale was used for a control run. The experimenter effect *skewed* this control scale from doing a true control run. This imprint on the control run scale was not in the best interest of the soybeans by causing the beans to retain *more* moisture.

ADDITIONAL CONJECTURE ABOUT THE CONTROL RUN

The faith-force acting as a placebo effect was wrong this time because *more* moisture was not the need. *Less* moisture was the need. Despite the prayer's moderating force on the first run of the test, on the second run of the test, the mind's push to force more water retention lingered and showed itself. The test worked.

The experimenter effect, the placebo effect, and the buildup of faith push in their own direction of intent. Why? As our culture teaches us, the more and the bigger something is, probably it's better. Spindrift conjectures that "the more the better, the bigger the better" is an ingrained cultural bias that leads the placebo effect, expectancy, and faith to move in the direction of bigness. This bias for bigness produced *more* water retention in the unprayed for soybean sprouts. (*Spindrift Papers*, p. 1-44)

MENTAL STEROIDS

The sprouting soybean test allowed a person's placebo expectancy thought, which acted like "a mental steroid," to be distinguished from the power in prayer which targets a need. This bigness effect is the faith of a person's mind at work thinking *more* moisture is better. In contrast, the need effect was to supply what was needed, *less* moisture.

COINCIDENCE OF DIRECTED WILL AND HOLY WILL

Sometimes a goal directed faith-thought or placebo effect is favorable. This is when its goal agenda happens to have the same motive as holy will has. The healing effect presumably can be more powerful because the holy prayer does not have to first "fight" to overcome the force of human will, the agenda of the placebo effect. In such a case, both the human will and the holy will forces are pushing in one direction as if they were one healing force. Such a coincidence of wills had to be avoided in Spindrift's test designs in order to measure separately the effect of each.

THE PERSONAL AND NON-LOCAL MINDS

Presumably there are two minds also. Just as there is a personal mind that each of us has, there is a non-local Mind some of us call the Divine Mind. Likewise, there are a faith-directed placebo thought with a will of its own and a non-directed holy thought that yields to a Will not its own. A willfully directed placebo thought had the answer to the need. Just ask it. A will-yielding non-directed thought submits to the solution the nonlocal Mind has for the need.

In our thinking we all use directed faith, and we could use more faith and expectancy. However, how often does this placebo thought go in the same direction as the more quality filled prayer thought? It appears the two types of thought-power do not align with each other often. **We presume that *if* a person had his consciousness disciplined enough so the agenda of faith (the placebo effect) moved along the same mental pathways as holy**

prayer thought, you would have a powerful spiritual healer or psychic. Why? Theoretically, there is an additive effect when expectant placebos and prayerful thoughts are working together rather than at cross purposes. (*Spindrift Papers*, p. 1-50) Enough theory. Back to the beans.

KNOWN TARGET / BLIND TARGET

Faith and the placebo effect are directed toward a goal. How can we say that quality holy prayers are not also goal-directed prayers since the need of the beans was known before the experiment began? A good question. This bean test was not a "blind" test. The power of the nonlocal Mind reflected through prayer presumably does have a goal: to meet a need. In addition, our experimenters were also aware of the need of the soybeans during a test. This non-blind test raises a question as to which kind of thought produces the effect. It is encouraging that this test shows mental action at a distance, but whose mental action? Is the action occasioned by the person's own human mind or the nonlocal Mind? This question was experimented with in the next soybean test.

DEEPER PROBING

Another test, one that generated considerable interest, pursues the question of whether **goal**-directed prayer or **need**-directed prayer is operating. A group of over-soaked soybeans and a group of under-soaked soybeans were prayed for together. There was a control group of the same makeup of soybeans away from the sight of the person praying. In this test, the person praying *did not know* which of the two soybean groups needed more moisture or less moisture. Nothing can entirely shield one individual's thought from what is going on in the mental world, but this was a "blind" test in that the researcher was unaware of the needs of the beans. **The hypothesis was that the nonlocal**

intelligence beyond the personal mind of the person praying would know the needs of the beans.

Prayer was applied to the subjects of the experiment. As results came in, they matched the hypothesis. Though the prayer provider did not know the specific need to pray about, the group of over-soaked beans gave off water and moved down toward normal, and the under-soaked beans took on water and moved up toward normal. The different needs were met.

RESULTS

The dual result was a move toward what was normal for the soybeans. The normalcy-reference point, the center point, was approached from two directions: the under-soaked beans becoming more properly soaked and the over-soaked beans becoming less soaked. This test was performed many times.

The operation of need-directed prayer, also known as non goal-directed prayer, was quantified by weight in the move toward normalcy for the two soybean groups.

Results showed different kinds of psi action at a distance occurring in the same time frame. The seeds' two different needs moved toward center or normal.[6]

A LITERAL FIELD TEST

What a relief for the Spindrift researchers to discover that a group of religious people in Ohio were field testing prayer on soybeans. An Associated Press story in the early 1980's reported that a church in Dayton, Ohio, diagrammed a soybean field owned by Mr. Maynard Bigamon, a farmer. The field was divided into twelve plots. Six plots were to be prayed for, and six plots were to be the control group. Ten church members did the praying. They had diagrams of the plots to look at. For forty nights at 11:30 p.m. they prayed, "sending love" to the six selected plots to be prayed for.

The project was set up by Gus Alexander of Wright State University. At harvest time county officials and the Green County agent's technical assistant were on hand to see the results. The technical assistant weighed the yields from all twelve plots. The completed test showed five of the six prayed-for plots of soybeans had heavier yields than the adjacent control plots. The test was successful.

I was glad I knew the Dayton church did this test. When I was a guest on a Chicago radio talk show, the host was incredulous about the Spindrift researchers praying for soybeans. When I mentioned this church group in Ohio praying for a soybean field, it stopped the host from being sarcastic about our tests.

The Ohio church's soybean field test was judged a success. Believers would say it proved the power of prayer. Parapsychologists would say it proves prayer at a distance. Mainline scientists would say, "I'll pack it away in a file for some future study." Debunkers would say, "The test is a magic trick or a fluke that can't be repeated in the presence of objective non-believers."

Gus Alexander, who ran the soybean project, said it was "similar to what people do through prayer and to the whole idea of spiritual healing. In this case, it's healing for the soybeans." The church pastor said the prayers were a "kind of nourishment" and "direct communication." As great as the test and those people involved were, Spindrift points out that the cultural bias of "more and more means bigger and better" was in the intent of the prayers for the soybeans.[7]

EXPECTING EXPECTATIONS

Prayer worked, but there were cultural expectations producing placebo effects in the prayer mix. The unconscious preconception that more and bigger were better for the soybeans showed in the results. That the experimenters also had plans *to increase through prayer* the milk production of cows as well as entire soybean fields indicates a strong preconception in the minds of those involved. As good Christians they proved prayer worked. As good capitalists of our culture, they proved that "more and greater means bigger and better."

Spindrift asks about the *kind of prayer input* in that experiment. Is the prayer directed at what is normal and best for a soybean crop, or is a prayer directed to push a crop beyond what is normal for it? Is more and bigger *always* better? The "biggest size" of a plant may not be what is the "best fitting size" for the plant.

Spindrift has spent much time on theories and the formulation of hypotheses before doing tests. It may be a surprise that real life scientists live by theories and hypothesis. A scientist just does not go over to a lab bench and do an experiment. The most important ingredient prior to doing an experiment is to conceptualize the hypothesis. Doing a test is not just looking for something to happen, but conceiving the kinds of effects which will be looked for in a test. A hypothesis predicts these effects ahead of time, and the experiment then either tends to confirm or disprove the hypothesis.

THREE PLANTS TESTED

Here is an example of a hypothesis followed by a test of the hypothesis. The following test has a controversy attached to it. You may have eaten some of the "giant vegetables" that are coming into grocery stores. They became giant through a plant gene that has been genetically manipulated. Growing big plants may be just fine to do and is a bargain for customers, but there again is this cultural bias that **"bigger is better."** Quantitatively it is better. Is bigger *always* better? While we are not vegetable spoilers, Spindrift asks if fooling around with natural vegetables, if pushing them beyond their "norms" is better?

Spindrift has not tested the giant vegetables, but Spindrift has tested a genetically-altered plant called "triticale." Its developers hoped that triticale would be a food that would grow under bad farming conditions and eventually feed starving populations. What is incredible about the triticale plant is that it is the first and only "new genus" created by man so far. Many species of plants have been developed but only one genus. "Botany is a branch of biology dealing with plant life."[8] A genus is a biological class, a head family name, with many subordinate species that are phylogenetically related to each other.

Triticale crosses rye grain and wheat grain. Triticale was created to blend the hardiness of the rye plant with the nutrition of the wheat plant. The question would not be if triticale would do good for mankind. Apparently it would. Spindrift thought that whether the universe, or indirectly the non-local Creator, approved of a new genus being created was a question that could be asked.

Spindrift took this question into the laboratory.

Tests were set up in which prayer was given to rye seeds and triticale seeds at the same time and to wheat seeds and triticale seeds at the same time. Control groups of seeds were also set up. All three types of seeds were stressed by less than favorable heat and humidity conditions. Thus, all the seeds were in a somewhat growth retarding environment while they were treated by prayers.

The hypothesis tested was this: if the intelligence in prayer and the spiritual virtuous ingredient in prayer were to **support the normal identity pattern** of each seed type, prayer would move the seeds toward normal growth for all three of the seed types. Otherwise, if the spiritual ingredient in prayer was supportive of the **growth identity pattern** of the wheat and rye seeds, but not supportive of the identities of the triticale seeds, then we would have produced some evidence that the moral and spiritual aspect of the universe disapproves of this particular genetic creation. We looked at whether all the seeds moved toward their normal identities in this experiment.

RESULTS

Results of the test showed that prayer *enhanced the growth* of the wheat seeds and the rye seeds as compared to the control run seeds. Prayer *inhibited the growth* of the prayed for triticale seeds as compared to the control run seeds. One person praying produced three psi effects. The hypothesis bore out. This test gives some evidence which apparently indicates that the universe says "no" to or doesn't recognize and penetrate triticale.

Perhaps collective consciousness will learn to cross a boundary and adapt to man made creations. Future tests like the triticale test may assist in determining original parentage. (*Spindrift Papers*, p. 1-36)[9] (The data is on pages 1-37 thru 1-41 of *The Spindrift Papers*.)

PRAYING FOR YEAST

If a person were to look over all the theorizing about, planning of, and executing of the tests themselves, one test would stand out as *fun* to do, once one got the hang of it. That is the yeast test.

As it went through several stages of development, and after it was run over 500 times, this test told participants more than they wanted to know about how their thoughts and prayers modulated psi effects. Within a two-hour period a person could see for himself how his prayer changed the amount of carbon dioxide (CO_2) given off by yeast. (*Spindrift Newsletter*, vol. 2, no. 1, Spring, 1985, and *Spindrift Papers*, p. 2-1)

Specialists known as yeast chemists were consulted. Interestingly there are a few people around who still argue that the cell structure makes yeast an animal instead of a plant. In any case, yeast was found to have life and needs that were testable. Yeast's well being can be measured in terms of the gas it gives off. As yeast gives off CO_2 gas, you know what is going on. It is easier to measure gas than to count bean sprouts.

HYPOTHESIS OF YEAST TEST

The yeast test was done to see if consciousness could affect yeast. Would prayer move yeast in the direction of greater freshness, which represents health for the yeast plant? Attempts were made through prayer to nullify stress and return the yeast to its normal range of freshness.

In this test the Klingbeils measured what happened to carbon dioxide gas production in both control and prayed for stressed yeast during a forty minute period. The hypothesis was that healing prayer would cause the yeast to act like *fresher* yeast, as compared to the control group. "The effect of spiritual healing was to cause less-fresh yeast to act more like fresher yeast."[10]

"Analysis of data should also show that qualitative [quality holy] thought *(Q)* and non-qualitative thought [faith] *(F)*, [produce different patterns], that the presence of one is proportionately the non-presence of the other."[11]

THE STRESSFUL LIFE OF A YEAST CELL

Here are some additional points about stress-testing the one-celled yeast plant.

1) The stress reactions of yeast to being mixed, heated in water, fed food, and so on can be monitored on a computer screen and graphed. (*Spindrift Papers*, p. 2-9 and 2-12, *Spindrift Tests*, 1983, p. 79)

2) Fresh yeast represented prime yeast, healthy yeast. A research problem was to find fresh yeast that would not overreact too quickly when activated in a test. Also, if yeast was not

fresh enough, it would under-react. Why? Because of its handling, the conditions of its frozen storage, and if it was too long on the shelf. (See endnote **12.**)

3) In line with 2), the Spindrift researchers had to come up with a yeast culture which exhibited a decent lag time. That is, the yeast did not react too fast when mixed in water, or it did not react much at all because it was too dormant. The proper yeast was found that performed well in the middle of these two stress ranges. (*Spindrift Papers*, p. 2-21, 22, 23)

THE FAITH-FORCE IN A FORTY MINUTE TEST

If the praying person's faith-force is stronger than the healing action that holy prayer is trying to carry out in the *first* twenty minutes, the force of his faith will cause the yeast to give off more carbon dioxide than the control container of yeast gives off. It was observed that this stronger faith phenomenon becomes apparent on a computer graph during the *second* twenty minutes.[13]

A person's faith-force displays itself on a graph as rising steps of buildup. *This pattern of buildup* is in contrast to the display of moderated, uneven, broken steps, *which is the pattern of the ordering-force in holy prayer.* The Klingbeils conjecture that a person's faith builds up an ascending pattern of gas release, because the force of his faith tends to follow the belief many of us have, that "bigger and bigger is better and better."[14]

USED IN LEAVENING BREAD

The *dry yeast* in the test is the same used in baking bread. It's a *non fast-acting* baker's yeast F53, a product of the Red Star Company from 1953-1984. (**A note to experimenters trying the test. F53 is now fast-acting, so for future tests, yeast in the slower-acting range could be prepared by a yeast chemist. That** is, after 1984, the proper product of yeast has been unavailable. A yeast chemist would have to calibrate yeast around the characteristics of the old F53 product of yeast.[15])

Before a test, yeast is taken out of refrigeration and adjusts to room temperature. Between day three and day eight out of refrigeration is the "window of opportunity" for doing the test. A test participant has to pray for the yeast in this time period to get usable computer measurements. The window of opportunity for the test occurs at a certain point as the stored yeast adjusts from being frozen to achieving room temperature. (*Spindrift Papers*, p. 2-16)

Hooked up to a computer are two electronic scales similar to scales one sees at the grocery store. When the two scales are used, two measured-out amounts of yeast are put in two measured-out amounts of lukewarm water in two containers; the containers are put on the two electronic scales. Two equal amounts of malt are poured into the two containers. It is feeding time for the yeast. Feeding is a type of stress.

After the lids go on the two containers, the computer program starts and one of the containers is prayed for by a volunteer or researcher. The pray-er can pray for the yeast for as much of the forty minute period as he or she wishes. A screen blocks the other control container of yeast from the eyes of the person praying.

As the yeast feasts on the malt, it releases carbon dioxide through two tiny holes in each lid. This release translates into *weight loss*. The scales transmit the losses in tenths of a gram to the computer.[16] Yeast may be luckier than human beings. It is an organism that can eat and lose weight!

MINUTE BY MINUTE GRAPHS

The test lasted for forty minutes. When the test began, yeast was under stress from the heat in the water and from feeding. Every minute, the carbon dioxide gas release was computer-graphed. The yeast test resulted in printed vertical bars on a graph that indicated intervals of time when the prayed-for yeast under stress gave off levels of carbon dioxide gas. The Klingbeils found that the division of the forty minutes of the test into five eight-minute intervals gave an adequate representation of the carbon dioxide being released. The Klingbeils determined that ten four-minute intervals was adequate for mathematical scoring purposes.[17]

CARBON DIOXIDE ALIAS CO_2

Depending on the need of the yeast during a particular time interval, the yeast would give off more or less CO_2 gas. As researchers John and Bruce Klingbeil explain:

> Theoretical considerations tell us that gas production will be moderated by patterning [quality] thought in terms of what is "good for" or "best for" the yeast. This means that in the moments of most intense feeding activity when the tendency toward over-action might be greatest . . . a moderating influence could possibly be seen in the treated [prayed-for] runs.[18]

> The effects of qualitative thought are seen more often in the patterns produced than in actual total increase or decrease of gas production. This is because, in contrast to goal-directed thought [or faith], qualitative thought adjusts the form and function of the system in accordance with the need of the system, the best interests of the system.[19]

A graph of this gas activity for both control group runs and prayed-for runs is represented in the following way. The X-axis on a graph represents time, the forty minute duration of a test. **The Y-axis** on a graph represents the amount of CO_2 gas given off during the forty minute test.

RESULTS

These four graphs of actual runs of the yeast test are based on Spindrift's "first" newsletter in 1984. Each graph is thirty accumulated test runs. The graphs are as follows:

1) The control groups' accumulated results are on **graph one.** This yeast was not prayed for. (Also includes random metabolic artifacts.)
2) Bruce Klingbeil's accumulated prayer results are on the qualitative graph, **graph two.** The graph's broken line, its up and down pattern of gas release, indicates the yeast is looking more like what fresher yeast looks like shown on **graph four.** The Klingbeils measured identity as a pattern representing normalcy.
3) A volunteer's accumulated prayer results are on the human faith graph, **graph three.** Faith and belief build an up hill pattern of bigger amounts of gas release.
4) **Graph four** is a reference graph of active fresh yeast. Its pattern represents health. When a test-participant's prayers can approximate *this pattern,* his thoughts have shaped the healing pattern that is in *the best interest* of the yeast. Then a modest example of healing at a distance has been recorded as a pattern on a graph.

Graph of Control Group Test Runs
With No Thought Applied

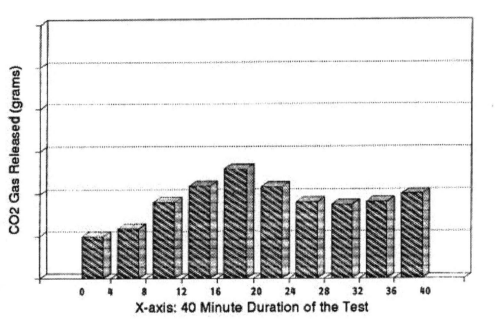

Qualitative Thought's Broken Gas Line
Production Greatest in 1st Half of Test

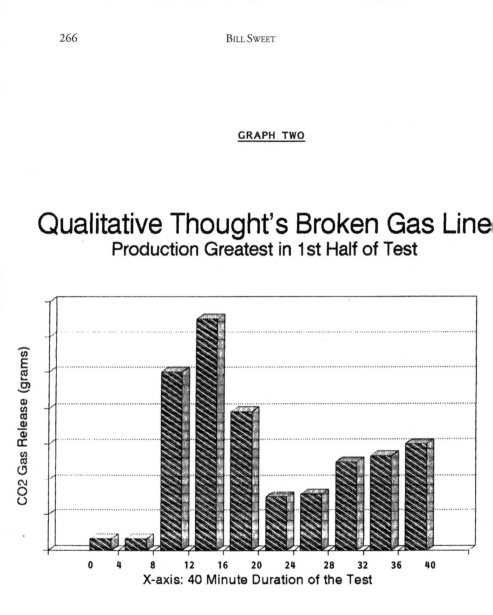

The yeast needed the most gas released during minutes 12-16. The bar in minutes 12-16 rises to a seventh level. The highest bar in Graph Three (minutes 36-40) only rises to a sixth level.

<u>**GRAPH THREE**</u>

Graph of Rising Gas Production Line
As Faith Builds Up

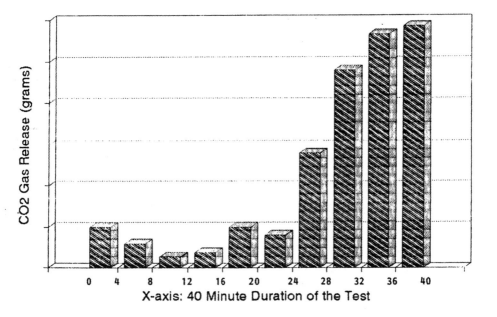

In tests of 44 to 48 minutes, the bars rise higher
to a seventh level.

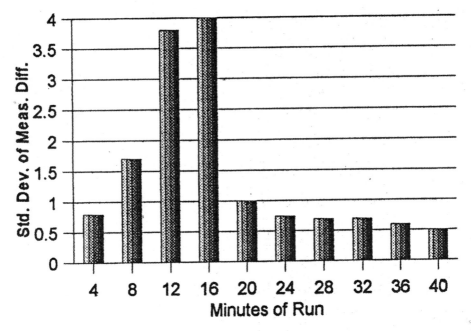

Freshest Yeast

This is a reference graph of fresh yeast after it has been mixed in water for a forty minute test run. No stress has been given and no treatment by prayer has been given to this yeast.

WHAT THE FOUR GRAPHS SHOW

The computer program monitored weight-loss over a 40-minute period. The 40-minute periods were divided into 10 four-minute periods—that is, into 10 groups.

EVALUATING TWO PRAYER PATTERNS

The Klingbeil's theorize, when prayer has an effect, a "Thy will be done" prayer produces what is "best," and a "My will be done" prayer produces what a person's expectancy "wants."

THE FAITH PATTERN

If ballooning faith predominates in the results (graph three), Spindrift would evaluate the person to have more tendency toward faith healing directed by his personal human mind. This result is more derivative of "*my will* be done." In fact, in some religious traditions, believers deliberately consciously and unconsciously *direct their faith and will* toward a goal to be achieved. This achievement of a belief or goal is their prayer preference. Most petitionary prayer is goal-directed.

MODERATING THE FAITH PATTERN

If the moderating agenda of a "Thy will be done" prayer predominates over the results of ballooning faith, the yeast organism gets what it needs. In the yeast test, the person who gets the prayer result in which *more*, instead of *less*, carbon dioxide is released early in the test would be evaluated to have more tendency toward spiritual healing (graph two).

For the need-driven-prayer to have a measurable effect, it first has to predominate over the "my will" force of faith and expectancy before going on to the need of the yeast. Spindrift presumes this need-driven-result is more derivative of "*Thy will* be done" and shows a semblance of order. This need-directed result draws a moderate uneven pattern of gas release on a graph.

We all have these two agendas of thought in us. They are different because they form different patterns which can be seen on graphs. *The yeast test is set up to have the quality power in prayer move in one direction and the quantity building up power of faith or the placebo effect move in another direction.* If the mind's willpower and faith supports the quality and direction of holy prayer, great, but the Spindrift tests are not conceptually designed that way.

To separate holy prayer working at a distance from the agenda of the mind's placebo effect faith working at a distance, Spindrift feels is something new to science and religion. This dual insight indicates the presence of the faith agendas in one's own thought and of moderation by the need driven agendas in one's own thought. This insight should tell us something about how prayer works when prayer works well.

POSITION OF ELECTRONIC SCALES

Here is another factor about faith in the form of the experimenter effect or placebo effect. **The Klingbeils found that the person praying develops *a mental imprint associated with the scale* used in runs of the test for which he prays. In control runs of the yeast test, the same scale which was used in the prayed for runs, carries over a *built up mental imprint.*** This imprint showed up in higher than normal results on that same scale when the yeast was **not** prayed for.

MENTAL IMPRINT

The Spindrift researchers surmise this mental imprint is the experimenter effect, one more psi effect to trace in the yeast test. Furthermore, someone else who walks in and takes the test may choose the other scale to pray for. That choice would eventuate in his developing an imprint associated with the other scale. **The experimenter effect would be displayed on whatever organism was on that scale.**

The Klingbeils traced the experimenter effect in the following way. The yeast on the control run scale was on the same scale previously used in a prayed for run. This control run scale gives off *more* carbon dioxide than a control scale should, than the control scale next to it. That is, the scale used previously to pray for, now being used for a control run, manifests higher results than the other control scale. A lingering associational linkage of thought is imprinted on the control scale that was prayed for earlier. Apparently thought not only *touches* the scale, but it also leaves an impression that lingers for awhile. (*Spindrift Papers*, p. 2-19)

AFTER PRAYER A REVERSE EFFECT

When a prayed-for scale is then used as a control scale, there is a lingering faith imprint adhering to the scale because even a holy prayer has a faith component. This faith component imprints as the experimenter effect.

There are two effects: after holy prayer benefited the yeast, the faith component of thought reasserted itself as the experimenter effect and imprinted the control scale of yeast. This experimenter effect not only *skewed* the control run, but it was not in the best interest of the yeast. (A similar imprint on a control run scale occurred in the soybean hot box experiment described earlier on page 252.)

EVALUATING HOLY ABILITIES

The final version of the yeast test evaluates how one prays. Generally a person who prays for the test registers, overall, either a holy thought result or a strong faith result. A third possibility is that a person might register no results at all. Twenty to thirty runs of the test would give enough *accumulated* data to work out a test score.[20]

THREE PATTERNS OF GAS PRODUCTION

The unique feature of the yeast tests is that they tended to show one of three distinct reactions to prayer.

1) If the prayer was ineffective, the prayed-for yeast would show a pattern of gas production that varied over time essentially like the control yeast (the yeast that was not prayed for).

2) If the pray-er was successful in achieving a holy, pattern-mending state and linking that state to the yeast, the gas production was significantly different from the control pattern and was repeatedly more productive in the *early* stages of the test period, when it was most needed by the yeast.

3) Sometimes the pray-er felt that he had not been able to achieve or maintain the desired holy state and to connect that mind-state effectively to the yeast. But he had felt a strong intention to "help" the yeast, and this goal-driven state showed up in a buildup of gas production *toward the end* of the test period. This buildup of gas was repeatedly more productive toward the end of the test period and was significantly different than the control yeast pattern (the yeast without prayer).

These prayer patterns seemed to correlate with the healing abilities of some of the participants. That is, some of the professional spiritual healers who had demonstrated in their lives an ability to help and heal persons through prayer, were apt to be those most able to achieve that healing effect in the yeast and produce the holy prayer pattern described in 2) above.

Some persons both experienced and inexperienced in prayer could achieve no demonstrable effect, and they produced a pattern described in 1) above.

Some persons who were experienced but untrained achieved the goal-driven pattern described in 3) above.

The fact that the patterns appeared to fall into one of the three types just described gave the experimenters confidence in their explanation of what was taking place.

(The data is on pages 2-3 thru 2-15 and 2-28 thru 2-29 of *The Spindrift Papers*.)

YEAST TEST THROWS A SWITCH AND TURNS ON A LIGHT

Here is a consciousness test that connects man's thought to machine through the condition of yeast. Man's mind influencing a machine is known as "psychotronics." One of the clever things done with the Spindrift yeast test was to put into computer memory a reference graph of one of the highest qualitative prayer scores that a prayer provider ever achieved in a past yeast experiment. An electric light bulb was hooked up to a switch outlet on the computer. A researcher prayed for the yeast. After the forty minute run of the test, his results have formed a graph in computer memory. If his graph was in the same amplitude range and similar to the reference graph already in computer memory, the light bulb would switch on. About one in six tries of praying for the test turned the light on. The yeast test is true psychotronics. A person's thought-pattern resulted in a light turning on. (*Spindrift Papers*, bottom of p. 2-20)

BY CHANCE OR
BY GOOD PERFORMANCE?

If two friends got together and played a game of tennis, one friend would be likely to play better than the other. Over a number of tennis matches, a pattern of each other's strong suits would show up. Spindrift found several individuals who could play the game of praying for the yeast test pretty well. These individuals could pray and occasion a **quality prayer** *signature*, a broken, up-and-down bar-graph pattern, the pattern of fresher yeast. **Prayer resulted in a recordable physical phenomenon, a computer graph of gas production that displays a distinctive pattern of fresh yeast.**

In the quality signature result range, differences in degrees of *amplitude* (amount) of quality prayer effects showed up on graphs from the efforts of these prayer participants. **That is, different participants' thoughts occasioned different amounts of gas production.** On graphs, the different heights of the amplitudes translate to how closely each participants' quality prayer result approached the height of the amplitudes of what fresher/healthier yeast looks like on a reference graph.

ISOLATING A TIGHTER CRITERION

By adding an electric light and an on-off switch to the yeast test, the Klingbeils sought to answer a question: How can a pattern of prayer-thought be isolated enough as the explanation for the light switching on? The Klingbeils explored this question experimentally. They experimented to find a range of bars on the reference bar graph put into a computer that would not be triggered by chance, experimenter effect, or other similar artifacts of psi in league with displacement effect and unintentional mental/visual cues and associations to the test.

DISPLACEMENT EFFECT DEFINED

Displacement effect occurs when the unconscious mind somehow fixes on a target other than the test target the conscious mind has chosen to concentrate on. This displacement effect is a type of experimenter effect. It is a drifting effect that has interfered with and garbled many parapsychological and prayer healing results. Here's an illustration. A psychic in a parapsychology laboratory is attempting to read a person's mind. The psychic is asked to guess what card a person is holding. The person holding the card concentrates on the image on the card. Instead the psychic's mind drifts to the color red which is shimmering. It turns out that the person holding the card saw a fire engine with lights flashing while driving to the laboratory. The psychic's mind drifted toward a tangential mental image. (Then there's the joke about the overworked school teacher who thinks about her little school children day and night. Desiring to be happier in her exhausting job, the school teacher prays, "God, please make me like other children of God." Suddenly she becomes short and little like the children she was dwelling on.)

DISPLACEMENT THEORY

Apparently the displacement of thought means that while you consciously think of one thing, your unconscious thought goes to something else. It is possible that displacement theory occurs when the mind and intuitive senses find other scenes or objects more engrossing to dwell on than the object at hand. Possibly the mind's defense mechanisms place twinkling images in front of a person's intuitive or spiritual or psychic senses to misdirect the objective at hand. Possibly the mind is made to link to many things, which shows how difficult it is to isolate thought enough in a parapsychology test.

PSI HITTING DEFINED

Parapsychologists test people to observe if they can affect the tossing of dice, guess cards, read minds, remotely view scenes, influence randomness in a machine, send healing to organisms, etc. In a series of tries, every time a psychic participant intuits the correct figure on a card, the correct position of dice, or a healer without any physical contact benefits an organism, these participants have made hits, psi hits. Such hits are called *psi hitting.* **Psi hitting is what parapsychologists and other researchers are interested in documenting.** When many psi hits build over time, beyond what is expected by chance, these hits show psi (or mental) processes may be at work.

The size of psi effect is shown by the magnitude of the departure from the expected result; the bigger the departure from chance, the bigger the evidence of psi. Many runs of the same test have to be made. Good psi hitting occasioned by enough tries of a test gives evidence that an anomalous mental force was present during a test. The more psi hitting data collected, the more convincing is the evidence that psi exists.

PSI MISSING DEFINED

Besides "psi hitting," parapsychologists look for evidence of "psi missing." Psi missing is when a psychic participant gets *too many misses* beyond chance. That is, when a person taking a test does not correctly guess a card or predict accurately *as often as would be expected*, this is called *psi missing.* Psi missing occurring beyond chance suggests psi was still involved in the test. John Klingbeil wrote, "J. B. Rhine pointed out in 1952 that, with an ESP deck, psi deviations were noted to be roughly equal in terms of psi-missing (low deviation) or psi-hitting (high deviation) in spite of the fact that a difference should (presumably) exist."[21]

Maybe displacement effect accounts for some occurrences of psi missing. Psi missing produced by a participant may not be what a person wants, because it may indicate lack of a *desired* psychic outcome or ability, but such *displaced* psychic effects show indirect psychic ability occurring anyway. These missing-the-mark-effects *should not be there* if the results were due only to chance.

PSI MISSING LABELED NOISE

The debunking skeptics say psi missing is the one thing parapsychologists are good at reproducing repeatedly. The debunkers point to *regular* psychology which tells us that human beings faithfully look for evidence to *support* what they already believe, no matter how far fetched it is. A debunker says, if a person feels psi missing is a type of psi, that is his personal belief system deceiving him.

There are enough believers and non-believers in psi to fill the world. However, it does seem some debunkers count the pot holes in the road, but they deny there is a road. They regard psi hitting as psycho hitting. The debunkers count the psi misses along the road but do not stop to smell the occasional flower of mathematical tracking of psi hitting.

PSI MISSING THROWS SHADOWS OF PSI

There is a trick parapsychologists use that skeptics (debunkers) feel is bogus to put in data analysis. The trick is to get negative marks on tests from psi missing data. As mentioned, sometimes psi missing in a test occurs above chance probability. As oxymoronic as it sounds, a person being tested might be "a good psi missing hitter." He gets too many misses beyond chance. A test participant does not get the psi hitting results he wants, but the data shows indirect evidence of the presence of psi effects. That is, a participant gets some unanticipated psi effects.

DIFFERENT WORLDS

The study of psi missing should not be so shunned. Science now knows the micro world of quantum physics is dramatically different from our everyday world. Likewise, the world of consciousness is likely to be different from our everyday world. Psi research has to start somewhere. Psi missing may be an important landmark.

The Klingbeils felt psi missing data should be tracked right along with other effects of psi. Some scientists may feel psi missing is noise, but as new ways to apply mathematics to psi effects evolve, having psi missing data on hand may become useful.

For Spindrift's contribution to parapsychology on psi hitting and psi missing experiments, see a talk and a companion scientific paper both called "Cards, Dice and Defense Mechanisms." The paper was written by the Klingbeils. The paper is on file at Spindrift, and it is published in *The Journal of the United States Psychotronics Association*, Summer, 1990.

TO TURN ON THE LIGHT
TO HIT, OR NOT TO HIT,
IS THE QUESTION

The Klingbeils wrote the following:

> The Spindrift [yeast] test separates patterning and volitional/intentional effects by observing their actions on a system at different points in time . . . . The basic thinking behind this test is the idea that early in the test (the first 20 minutes) feeding stress will make the patterning effect more pronounced than the goal-directed effect and that

late in the test (the last 20 minutes) the goal-directed effect will be more pronounced.[22]

In inventing the protocols for the turning-on-the-light test, the Klingbeils had to figure out what numbers on a graph would be necessary to hit a target on a graph. They had to arrive at a range on an emerging graph of qualitative psi effects that could fit in and closely match a graph already in computer memory. Individual segments of the emerging graph are printed after every four minutes of praying. The graph already in memory represented a fairly good recovery of yeast from heat stress. Could emerging prayers match the graph?

COMPARING PSI PATTERNS

In this test where a light turned on, patterns of thought were compared. Two graph-patterns must be a close match for the light to switch on.

The Klingbeils ran a battery of yeast tests as a series of control runs alone. In the control runs no intentional or displacement thoughts would be consciously linked to the yeast. Fifty control runs were laboriously done. Each control run consisted of two scales holding two containers of yeast in heated water. Of the fifty control runs, forty nine stayed clear of the range of bar formations that would match a graph in computer memory which would then trigger a light switch to turn on. One control run in the fifty runs did come in range close enough to trigger the light switch. Variations like this are expected. These side effects may include experimenter effect and an occasional metabolic effect when yeast is activated in the water.

Experimenter effects were not much of a problem in previous uses of the yeast test. Over a series of yeast tests that were prayed for, such side effects in the control runs could be averaged down mathematically. Checking the results of a series of prayed for yeast runs *against* a series of control group yeast runs is how experimenter effects and psi hitting effects are found and distinguished. The psi hitting evidence presents itself as a distinct pattern on the prayed-for side, the targeted container side of the test. The experimenter effect pattern presents itself on the control run side of the test. The two patterns are as different as apples and oranges.

CONTROL RUN NEGATES
PSI HITTING AS CATALYST

The Klingbeils had to find out how to hit a target (a light switch) without a control group run hitting a target (turn a light switch on). They had to put in a better target graph. The graph would have to be *a target out of range* of the control run blips/artifacts. The exaggerated control run blips/artifacts/experimenter effects would be the key variable to keep at bay. Why? Because having a control run occasionally turning on a light would weaken the strength of the evidence. Was it chance or prayer that actually switched the light on?

TO TURN ON THE LIGHT
BETTER PRAYER
PERFORMANCE NEEDED

The Klingbeils discovered they had to raise the standard of quality mental input to turn on the light. They had to raise the standard of prayer performance so high that a control run could not get up there. The new graph in computer memory would have to be a very excellent example of the recovery of yeast from stress. Previous graphs were studied. An impressive example of a person's qualitative prayer performance on stressed yeast was chosen. This impressive performance amounted to a significantly larger qualitative effect elicited by prayer.

DOING THE TEST WITH THE NEW GRAPH

The chosen graph was installed in memory. The Klingbeils would be looking for a hit or missed target. The target was the reference graph. A hit would switch on the light. Would a control run turn on the light?

A number of yeast tests were conducted of both prayed-for runs and control-group runs. The measured results of CO_2 loss and gain in prayed for runs accumulated and formed graphs. The measured results of CO_2 loss and gain in the control group runs accumulated and formed graphs.

RESULTS

The Klingbeils were pleased. Comparing prayer effects against the pattern on the new reference graph worked well. Prayer occasioned a qualitative graph match in about one in six tries of the yeast test. A psi hit like that reminds a person of a Western movie where a cowboy has a six shooter with only one bullet in a chamber and five empty chambers. This one psi hit, about one in six, turned on the light. In the numerous control group runs of the yeast test, no control group run ever turned on the light. The test worked.[23]

CLOSE BUT NO PSI-GAR

Does psi hitting happen often enough? In the upgraded turn-on-the-light yeast test the level of difficulty to achieve a target match, a psi hit, was raised. A scientific dissenter to the test might say, "Your test isn't good enough. Your test works less than twenty percent of the time. The test should work all the time."

This kind of criticism misses the point. How often does an experiment have to work to show the presence of psi? One psi hit out of six is not bad. **Hitting the target, a light** switch, with the energy in prayer, even if it takes many attempts, is a scientific breakthrough.

POPULATION PROVIDING TEST PARTICIPANTS

The Spindrifters feel that effective pray-ers are psi users and do not know it. Considering that millions of people practice praying daily, it seems reasonable to assume that there are a number of pray-ers with potential psi hitting abilities in the world's population. Are there not many faith effects, healing effects, and psi hitting effects that can be tested, using these experienced pray-ers? The Spindrifters hope a lot of people will be tested in the future. Why? So many people will have the opportunity to see their psi hitting and prayer hitting effects, or lack of them, catalogued by the scientific method.

MOTIVES RIDICULED

Praying for a plant in a laboratory has drawn ridicule. It is not easy for any of us to think outside the norm, especially when it comes to an emotional subject like religion. If the experiments spark more interest in investigating the inner qualities of a human consciousness, perhaps those religious people who are bothered by the experiments might reevaluate their worth.

The motive of a person praying under scientific conditions is not directly to get a score or a high enough score to turn on a light. The motive is to pray to support the identity of the yeast cells, or to benefit the needs of the yeast cells, or to express some similar loving motive. If a measurable result ensues, a faith pattern or a qualitative pattern emerges on a graph. If a very strong qualitative prayer result ensues, a pattern emerges that is distinctive enough to flip on a light switch. People should pray as they normally do. The scientific method just monitors to see what prayer does to an organism.

DNA RELATIVES?

Genetic scientists have discovered that deep down in the tiny corridors of a yeast cell's genetic code is a DNA component that is a common ancestor to human beings. Much of a yeast cell's genetic code is the same as that in human beings. Whether this surprising genetic kinship has anything to do with why yeast is such a sensitive organism for tests of thought and prayer is pure speculation.[24] Spindrift has tested prayer on many plant organisms. Yeast was the easiest to work with experimentally, revealing the most information by being a sensitive indicator or medium or reflector of thought. From the Spindrifter's experimental experiences, yeast could really be called a fun fungus.

YEAST IN REVIEW

To acquire testable yeast, yeast chemists should be consulted. The yeast test recorded two psi outcomes: 1) the yeast mending-effects occasioned by goal-free prayer. These CO_2 effects reflected what was best for the yeast under the circumstances. 2) the continually increasing effects of placebo faith occasioned by goal-directed prayer. These faith building up effects occasioned the yeast to give off more CO_2 than was needed for the circumstances of the yeast.

Yeast testing illustrates a nurturing and identity-supporting power in prayer. How? Prayer helps stressed yeast act more like fresher, healthier yeast.

If a person's faith-bias of what the yeast needs is the strongest ingredient in prayer, a building up pattern of CO_2 dissipation is formed. This pattern is not what the yeast needs.

The yeast test shows several consciousness effects:

1) **The presence of a psi effect,**
2) **the quantity of the psi presence,**

3) the ordering-quality of prayer-psi,
4) the building up of faith-directed-psi, and
5) psi hitting a bull's eye target—a computer graph of healthy yeast.

Regarding the holy or quality ingredient in prayer, the Spindrift yeast test looks at two things:

1) the order-mending effects that approximate ten different norm intervals during a forty minute test, and
2) the degree of amplitude, height, of the order-mending effects.

The yeast test gives evidence that a person can achieve a quality prayer result, a result that is best for the yeast. The yeast test can also show amplitudinal degrees of quality psi effect. One way this quality is calculated is by comparing a person's prayer results against a graph of what fresher yeast looks like. That is, a person's prayer results are checked for coherency (logically connected) with a graph of yeast in better condition. A person who has prayer results projected on a graph that comes closer to the fresher yeast graph scores higher marks. Prayed-for graph results are compared with the control group runs of the yeast test.

THREE RESULTS

Three kinds of results are recorded on the yeast test.

1) Some people record no prayer or psi results. No results would mean their prayer results would appear the same as the control group results.
2) Some people record qualitative (quality) prayer results which translate into the yeast receiving what it needs for its stressed circumstances.

3) Some people record a faith building up component of prayer, the placebo effect component, that apparently has its own idea of what the yeast needs, more gas released. (*Qualitative Research*, p. 101)

VISUAL COMPARISONS

Check the graphs of the yeast test on pages 148-151. Visually please compare the following:

1) A control group graph of yeast has *differences* in peaks and valleys *compared to a faith* graph of yeast. Faith builds up higher steps.

2) A control group graph of yeast has some *similarities* in peaks and valleys *to a non goal-directed* graph of yeast. Why? In a sense, a control group is a normal curve of yeast that is **depressed** by the addition of stress to the yeast. In a non goal-directed graph, *prayer helped overcome the stress* in the yeast. Without prayer, the stress depressed the curve of yeast.

3) The CO_2 highest peak of a non goal-directed prayer for yeast is actually **higher** than the highest CO_2 peak of a goal-directed faith peak that builds up on the faith graph. **Notice that the qualitative graph uses seven spaces (more headroom) than the six spaces used on the faith graph.** This early non goal-directed peak occurring in the first twenty minutes is approximating what fresher yeast looks like.[25]

4) The *comparison* of control group CO_2 release with prayed-for CO_2 release reveals the mending-effect of non goal-directed prayer, or the faith building up effect of placebo-driven prayer, or no effect discernible from any prayer. John Klingbeil adds, "For the actual evaluation [of the graphs] the minute-by-minute number of grams difference between the two balances (in tenths of a gram)

are used as the basis for the evaluation." (*Qualitative Research*, p. 97, *Spindrift Papers*, p. 2-19)

AN ODD USE OF YEAST AND PRAYER?

The yeast test is a psychotronics test, a parapsychology test, and a religious test. A person taking the yeast test can be described as undergoing **psi-CO_2analysis.** Why? Because measuring the effects of consciousness on carbon dioxide release is psi-CO_2analysis. The test participants' graphs are on file.[26] For the computational PC program that scores the yeast test, see *The Spindrift Papers*, page 2-32.[27]

CO_2 AND PSI

In 1984, Spindrift's first newsletter included an article by John Klingbeil:

A Note To Our Readers

It is probably appropriate that Spindrift's first newsletter be devoted to Spindrift's first major research project—*The Yeast Test.*

The Yeast Test is the first controlled repeatable test of spiritual healing of its kind. The data and mathematical analysis show that it works . . . .

Spindrift has put almost all of its efforts since its inception into this project. It was felt that because Spindrift works in an area that most people find strange that it needed to have a complete package to put forth—the theory, the data, the mathematical analysis, and the knowledge that it is ready, willing, and able to replicate these tests.

This is a milestone for Spindrift. It is Spindrift's coming of age. With the repeatable test it leaves the realm of conjecture and meets the hard sciences on their own ground.

The existence of these tests is itself a challenge to the materialistic view that science holds, but Spindrift is comfortable making that challenge.

The math and data will not be gone into in this newsletter, but on the last page there is an order blank for a copy of *The Spindrift Tests* [1983] which contains all the information.

The balance of this newsletter is composed of the reactions of some of those associated with Spindrift to the tests.

The first newsletter included an article "The Yeast Test" by Spindrift's president, Gladys Myers.

The Yeast Test

Spindrift announces *The Yeast Test*, a series of experiments in which conscious thought affects matter. *The Yeast Test*, an outgrowth of nine years of research, is a *repeatable, controlled* series of tests in which mental input, prayer, alters the amount of gas released by yeast as measured by electronic balances interfaced with a computer.

An intriguing by-product of the research with yeast is the ability to activate a physical mechanism—to turn on a light—through mental means alone. The yeast test was set up to distinguish between two modes of consciousness that appeared in our earlier test: first, strong faith or belief, goal directed (the placebo effect); and second, qualitative thought, thought imbued with God-like qualities, which does not outline response. In practice, there is some overlapping; however, one type of consciousness usually predominates.

The yeast tests were successful in differentiation: faith results in a rising gas production line (as faith builds up), qualitative thought results in a broken gas production line, which, from earlier tests, indicated response to an organism's need rather than the thrust of belief.

Faith moves an organism in the direction of belief and can force growth that is not always in the best interest of the organism. Conversely, qualitative thought returns an organism to its normal state, be that return a slowing down or acceleration of growth.

Just as faith healing with its rising line pattern in the yeast tests was easily distinguished from qualitative healing with its broken line pattern, so patterns were found in qualitative runs that were not in control runs. Gas production from the balances, monitored by the computer, fitting those non control patterns created by qualitative prayer, activated the light.

INORGANIC PSI TESTS

Praying for simple biological organisms relates more directly to healing or measurable improvement in people's minds than do Spindrift's inorganic experiments. The inorganic experiments study how thought and prayer affect random action in card and picture guessing, dice throwing, and numbers accumulating in **supposedly** a random fashion in a computer. In line with the work of other parapsychologists, these tests provide new clues on how thoughts affect physical things. Also the tests show how our mind's defense mechanisms affect psi. The tests give evidence that prayerful thought can subtly touch and affect physical targets.[28]

⚜

SPINDRIFT IN REVIEW

Bruce and John Klingbeil experimented with the premise that a person's consciousness projects patterned effects into the physical world. In this interaction of consciousness with the world, some patterned effects are projected by human faith and goals. Other patterned effects are projected as pattern-mending effects because they brought more order to the organisms. The organisms' need was for more order.

Healing effects of order were thought to be what a quality prayer would produce. A quality prayer's holy ingredient that creates order was thought of as the prayer's *qualitative force*. Presumably the holier a person is, the more qualities of order and love he or she can radiate through prayer.

The Klingbeils contemplated that a prayer-filled consciousness *of compassionate qualities* elicited pattern mending ordering-effects. Quality ordering-effects would affirm the identity or target prayed for. Results showed that open goal-free prayer promoted the best solution for the circumstances. The Klingbeils viewed prayer as a voice in thought, a focused form of consciousness and quality prayer as radiating at the holy end of the spectrum of consciousness and psi.

Goal-free prayer is a breath of fresh care. Prayer that emphasized the qualities of good, purpose, love, support, compassion, forgiveness, and so on, which one cultivates in consciousness, brings out qualitative effects that are scientifically measurable. A researcher or volunteer provided his or her prayer thoughts for the tests in the search for consciousness-effects. A prayer provider's consciousness acted as a conduit for psi effects to be tested. Incidents of prayer reproducing order in an organism could be called subtle examples of spiritual healing.

The Klingbeils felt that plenty of people practice prayer in the general population, which meant an abundance of prayer providers could be potentially tested. Spindrift feels that prayer is likely to be the **most consistent** tool for the study of psi.

The Klingbeils began Spindrift in the hope of finding evidence for a psi force in prayer, especially a qualitative healing psi force. They researched ways to link prayer to spiritual healing results. Their religious training was that spiritual healing occasioned by prayer acted at a distance differently than the forces of directed will-power and human faith. Their research indicated that non goal-directed prayer, "Thy will be done," produced different test results than goal-directed prayer, "I want my goals." In wanting "my goals" and asking in prayer for material things, mortals should be more watchful that they're not using God as a **Mystical Cosmic Bellhop** to get what they want. For generalization's sake, non goal-directed prayer affirms what is closest to the natural order. Goal-directed prayer manipulates outcomes to follow a force-fed strategy.

The Klingbeils were the first to demonstrate this goal distinction experimentally. As far as is known, they were the first to introduce the terms *ordering-force, ordering-effects, faith-force, faith-effects, goal-directed thought* (creates *particle prayer*) **and** *non goal-directed thought* (creates *wave prayer*). **The Klingbeils also introduced the theory that the mind's defense mechanisms throw up a wall of resistance to keep man in the dark,** *so man cannot remember accurately* **details of his paranormal and spiritual experiences.**

⚜

MEASUREMENTS

John Klingbeil defines spiritual healing as "**The mental process that involves the acknowledgment of a system's** original identity for the purpose of producing or maintaining that system's order and normalcy."[29]

He explains the three steps in the measurement of prayer and healing.

> 1) the deviation of an organic process from normal,
> 2) the application of spiritual healing [prayer],
> 3) measurement of the return of the process to normal. From tests done in this way, equations can be developed. The fact that this can be done tells us that qualitative experience is capable of flowing into human life in patterns that can be quantitatively described.[30]

UNCONSCIOUSNESS, PSI EFFECTS, AND PSI BLOCKERS

The Klingbeils felt the realm of the unconscious is where the action is, is where psi action mostly takes place. The Klingbeils experimented with how unconscious intentions manifested psi effects. Why the unconscious realm? Conscious efforts to occasion psi did not produce much in the way of results. The virtuous qualities of thought, the mental associational links to persons, places, or things, and how a person really thinks and really feels evolve mostly in unconscious thought. Psychology backs this view up somewhat. The Klingbeils started pondering and praying, drawing from unconscious qualities of thought. One's goals are not being outlined, but qualities of compassion, concern, and care, etc., are pondered.

In our unconscious realm are the defense mechanisms of the mind. Some defense mechanisms function to protect us human beings from distraction so we can concentrate and survive in our human existence. The Klingbeils proposed that other defense mechanisms operate as psi blockers to conceal from us our experiences of psychic and spiritual phenomena. They hypothesized that there are psychic experiences going on around us, but we're not aware of them. We are not aware of psychic experiences because our defense mechanisms **neutralize** psychic experiences in our **conscious awareness.** The Klingbeils researched ways to circumvent the defense mechanisms of the mind through applying randomness theory. In some experimental designs the Klingbeils were able to support their theory that our minds won't permit us to discover too much about the subtle but vast nonlocal interactions of our minds with our daily lives.

PSI IN THE NEW CENTURY

Within the parameters of their experiments with non goal-directed thought, prayer was found to exhibit psi effects of a qualitative nature. Put another way, within test protocols, a person's consciousness occasions qualities that can be quantified indirectly. Put one more way, within Spindrift's experimental design limits, *qualities and virtues of a person's consciousness can be quantified, can be numerically represented, as eliciting ordering-effects.* Ordering-effects are occasioned by qualitative thought or holy prayer. Ordering-effects influence organisms and simultaneously produce patterns.

What is a theory or concept of holy prayer? Prayer brings evidence of increased order to a laboratory situation. What is a theory or concept of God? God is the Ordering-Force, the Ordering-Consciousness, the Ordering-Principle.

Bruce and John Klingbeil walked into a buzzsaw trying to link science to religion. The Klingbeils sharply felt that if there was attention given to the tests, more attention was centered on the gall or even the evil of attempting the tests in the first place, than on inquiries about any particular test finding. Reactors to the tests have seldom sought details of the tests. Rhetoric was substituted for inquiry. However, the future for prayer and healing research may have potential. One hint is that people are not making fun of prayer research and not belittling it nearly as much as they used to do. Another hint is that the taboo subjects of researching prayer, spirituality, messages from the brain, and the nonlocal actions of consciousness are being talked about by some researchers and physicians who would not have commented on these subjects in the last century.

KLINGBEIL OBJECTIVES

Bruce and John pursued four objectives.

1) To raise the questions and implications that would help society focus on the importance of testing human consciousness and prayer on healing.
2) To develop hypotheses about human consciousness and prayer.
3) To perform tests of the hypotheses.
4) To develop ideas for a theoretical explanation of how prayer acts nonlocally (at a distance).

Bruce and John did unique preliminary work on these objectives above. In objective 1, raising consciousness, they were pioneers who broke barriers in research. The fact that the Klingbeils met so much opposition may indicate how successful they were at measuring the nonlocal effects of prayer.

A CONCLUSION

Both goal-directed and non goal-directed thoughts produce effects at a distance. Non goal-directed thought produces "ordering-effects" which tend to fit a tighter criteria of "a return to the norms."

In this context of prayer returning to the norms of a system, the evidence suggests that non goal-directed prayer is more effective than goal-directed prayer. The ordering-effects of non goal-directed prayer enhance a system to attain healthier conditions which are nearest best for its circumstances. Goal-directed prayer often pushes a system around without realizing the need to realign a system to its natural healthy state.

For effective prayer, experiences in the laboratory suggested that experimenters should quiet the agitation and ego goals in thought. For example, a female volunteer said in effect, "I just surrounded the plants with love, knowing it was God's Love, and I knew that the plants would be reached by that Love."

A conclusion about some of the approximately seventy experiments the Klingbeils have done might be the following. The effects of prayer often subtly imprinted and sometimes even improved the circumstances of a targeted system. The test results suggest that as a source of psi, prayer is "an abundant reservoir of testable thought" as Bruce Klingbeil put it. Why? Because the test results suggest that holy intentions in prayer act as a subtle "ordering-mechanism that changes physical systems" as John Klingbeil put it. In a 1984 letter, John proposed that prayer is the best resource of psi for scientists to test the actions of consciousness.

CLOSING COMMENTS

Here is an excerpt from the Summer 1991 newsletter written by John Klingbeil:

> We at Spindrift have found our experimental work to be easy, the articulation of our work to be difficult, and our efforts to secure serious consideration of our work the hardest thing of all.

Beyond the use of basic scientific techniques applied to thoughts and prayers is this repeated complaint. How can your Spindrifter's thoughts and prayers help or heal a cell of yeast, a mung bean or soybean, a fungus, etc.? It sounds too absurd to consider. Spindrift would say that it may sound absurd at first, but something botanist Luther Burbank said may help. "Plants are as responsive to thought as children." *Spindrift is a new approach to botany.*

Gladys Myers wrote about the excitement the Spindrift team felt in the first Spindrift newsletter in 1984:

> We, at Spindrift, think we have a breakthrough in man's knowledge which will impact on the foundations of the fields of science, theology, and medicine. It reminds one of Charles Darwin, the impact of his discoveries, and the now amusing remark made, upon listening to Darwin's preliminary explanations, by the president of the Linnean Society, that the year "has not been marked by any of those striking discoveries which . . . revolutionize . . . the department of science on which they bear."
>
> It is easy to concur with the world's recognition of achievement. It is a rare quality, indeed, to be able to perceive the future significance of a discovery.

If society becomes startled by the scary potential that psi, prayer, and quantum weirdness may actually be real, would society react as did the Bishop of Worcester's wife when she became cognizant of Charles Darwin's theory of evolution. The Bishop's wife supposedly said, "Descended from the apes! My dear, let us hope that is not true, but if it is, let us pray that it will not become generally known."

ANECDOTES HERE

DATA THERE

Bruce commented on how society may require shifts in religion and science for a harmonious convergence of science (quantity), spirituality (quality), and psi (nonlocality). Bruce explained in effect: "A convincing paranormal testimony of healing is the experience leading the data . . . . A person who has a spiritual healing feels the healing is proof for him. Personal proof in one's life is important. Repeating the testimony about the healing may reach people who are already personally convinced of healing by prayer. Healing is part of their *spiritual* belief systems.

"Someone with a *physical* belief system hears the same testimony and says, 'You can't prove that's what happened,' and that's probably true; the testifier probably can't prove it. *If* the [skeptical] questioner is sincere, he is only reflecting our culture's scientific orientation. Our culture is both religious and scientific, but today's culture is more influenced by science than religion. We who have religious mindsets should learn to speak the language of our culture.

"In our scientific age, testimonies of healing don't translate into tangible, modern scientific proof. A healing is valid for the individual, but calling our testimonies *the only proof we need* often sounds stupid to people trained in science. They understand how proof is determined.

"A deeply felt testimony may be beneficial to repeat to someone who needs to hear it. I don't mean to take anything away from a person's testimony or his personal experiences of God, **but our culture has changed.**"

Charles Darwin wrote "It is not the strongest of the species that survive, nor the most intelligent, but one most responsive to change."

Endnotes

Chapter One:

1   The novel, _The Healer_, by John Klingbeil, 1980, 1984, and 1985, p 1.
2   Conversations with the Klingbeil family and _The Healer_ by John Klingbeil.
3   _The Healer_ by John Klingbeil, 1980, p. 69.
4   Lyrics by Ira Gershwin from _They All Laughed_, copyright 1937.

Chapter Two:

1   _"Interaction: The action of the qualitative calculus or good-ordered system pattern on the qualitatively opposite or evil-unordered non-system. This interaction leads to semi-ordered states which appear as conditions of matter, energy, and space-time." From the book _Qualitative Research: The Early Years_ by John Klingbeil, 1984, p. 158. **Parapsychologists call Spindrift's prayer on plants DMILS "direct mental interactions with living systems."**_

2   A system can be a "person being prayed for, a seed, a plant, a circumstance, a device, or individual and collective beliefs. All can be the objects of prayer." Notes taken from a 1985 conversation with the Klingbeils.

3   For examples, see Exodus, Chapter 21:12-17, 22:18-24, 32:27; Leviticus 26:8 and 17; Numbers 16:29-33, 21:23-26, 21:32-35, 26:9 and 10, 31:5-17, 35:15-21.

4   Quotes about the word "Quality" from _Zen and the Art of Motorcycle Maintenance_ by Robert Persig, Bantam Books, 1974.

> "A photograph can show a physical image in which time is static, and a mirror can show a physical image in which time is dynamic, but I think what he saw on the mountain was another kind of image altogether which . . . did not exist in time at all . . . . Quality . . . you know what it is, yet you don't know what it is . . . . Quality is a characteristic of thought and statement that is

recognized by a non-thinking process . . . . He singled out aspects of Quality such as unity, vividness, authority, economy, sensitivity, clarity, emphasis, flow, suspense, brilliance, precision, proportion, depth and so on . . . . If . . . a world without Quality functions abnormally, then we have shown that Quality exists . . . . At the center, generating the waves, was Quality."

These quotes above are from pages 82, 178, 200, 202, 210, and 204.

[5]   *Luke 6:19.*

[6]   *Luke 8:46 and Mark 5:30.*

[7]   *See The New English Bible and The New Testament Modern English by J. B. Phillips. Cultivating more quality or virtue in our prayer thoughts amounts to adding more of it to our life. Some fruitful qualities are "love, joy, peace, long-suffering, gentleness, goodness, faith, meekness, temperance . . . ." (Galatians 5:22-23). Such* **"qualities"** *as these go into a holy or "qualitative" prayer.*

[8]   *The Spindrift Newsletter, Summer 1990, Number 1, p. 5. Also from p. 5, "In . . . distributions formed by calling cards and throwing dice we have been able to study the psychodynamic tension between [ordered] thought and the activity of the human mind acting to conceal the action of [ordered] thought." See a 1989 paper by the Klingbeils titled "Cards, Dice, and Defense Mechanisms."*

[9]   *The Journal of the American Society for Psychical Research, Vol. 90, January 1996, p. 71.*

   In the ASPR American Society of Parapsychology Research Newsletter, Volume XVIII, Number 2, 1993, p. 10, Theodore Rockwell describes the Klingbeil theory of the mind's manipulation of psi. "The conceptual basis for the Spindrift work is that there are competing processes at work in the interaction between the mind and the environment: 1) a perceptive process, which perceives how the dice or the cards will fall; 2) a defense mechanism, which tries to hide our perceptive abilities from us; 3) a PK (psychokinetic) process, which can affect how the cards and dice will fall; and 4) a defense mechanism, which tries to undo the effects of the PK process."

[10]   *A fun speculation was that some gifted actors and comedians might make excellent participants in tests of psychic and spiritual phenomena. Some actors and comedians are able to get out of their own skins, their own selves and egos, and shift into an auxiliary personality of someone else they are imagining. It might be a way to get around the brain limiting one to his or her own perspective, bias, and ego temporarily. Perhaps the brain shuts down barriers and defense*

mechanisms when a gifted actor forgets self and is supplanted by another self dictated by the acting.

11 *One reason religious people reject taking a test is that participation might be contrary to a person's belief system to pray in a laboratory or controlled setting. Another reason is people might be apprehensive about whether their prayers work or not. Another reason is people might conceive of any tests of one's mind or consciousness as psychic, and they feel the psychic realm is evil and has no common ground with prayer.*

12 *"Although this observation seems rudimental, it has never appeared in the research literature available in this area, nor has this characteristic of thought previously been experimentally investigated." The Spindrift Tests, 1983, p. 4.*

13 *An example of how a person's faith, beliefs, and visualization of a situation misconstrued the way a need was met was printed in The Reader's Digest of September 1997, p. 16. "On her way to the church for my wedding, one of my bridesmaids had car trouble. My dad, a minister, spotted her and stopped to help. After assessing the situation, Dad placed the palm of his hand over the air-intake pipe, which created a seal, and instructed Tina to start the car again. It worked. Tina was amazed. So amazed, in fact, that when she reached the church, she ran up to me and told me about the miracle my dad had performed—he had laid hands on her car and healed it." Pauline Schneider (Kitchener)*

14 *As far as is known, the Klingbeils were the first to introduce the terms, ordering-force, ordering-effects, faith-force, faith-effects, goal-directed thought and prayer, non goal-directed thought and prayer, particle prayer, and wave prayer.*

15 *On p. 145 of Be Careful what You Pray For . . . You Just Might Get It, author Larry Dossey, M.D., writes: "Even the simplest bodily processes are dauntingly complicated. In view of our appalling ignorance of the human body, asking for a 'return to the natural order and harmony' appears to be a sound strategy in praying for healing. This approach does not require us to know the ins and outs of apoptosis. We can let the body figure out which cells should live and which should die. Our role may be to set the process in motion, not to tell the body in detail what to do. If we forget this, we may find ourselves inadvertently participating in negative prayer."*

16 *Luke 22:42.*

17 *John 5:30.*

Chapter Three:

1   *The Spindrift Newsletter*, Spring/Summer 1991, Number 5, p. 11.

2   *Science and Health with Key to the Scriptures*, by Mary Baker Eddy, p. 399.

3   *Miscellany*, by Mary Baker Eddy, p. 302.

4   *Christian Science*, by Mark Twain, Book II, Chapter I, paragraph 11.

5   *The Years of Authority*, by Robert Peel, p. 248.

6   *The Years of Trial*, by Robert Peel, p. 126.

7   *The Years of Discovery*, by Robert Peel, p. 138.

8   *The Christian Science Monitor*, October 20, 1965, reported by Paul Seely. Part of Mary Baker Eddy's description of "Elementary electricity" is the following. "Electricity is not a vital fluid, but the least material form of illusive consciousness . . . . Electricity is the sharp surplus of materiality which counterfeits the essence of spirituality . . . ."

9   *Science and Health*, p. 484. Also see **On Einstein's Interest in the Metaphysics of Mary Baker Eddy** by William S. Cooper, Professor Emeritus, SIMS, University of California, Berkeley.

10 *The Universe and Dr. Einstein* by Lincoln Barnett, chapter 1, p. 11.

11 *The American Heritage Concise dictionary*, p. 642.

12 *The Christian Science Sentinel*, February 24, 1968, *The Home Catacomb*, Volume 7, number 2, 1993, p. 22.

13 The following point has caused many people to be upset with Bruce, John, and Spindrift. The commotion was that Spindrift was attempting tests of holy prayer. Why attempt it? Because one's subjective interpretation of a spiritual healing, even to the person involved, often changes in detail and is unreliable as "hard" evidence. Empirical failures of spiritual healing make other claims of good healing look suspect. Scientific monitoring of prayer bringing healing might establish harder evidence for healing than a person's interpretive testimony about a healing. Also scientifically controlled tests might establish insights into some of the healing aspects of prayer and consciousness.

14 *Science and Health*, p. 331.

An increase in spiritual qualities influencing our prayers parallels well with Heresy's Phenomenonic Theory. The theory states that everything we do in life accumulates toward something better. Like other aspects of life, once a new quality is cultivated, or a new talent is learned, or a new

car is bought, a return to one's previous condition is undesired. We get used to the new condition and do not want to go back to the old condition. For example, if a man hated, and he learned to love, would he want to go back and hate again? Probably not because he grew better in virtue and quality.

15   *Justa Smith's work in* The Quiet Revolution, *1980, p. 73.*

16   *Immediately after notification of his expulsion, Bruce wrote two letters to the church directors concerning the scientific issues which brought about his punishment. The director's letter in return said in effect that they now had enough information about Bruce to stick with their decision to keep him out of the* Journal.

17   Church Manual, *Mary Baker Eddy, p. 44.*

18   *A few church people have not been against experiments per se. They feel that God allowed only Mary Baker Eddy to do experiments. She was guided to discover what she needed and that was the end of her experiments. The Spindrifters did not have the same Divine permission or assigned mission to do tests. The position that only one person can do experiments sounds similar to substitutionary atonement theology, where all the work is done for you by one person.*

Other church people feel that scientific investigations are not very productive. The needed truths have all been worked out years earlier. "Why reinvent the wheel" and do more experiments? Enough information is already known.

In 1980, Beverly Rubik, a Ph.D. in bio-physics, met with church officials in Boston about possibly funding and doing comparative studies of "hands-on" faith healing with "distant" spiritual healing. Dr. Rubik thought the church would be interested in scientific studies of prayer because it was called Christian Science. In laughter, "Oh, no. That [testing] is not what it's about," was the response. Maybe it was sincere laughter, but essentially Dr. Rubik was laughed out of the building. (Told to me by Beverly Rubik. I imagine that the Klingbeils' research was the elephant in the room nobody mentioned.)

In the mid-1990's, with society's growing interest in alternative healing and the new quantum-scientific ways of looking at reality, some church people did start believing that scientifically investigating the nature of holy prayer, spirituality, and healing was a right pursuit. At a 1996 symposium on "Spirituality and Healing in Medicine II," a church official said, "If today's conference had occurred in Mary Baker Eddy's time, I feel she would surely have been here, explaining her own experiments and findings, observations, and discoveries." From The Christian Science Journal, March, 1997, p. 23.

[19] *Mary Baker Eddy wrote, "Spiritual ideas, like numbers and notes, start from Principle, and admit no materialistic beliefs." Science and Health, p. 298, line 21. She also wrote "Through astronomy, natural history, chemistry, music, mathematics, thought passes naturally from effect back to cause." Ibid., p. 195, line 16.*

Chapter Four:

[1] *The Spindrift Update Newsletter, Volume 1, Number 1, September 1988, p. 2.*

[2] *In Westword, reported by Mike O'Keeffe, October 3-9, 1990, p. 6.*

[3] *Quantum Reality: Beyond the New Physics, by Nick Herbert, p. 15.*

[4] *For the data on this mung bean test, see the Appendix, the first test described.*

[5] *One's belief can cause political turmoil though. A talented science writer held an unpopular belief. Look what happened to him when his belief was found out.*

> *A Chicago Sun Times newspaper of November 14, 1990, editorial reports: Freedom of Belief? Stop Presses.*
>
> *On Tuesday, we mentioned that the Stanford University athletic department had suspended the university band from playing at school football games because it had lampooned the spotted owl environmental controversy. It's the latest example of the growing tides of intolerance on university campuses of speech that is not politically correct.*
>
> *Now we discover that Scientific American magazine has taken the idea of politically correct speech to even grander depths of absurdity.*
>
> *As the New Republic magazine reported, Scientific American was prepared to hire Forrest M. Mims III to write a column for laymen called "Amateur Scientist."*
>
> *The magazine had liked Mims' work, but at the final interview Mims made the fatal mistake of saying he had written for some—gasp!—Christian publications.*
>
> *An editor—apparently appalled at the notion that people hold religious beliefs, especially those kinds of beliefs—asked Mims for his views on abortion and evolution.*

Mims said he was anti-abortion and was a creationist (although as it turns out later not a literal one, but someone who simply believes that God created man).

That did it. The magazine withdrew the job offer, even though previous columns Mims had written were considered "fabulous," even though they presumably were not laced with subliminal anti-abortion and creationist propaganda and even though the magazine's editor considered Mims a man of honor and integrity.

Like we say, this goes even beyond politically correct speech. Now, it appears that the folks over at <u>Scientific American</u> think that to objectively write about science, you must also hold politically correct beliefs. (Reprinted with permission, <u>The Chicago Sun-Times</u> c 1996)

Chapter Five:

[1]   *Kate Buck addressed The Century of Progress exhibition on October 8, 1934. She said descriptive words on how to model one's thoughts after the invisible Spirit realm. She spoke of writer Phillips Brooks writing to her as a teenager. "I ran across a letter from him in which he said this, 'Little girl, someday we shall leave the symbols for the reality.' Probably this meant nothing to me at the time; but when I read it about a year ago, it seemed like a flash of light. Shortly after, I opened the Bible to those words of Jesus, 'When you pray, believe that you receive, and ye shall have.' Uniting this with the message from Phillips Brooks, it seemed to bring a new interpretation, namely, this: 'When ye pray, believe that ye receive in the world of realities, and ye shall have in the world of symbols.'... When we gratefully realize something of what we really have in the kingdom of God... our consciousness of the abundance of good will naturally objectify itself in the world of symbols."*

[2]   <u>Science and Health with Key to the Scriptures</u>, p. 248.

[3]   <u>Ibid.</u>, p. 595 and 596.

Chapter Six:

[1]   *<u>The Conscious Universe</u> by Dean Radin, Ph.D., is a book about the legitimate quest of doing scientific research of psychic phenomena. On page 205 is a chapter titled "A Field Guide to Skepticism," which discusses the pros and cons of skepticism.*

[2]   *The Spindrift Update*, September, 1988, p. 12.

   In his paper, "Ten myths of science: Reexamining what we think we know . . . ," William McComas of the University of Southern California examined how students tend to learn a misconception about science. The misconception is that a person can do research, applying the scientific method in only one strict and uncreative way. Students didn't consider thinking "outside the box" that there might be another way to apply the scientific method. This paper is copyrighted, 1996, by the School & Mathematics Association, Volume 96, 01-01-1996, p.10.

[3]   A United Press International (UPI) story of July, 29, 1985.

Chapter Seven:

[1]   *The Spindrift Newsletter*, summer 1991, number 5, p. 11.

[2]   *Out of My Life and Thought* by Albert Schweitzer.

[3]   *The Home Catacomb*, Volume 7, number 2, 1993, p. 17.

[4]   *Ibid.*, p. 24.

[5]   Quoted from letters dated November 30, 1983, and May 23, 1989.

[6]   In the early 1980's, Gladys Myers gave a talk at a neighbor's house after a Bible study group. Gladys found she was the only one who was enthusiastic about researching prayer. The hostess said to Gladys that if I didn't know you as a neighbor, I would think you were weird and couldn't really be serious about what you were saying.

[7]   Spindrift seeks to package itself better. The following example illustrates what better packaging can do. Computers and simple (less technical) skill has made communicating via the Internet a world phenomenon. I have tried to get friends interested in becoming ham radio operators. I failed. Yet the Internet is a glorified form of ham radio. A person can contact people from around the world and exchange information. The Internet is packaged in a more appealing way than is ham radio.

[8]   The book, *Pulpit and Press*, by Mary Baker Eddy, p. 63. Mrs. Eddy prayed for plants her students dubbed "floral demonstrations." In front of her students and at least one visiting journalist, Mrs. Eddy's thought encouraged flower buds to blossom right away.

[9]   Author's notes.

[10]   Author's notes.

[11]   *The Home Catacomb*, Volume 7, number 2, 1993, p. 24. Bruce and John Klingbeil also told me the details.

12 *The Spindrift Update Occasional Newsletter*, Volume 1, number 1, September 1988, p. 3.

13 *The Home Catacomb*, May 1996, Volume 10, number 1, p. 14-16.

14 *Reported to me by Bruce and John Klingbeil.*

15 *I had a dream in July, 1997, which may have a message in it. I dreamt I was giving a talk about the prayer tests. An audience person raised her hand and asked me to tell about negative prayers directed toward Spindrift. I gave her some examples of negative prayers. I finished speaking.*

A religious group in the audience was given the floor to respond to what I had said. One man said about his group's negative prayers against Spindrift, "It's not negative prayer when you know you're right."

In 1996, a close relative of mine was in turmoil with her boss. A small group held hands and prayed for her. The prayer leader prayed aloud, "I'm not telling You what to do God, but I'd break his legs."

An adventure occurred in the 1980's that spooked us at Spindrift. Richard Oakes, a writer friendly to Spindrift, traveled to England to interview Dr. Glen Schaefer, a scientist and professor doing research tracking with radar the flying patterns of insects. Dr. Schaefer was a Christian Scientist. Mr. Oakes had an appointment to interview Dr. Schaefer about his research into how Christian Science's scientific side was an unknown to virtually everyone. When Richard Oakes got off the airplane, he found out that two weeks earlier Dr. Schaefer had died. When Mr. Oakes returned to the United States, he cried on the phone as he told me about it. We at Spindrift felt paranoid because of the timing. It seemed like a force was working against us.

16 *The Home Catacomb*, Volume 7, number 2, 1993, p, 24.

17 *Ibid.*, p. 24.

18 *From a copy of The Quiet Revolution John Klingbeil signed on December 15, 1981. On p. 100-102 of his book, John has written a list of seventeen reasons that indicate why religious people have problems with the natural sciences and scientists have problems with religion.*

19 *A lawyer was retained to read The Healer before it was published. Though a work of fiction, the lawyer advised eliminating some religious characters' imaginary dialogue.*

Though in juxtaposition, the events mentioned in The Healer had taken place. Healer and author Rev. Walter L. Westin of Wadsworth, Ohio, told me he cried several times while reading the book. The events mentioned reminded him of the struggles he experienced as a Methodist minister trying to introduce his healing prayer discoveries to other ministers. Rev. Westin has written PrayWell: a Holistic Guide to Health and Renewal and The Self-Healing Pocket Guide.

[20]   *Chicago appearance notes.*

[21]   *Letter on file.*

[22]   *U.S. News & World Report of May 12, 1997, p. 22, reports the following. "Anyone who says 'God bless you,' after you sneeze is trying to deprive you of your constitutional rights, according to Free Inquiry . . . ." Free Inquiry feels the same way about "saying grace at a dinner party in your own home."*

[23]   *The Spindrift Quarterly, Spring, 1992, p. 7.*

    One example of someone getting furious at Spindrift's religious roots would be an experience of Bruce Klingbeil's in 1991. A man in Detroit was writing a book about prayer. Spindrift was mentioned in a lecture he heard. He wanted to know more and was thrilled when he got in contact with Bruce.

    Upon learning Bruce Klingbeil was a practitioner of Christian Science, the man wrote Bruce a letter accusing Mary Baker Eddy of being a thief and her followers of being fresh food for a charlatan. Bruce wrote him back, but he was not heard from again.

    Bruce commented to me that emotionalism and biases have stopped cold many people from further investigating Spindrift. Some people were definitely emotional. I mentioned in a 1991 speech written by Bruce that "Christian Scientists were outraged at the proposition that the things of the spirit could be reduced to examination by the things of the flesh . . . However, and paradoxically, outrage exists among other church groups here and there that the new discoveries weren't made within their particular denomination." From an address to The Archaeus Project Meeting in St. Paul, Minnesota.

Chapter Eight:

[1]   *Essentially from The Spindrift Papers, p. G-1—G-6.*

[2]   *About the placebo effect: "The tensions are especially great when one attempts to move between the divide that separates the explanatory strategies of the so-called cultural or hermeneutic sciences (roughly concerned with 'meaning') and the so-called natural sciences (roughly committed to explanations in terms of 'mechanism').*

Because placebos as a phenomenon seem to hover ambiguously at the crossroads between these two perspectives [of meaning and mechanism], they are at once a frustration and a wonderful challenge." From The Placebo Effect, *1997, edited by Anne Harrington, Harvard University Press, p. 7 and 8.*

Norman Cousins, longtime editor of The Saturday Review, *described the placebo effect as the "doctor who resides within."*

3 *The quote is from the front cover of* The Spindrift Papers.

4 The Spindrift Tests, *1983, p. 70.*

5 The Spindrift Papers, *p. G-3.*

6 Ibid., *p. G-3.*

7 Ibid., *p. G-4.*

8 Ibid., *p. G-4 and G-5.*

9 The Placebo Effect, *1997, edited by Anne Harrington, Harvard University Press, p. 2.*

10 Healing Beyond the Body, *2001, by Larry Dossey, M.D., p. 132.*

Chapter Nine:

1 *An unpublished paper titled, "Science and the Contemporary World in the View of a Theologian." The paper is in the Harvard Divinity School's Tillich-Archives.*

2 *I was a seminar leader for the "ReDiscovering Cosmos Conference," a conference about religion and science held in Syracuse, New York, in August 1997. I met scientists and theologians who were exploring avenues of mutual respect between science, religion, and consciousness research. During the conference, my opinion formed that the future leadership in discovering common interests between science, religion, and consciousness research was coming from the Lutheran Church (ELCA Synod), the Episcopal Church, and from some Presbyterians. It was strange to me that the Christian Scientists weren't at the forefront of the science/religion connection.*

A Dallas Morning News *article about the conference initiated a September 12, 1997, letter to me from my church. The letter included, "In the future, if you have occasion to go to similar events, we would ask that you would make it clear—especially if you speak to a reporter—that you are not a spokesperson, official or unofficial, for the Church of Christ, Scientist. If your being a Christian Scientist must be mentioned at all, please consider, if you haven't already, how natural it would be for your listeners to assume you are representing the church.*

We would, therefore, be grateful if you would make clear that you are speaking only for yourself or, perhaps, for Spindrift."

[3]   *In 1995 and 1996, the CIA and Defense Department revealed their psychic experiments which included their uses of "remote viewing." In 1997, a military remote viewer claimed that, during the Gulf War, members of his psychic war group mentally harassed Saddam Hussein to drive him crazy and to make him appear untrustworthy to his followers. The military remote viewer is David Morehouse and his book is* Psychic Warriors. *Morehouse's claim about Hussein is disputed, but it's true that Morehouse's military remote viewing unit was tasked to find mobile SCUD missile launchers in Iraq.*

During President Jimmy Carter's administration, through the parapsychological community grape vine, Bruce and John Klingbeil and I heard that psychics including remote viewers were being tested by the government for national security projects. John and I mailed twice to the Central Intelligence Agency John's draft of his book about his psi experiments including John's remote viewing experiment with tagging the hidden location of growing beans. John's hidden bean experiment could be used to see if psychics could tag and spot the location of missiles in underground missile silos. Spindrift never heard from the CIA, but in 1995 it became publicly known that tests of psychic talents for national security reasons were funded by the government for several decades. In some experiments of remote viewing, psychic remote viewers did try to tag the locations of underground missiles hidden in silos.

For more information on "RV," read Jim Schnabel's book Remote Viewers *(published by Dell), and* Captain of My Ship, Master of My Soul, *by F. Holmes Atwater.*

[4]   *The participant's "touching thought" caused just enough change in the orderliness of the randomness to be mathematically tracked and illustrate that subtly something was going on besides randomness alone. The known quantum physics theory that the observer is not a passive observer applies. The observer subtly affects what he observes.*

Bruce and John developed evidence that the mind is involved in the shuffling of cards which biases an outcome. It's also true for the tossing of pairs of dice. The Klingbeils proposed that our defense mechanisms set us up to deny or wipeout any recognition of most events which were too extraordinary from normal experience like a psychic event in one's life.

The Klingbeils also did their fair share of randomness testing using devices called random number generators RNGs. These generators delivered a constant flow of zeros and ones which were acceptably random to test against chance occurrences. Based on the work of other researchers, the Klingbeils had four circuit boards programmed to produce random numbers. Thought and prayer were applied to these boards. Over time the loop circuit numbers that were prayed for began stacking up in patterns which illustrated that they were no longer randomly produced sequences of zeros and ones. Thought had subtly interacted with the looped numbers on the circuit boards.

5 Bruce and John had their photograph taken by Brian O'Leary, a former United States astronaut who is an author of books on New Science.

Chapter Ten:

1 The verified quote was about the theory of evolution from <u>Christian Science: Its Encounter with American Culture</u> by Robert Peel, p. 91. A couple of weeks later another quote that happened to be the motto for Spindrift was finally verified. Bruce and John would have been pleased that electrical wizard Charles Steinmetz's quote was published in <u>Church Federation</u>, June, 1930. The quote was also published in <u>Mary Baker Eddy</u> by Rev. Lyman Powell, p. 280; <u>Answer Without Ceasing</u> by Margaret Lee Runbeck, p. 36 and 330, and <u>Autobiography of a Yogi</u> by Paramahansa Yogananda, bottom footnote p. 516-517. The Steinmetz quote is "I think the greatest discovery will be made along spiritual lines. Here is a force which history clearly teaches has been the greatest power in the development of men and history. Yet we have been merely playing with it and have never seriously studied it as we have the physical forces. Someday . . . the scientists of the world will turn their laboratories over to the study of God and prayer and the spiritual forces which as yet have hardly been scratched."

2 For more information about this **mung bean experiment,** see the Appendix, the first experiment described.

3 A reporter from Portland, Oregon, asked me about John, "Isn't there anything that a 35 year old man would look forward to living for?" I said, "Yes, but my answer under the circumstances is obviously incomplete. I need to find out more information myself." A <u>Boston Globe</u> newspaper reporter wanted my opinion on the Klingbeils having been murdered. The physical evidence did not point to murder.

4   *Bruce had an opinion about the stock market crashing that wasn't anything new. However, in a March 1993 phone call, Bruce expressed the same opinion in such depressing dark terms that I noted it. Bruce said a stock market crash was due, because people had too much faith in rising stock prices as being their salvation. In addition, there was a general heading of the coming generation into a moral and educational decline which would compromise the future security of the nation and the stock market. Perhaps Bruce's opinion was in part his mood.*

5   *The Spindrift Quarterly, Winter, 1993, p. 7.*

6   *In 1993, I wonder why selling the scientific equipment didn't bother me more and trigger something in me. Selling the equipment did bother Gladys Myers who, like several of us Spindrifters, put time into selecting the equipment and contributed chunks of money toward purchasing the equipment.*

7   *In a letter on file Dean Radin wrote, "I thought for a while that my last letter to them may have been partially responsible for their despair . . . . But they certainly did not have to feel bad about their statistical mistake. It was a very subtle artifact that took me several months of effort to spot, and then several more months to figure out how to correct. This sort of error creeps into leading-edge scientific work all the time . . . .*

     Dean Radin's work in parapsychology has had its strange moments for him. A reporter once asked Dr. Radin if the television show "The X-Files" was true. (Art Bell interview of Dr. Radin on the "Dreamland" radio show, August 24, 1997.)

8   *One person Bruce contacted in April, 1993, was a practitioner. After listening to her attempts to communicate with the church followed by her removal from Journal listing as a practitioner, Bruce told me he felt sad over her unhappy experiences which had parallels to what he went through himself. (name on file)*

9   *To contact a number of organizations that are finding ways to bridge aspects of religion and science, the John Templeton Foundation compiles and edits editions of a book titled Who's Who in Theology and Science. The book contains biographies and bibliographical guides to people and organizations interested in the "interaction of theology and science." For similar information also see the quarterly publication Science & Spirit published in Concord, New Hampshire, and the monthly publication of the Center for Faith and Science Exchange, the FASE Notices, published in Newton Centre, Massachusetts. Also see the journal Zygon, a publication of the Center for Religion and Science located in the Evangelical Lutheran Church of America (ELCA), Lutheran Center in Chicago, Illinois.*

¹⁰   <u>Miscellaneous Writings</u>, p. 289, line 8.

¹¹   <u>The Oregonian</u>, June 21, 1993, p. B1, reported by Cheryl Martinis.

¹²   The following is a humorous story I recall Bruce told me approximately a month before the suicides. A news report stated that Oregon's gay community was selling T-shirts. The T-shirts' epigram read, "I Can't Think Straight." Bruce and I laughed about that epigram.

There is a cartoon which always caused John Klingbeil to laugh and is a bit of Spindrift's early history in the 1970's. John liked a Sidney Harris cartoon so much that John wrote to Mr. Harris for permission to reprint the cartoon in Spindrift's literature. John paid a fee, and Mr. Harris gave written permission for Spindrift to use it. The cartoon has two mathematicians looking at mathematical equations on a black board. In the middle of the equations is one equation the mathematicians can't figure out, so one of them wrote into the equation, "Then A Miracle Occurs." John had a print of the cartoon put on a white sweat shirt of his. After the suicides I was given that sweat shirt.

¹³   Cleve Backster said he believes "The simplest living entities have perceptions." Also he added that some entities people aren't aware of as living have perceptions. "All the biology-related research Bruce and John Klingbeil have done parallels my research especially as it relates to living cells and plant perceptions. The Klingbeils' healing of plants through prayers is another wrinkle of thought to be fathomed." Approved quotations obtained on September 6, 1995.

Cleve Backster's experiments with plants wired to lie detectors are legend. Backster was able to detect the responses of plants to human intention toward the plants. Cleve Backster was written up in the book <u>The Secret Life of Plants</u>. One of the co-authors, Christopher Bird, (and Backster too), were suspicious of the official explanation of the Klingbeil suicides. Christopher Bird said he was going to investigate and write about the Klingbeil suicides.

¹⁴   In his book <u>Making Miracles</u>, p. 137-139, psychologist Paul Pearsall has "formulated, based on the Spindrift research" what he celebrates and presents as "The Ten Commandments of Prayer."

¹⁵   Rev. Karl Goodfellow said that Bruce's comment stayed with him because it meant something personal and had a ring to it of the Star Trek theme of man exploring where no man has gone before. Rev. Goodfellow added, "If it wasn't for the work in the laboratory that the Klingbeils did, I wouldn't be able to do what I am doing." At that point Karl was tracking the effects of 4,000 people praying for the welfare

of farms in the state of Iowa. Approved quotations obtained on September 22, 1996.

[16] *Bruce Klingbeil felt that once he could correct the church's misconceptions about the tests, the church would reinstate his name in the <u>Journal</u> as a practitioner. Bruce was mistaken. After his name was removed in 1983, several so-called dissidents circulating lists of practitioners suggested Bruce list with them. Bruce did not because he thought listing would hurt his prospects for being listed again in the official <u>Journal</u>.*

[17] *Historically, if called on, the church took care of elderly nurses and practitioners. By losing his practitioner standing, Bruce was cut out of that program.*

[18] *That Spindrift was unable to obtain funding/grant monies did not only depress Bruce and John but some of us other Spindrifters as well. In one of the last conversations I had with Bruce, he, John, and a Spindrift board member, Laura Schunk, were preparing yet another research grant proposal to a foundation.*

Laura Schunk was close friends with John and Bruce. She had a rough time getting over the suicides. Laura was the legal board member who held onto the Spindrift data files meticulously created by the Klingbeils. For nine years after the suicides, Laura moved frequently. She moved to Pennsylvania, Florida, Southern Oregon, Northern California, Arizona, and even England. Laura drove a trunk of crates containing the Spindrift data files around the United States. When she arrived, Laura placed the crates in rented storage bins. In June 2002, she had decided to get free of her unsettling life and sad memories. Laura shipped me 17 boxes of data files. Laura felt such an emotional release that she didn't mind spending over $500 in shipping costs. I gave these files to Deborah Klingbeil to preserve.

[19] *Publicity from Spindrift was usually sent to news organizations. One newspaper in the Chicagoland area carried an article which was suspicious of raising money to test prayer on yeast. The gist was that Spindrift was a scam. It was Christmas time, and the article suggested readers give their monies to more worthy causes. The article ended with "On the other hand, there's nothing more heart rending at Christmas than a yeast on the skids." "John [Klingbeil] laughed out loud at the article, framed it, and kept it on his desk next to his Far Side calendar by Gary Larson." From <u>The Home Catacomb Newsletter</u>, Volume 7, number 2, 1993, p.*

26. This issue of <u>The Catacomb</u> carries additional history, insights, and interpretation of the Klingbeils' circumstances.

A curious allegory can be found in <u>The Catacomb</u> of January/February 1997, Volume 11, number 1, p. 8. The following is an excerpt:

Two monks lived on a mountain in a world where no one knew how to climb mountains. The two monks spoke only an ancient language. The people around their mountain spoke Chinese.

The monks wanted to share what they had learned about the techniques of mountain climbing with the people. So the monks taught themselves to speak Chinese as best they could. The monks presented their findings to the people.

The people responded, "Yeah, sure. Let's capture these two guys and force them to tell us what they're really up to."

But the monks had disappeared.

[20] *The local Portland, Oregon, PBS television station had planned two thirds of a program with two unorthodox doctors when a producer called the Klingbeils and said she was intrigued with their experiments with prayer and consciousness. The last part of the program was to be an interview with Bruce and John taken from a ninety minute interview which was video taped in the Klingbeil's first floor laboratory in their townhouse. Even though the producer and staff were thrilled with the Klingbeil interview, someone said something about Spindrift being too controversial. The Klingbeil interview was cut a few hours before the program aired. See the chapter "Politics and Prayer" for more details on the Klingbeil television cancellation.*

[21] *Communication became a shouting match of written words: a hundred pages of letters back and forth. It was as if, shown the speed of light, the skeptics asked to be shown instead the speed of dark.*

[22] *There is only one other time that I heard about the Klingbeils being linked to guns. In the early 1950's, Bruce and his young family lived in Rhinelander, Wisconsin. Bruce started to become a practitioner, which required gradually giving up other occupations. Bruce did not have enough money to feed his family. He felt the responsibility to feed them. The answer to his prayer meant putting aside his personal feelings about killing animals. Venison could feed a family for a long time. Bruce went into the woods to shoot a deer. Spotting the deer he was after, he raised his rifle and took aim. He pulled the trigger. The rifle misfired. At*

> *that moment Bruce felt that he had fulfilled his obligation to his family and to his prayerful guidance to go ahead and shoot. He fulfilled the obligation but did not have to kill the deer. After this hunting episode, the finances of the Klingbeil family began to improve.*

23   *Edwin Howard Armstrong, "on July 18, 1939 . . . began broadcasting [in FM] from his own station, W2XMN, in Alpine, New Jersey. Although Armstrong provided program material that helped hi-fi succeed, it became Armstrong's nemesis." Distraught over the patent lawsuits, he jumped from a window on January 31, 1954. Armstrong's "widow, Marion MacInnis Armstrong . . . pursued the litigation that continued for another 13 years and ultimately won." From* <u>Audio</u> *magazine, May, 1997, p. 46.*

24   *Dr. Ignaz Semmelweis' hand washing program brought the baby mortality rate down. During 1847-1849 Dr. Semmelweis "proved that puerperal fever is a form of septicemia, thus becoming the pioneer of antisepsis in obstetrics." From* <u>Dorland's Illustrated Medical Dictionary</u>, *26th. edition, p. 1187.*

25   <u>*Science and Health with Key to the Scriptures*</u>, *p. 215, line 27.*

26   *The irony must be that the church has not "connected the dots" between the Klingbeils' tests and the tests they now participate in. I received a September 12, 1997, letter from the church which includes, ". . . . though we don't doubt the sincerity of your views, we really can't endorse the kind of experiments, or 'tests,' that you advocate. Mrs. Eddy's proving ground was not a laboratory but daily life, based on Jesus' own model of [healing] (Matt. 4:23). We understand that this should be our primary, if not our only, "test site.". . . We appreciate your interest in the significant changes going on in world thought regarding prayer, healing, religion, and the sciences. We're confidant that individual practice of the spiritual laws of healing . . . will continue to bring about such changes for the good for mankind."*

27   *A lengthy January 13, 1985, letter to two Spindrift members.*

28   *The last chapter of* <u>The Demon-Haunted World: Science as a Candle in the Dark</u> *by Carl Sagan.*

Chapter Eleven:

1   <u>*How to Pray: Tapping Into the Power of Divine Communication*</u>, *by Helene Ciaravino, Square One Publishers, 2001, p. 24.*

² *A May 1987 letter to the Spindrift Board of Directors.*

Epilogue Endnotes:

¹ *"The Effect of Prayer on Physical Health," in The Journal of Religion and Health, Volume 33, # 3, Fall 1994. By Paul Duckro and Philip Magaletta of the St. Louis Medical Center.*

² *The People's Idea of God: Its Effect on Health and Christianity, a sermon delivered in Boston by Mary Baker Eddy, p. 3.*

The Botanical Experiments Endnotes:

¹ *The Spindrift Tests, 1983, "Tests of Cumulative Effect," p. 19 and p. 131-132, Qualitative Research, p. 75, Identity Field Theory, p. 47, and The Spindrift Papers, p. 1-35 and H-4.*

² *Matthew 18:20.*

³ *Spindrift's 1981 brochure, test example # 2.*

⁴ *Qualitative Research, p. 104.*

⁵ *Spindrift Newsletter, Volume 2, Number 1, Spring, 1985, p. 11.*

⁶ *This dual-direction soybean test can be found in Qualitative Research, p. 87, Identity Field Theory, p. 69-72 with the data following, The Spindrift Tests, 1983, p. 49, and The Spindrift Papers, p. 1-31, C-3, F-3, J-2.*

⁷ *The Chicago Tribune of January 16, 1997, Section 2, reports the following: "A century ago, a driven hunter of dinosaur bones named Edwin Drinker Cope came up with a particularly American twist on natural selection: Plants and animals evolve into ever-larger sizes. This bigger-is-better view of evolution has become known as 'Cope's Rule' and has been taught in high schools and universities ever since." A Chicago based paleontologist, David Jablonski, feels he has debunked Cope's Rule by measuring the fossil collections of mollusk that represent millions of years of evolution. Results: "About 30 percent of the lineages did indeed evolve into bigger body sizes. But about the same number evolved into smaller sizes. And about the same number of lineages show that the largest species got larger, but the small got smaller." The article answers the question why no one had tested Cope's Rule before. Because there was a bias that it was true. See David Jablonski's article for Nature of January 16, 1997.*

8   *Merriam-Webster's Dictionary*, Tenth Edition, 1998, p. 134.

9   *Spindrift applied for grant money several times for this three-seed experiment which
     included triticale seeds and was turned down. The Spindrift team reaction was that
     if grant money was not forth coming with this seed test, you can almost give up trying
     to get grant money for an original experiment.*

10   *The Spindrift Papers*, p. 2-23.

11   *The Spindrift Tests*, 1983, p. 79.

12   "*The yeast test requires active, dry yeast. Dry yeast is needed because the gas production
     of compressed yeast is not sufficiently stable for our testing purposes.*" *The Spindrift Tests*,
     1983, p. 81.

13   *John Klingbeil writes, "The gas production of the last 20 minutes tends to be more
     stable than the gas production of the first 20 minutes. . . . The early differences may be
     due to water temperatures or room temperatures, factors which can vary somewhat
     from run to run, as well as being a reflection of the freshness and the storage conditions
     of the yeast . . . As a result of this circumstance a ratio can be drawn that throws light
     . . . on the effect of thought. If we take average gas production of the last 20 minutes of
     a run and divide it by the average gas production of the first 20 minutes of the run,
     a ratio of increase is found." For more explanation see* The Spindrift Tests, *1983, p.
     101.*

14   "*In our **earliest** exploratory yeast tests, we saw a characteristic pattern modified in the
     direction of greater gas production because of a barely recognized assumption on our
     part that our prayers would increase gas production. (The belief that our prayers are
     beneficial is usually consciously and unconsciously linked to the more/bigger/faster
     concept of good which prevails in our culture.)*" "**The more/bigger/faster is better
     syndrome seems to be somewhat entrenched in our belief systems.** *Not only does
     this show up in our yeast tests but it has been found in other research as well. For
     example, a paper by Carrol Nash presented at the 1981 Parapsychological Association
     Convention reported on the efforts of ungifted college students to selectively accelerate or
     inhibit the growth of bacterial cultures in test tubes. Although overall results were
     significant in the predicted direction, acceleration was more successful than inhibition.*"
     The Spindrift Tests, *1883, p. 79 and 89.*

     *In contrast to "**bigger is better**," in the Orient the cultural bias is often for less,
     not more, as better. For example, the forced miniaturization of plants is called bonsai.
     Bonsai can be very beautiful. Bruce Klingbeil felt the bonsai process prevented a plant
     from becoming its potential natural identity. Stunting the growth and cutting the*

root system was not letting the plant develop normally. On that basis Bruce felt bonsai was not the best outcome for a plant. It's not less than or more than what a plant needs, but what is normal and natural is the point the Klingbeils tried to get across in their healing tests on plants.

    Not all cultural biases raise questions like the above. I had a memorable experience of learning "less is better" when I attended a quantum physics conference at a Buddhist monastery in 1989. I asked if I could have seconds on the food. A monk affirmed to me, "Yes. You can have as little as you want." I then learned that the monk used the word "little" in place of the word "much."

[15] *A graph of the slower acting range needed for testing yeast by prayer is described on p. 2-23 of The Spindrift Papers.*

[16] *After gathering the data, the computer calculated "(1) The standard deviation ratio (the percent by which the standard deviations of [prayed for] yeast exceed the standard deviations of control yeast), and (2) The +/—ratio (the number of times the [prayed-for] yeast measurement exceeded the control yeast measurement divided by the number of times the control yeast measurement was less than the [prayed-for] yeast measurement)." For more explanation, see The Spindrift Tests, 1983, p. 90.*

[17] *The Spindrift Papers, p. 2-18 and 2-19, and The Spindrift Tests, 1983, p. 90 and 96.*

[18] *The Spindrift Papers, p. 2-22.*

[19] *The Spindrift Tests, 1983, p. 94.*

[20] *Ibid., p. 89, Qualitative Research, p. 93, The Spindrift Papers 2-18 through 2-20. Bruce and John told me 20-30 accumulated runs would be enough to get a fair reading of a person's ability to produce results which showed a faith-direction of his prayer effect or an identity-supporting-direction of his prayer effect.*

[21] *Identity Field Theory, p. 91. The Klingbeils felt psi missing carried over to prayer experiments as well. They postulated that our minds do not often permit us to witness the occurrence of a psychic or spiritual phenomenon because learning that one has such powers can be scary. A person may participate in a prayer experiment, but instead of getting the expected positive result, his self-doubt creates instead a negative, psi missing, result. John writes, "Psychology would suggest self-doubt as underlying the early negative effects of the healers (possibly negative effects are akin to some of the psi-missing effects of parapsychology) . . . . " The Spindrift Tests, 1983, p. 106.*

[22] *The Spindrift Papers, p. 2-20 and 2-21.*

[23] *"Because we were able to find patterns in the qualitatively treated runs that were not*

in the control runs, we were able to use these runs to turn on a light with a mental signal. We placed the search patterns in the program that monitored gas production from the balances, and when a stored pattern appeared, the computer turned on a light." From The Spindrift Tests, *1983, p. 94.*

24   *Religion & Genetics exchange column editor for the Faith and Science Exchange newsletter* FASE, *the Rev. Dr. Demetr Demopulos, wrote the following for the May 1996 issue. "Yeast . . . has been a major research organism in the study of genetics. As strange as this may sound, it is true. The genes are similar [to human genes], and the proteins they encode are almost identical." Also see the article on the sequencing of DNA in yeast by Richard Saltus in* The Boston Globe *of April 25, 1996, p. 29.*

25   *Different types of stress change the need the yeast has, which helps define the height of the early peak or quantity of gas released. That is, "The response of the yeast reflects the stress the yeast is under. . . . In the activation of yeast [stirring in lukewarm water] the response of the treated yeast to [quality prayer] is initially to produce less gas than the control, then to produce more. In the feeding of yeast the response of the treated yeast to [quality prayer] is initially to produce more gas than the control, then to produce less." From* Identity Field Theory, *by John Klingbeil, p. 56.*

26   *One source for graphs of tested volunteers whose thoughts-prayers changed stressed yeast can be found in* The Spindrift Tests, *Copyright 1983, by John Klingbeil, p. 96-118.*

27   *Leavened and unleavened bread has many literal and symbolic uses in Bible history. Often the word leaven is associated with the yeast fungus which makes baked goods expand and wine ferment.* The Abingdon Bible Commentary, *published by The Abingdon Press in Nashville, Tennessee, 1929, p. 978, comments, "When placed under the microscope the working of leaven in the meal looks like a veritable battlefield: there is assault and penetration in the face of determined resistance [types of stress] until peace descends after the whole has been conquered."*

28   *The inorganic experiments with thought and prayer can be found in John Klingbeil's books* Qualitative Research: The Early Years, The Quiet Revolution, The Spindrift Papers, *and* Identity Field Theory.

29   Spindrift Newsletter, *Volume 2, Number 1, Spring, 1985, p. 11.*

30   The Quiet Revolution, *1980, p. 24.*

Index

A

Aaron, Priest, p. 116, 117
ABC News, p. 16, 32
Agnew, Spiro, p. 102
Ahithophel, p. 220
Albuquerque Journal, p. 28
Alexander, Gus, p. 256
Allen, Steve, p. 148
American Society of Parapsychology Research Newsletter, p. 298
Andrews, John, p. 79, 86, 102, 103, 107, 108, 109, 140
Andrews, Sperry, p. 15, 202, 208
Apple Computer Applications, p. 77, 332, 335
Archaeus Project, p. 187, 189, 306
Aristotle, p. 347
Armstrong, Howard, p. 219, 314
Armstrong, Marian, p. 314
Associated Press, p. 103, 255, 360
Atlantic Monthly, p. 73
Atwater, Holmes, p. 308
Aurelius, Marcus, p. 369

B

Backster, Cleve, p. 15, 172, 204, 213, 311, 327
Barnum Effect, concept, p. 343
Barsabbas, Joseph, p. 117
Barnett, Lincoln, p. 300
Bay Area Skeptics, p. 105, 132, 133, 140
Belk, Henry, p. 139
Bell, Art, p. 310, 331
Benor, Daniel, p. 328
Benson, Herbert, p. 19, 168
Bigamon, Maynard, p. 255
Bockris, John, p. 108
Borysenko, Joan, back cover, p.15
Boston Globe, p. 197, 309, 318
Brooks, Phillips, p. 303
Broughton, Richard, p. 108, 206
Bruce, Lenny, p. 102
Buck, Kate, p. 303
Bullock, Bob, p. 108
Burbank, Luther, p. 241, 295
Burnett, Ron, p. 15
Burns, George, p. 184

C

Caltech, p. 130

Calvin, John, p. 155

Cambridge Psychological Society, p. 225

Carter, Jimmy, p. 308

Carver, George, p. 337

Cayce, Edgar, p. 327

Center for Religion and Science, p. 310

Center for Theology and Natural Science, p. 181

Central Illinois Skeptics, p. 132

Central Intelligence Agency, p. 172, 187, 308

Century of Progress, exhibition, p. 303

Chemistry of the Blood, p. 116

Chicago Sun Times, p. 302

Chicago Tribune, p. 130, 131, 315

Chopra, Deepak, front and back cover

Christ, Jesus, p. 52, 65, 66, 71, 72, 85, 91, 110, 117, 118, 138, 149, 166, 220, 303, 314, 349, 350

Christian Science, p. 22, 23, 25, 64, 70-73, 86, 91, 92, 94, 149, 167, 186, 301, 309. *See also* Eddy, Mary Baker

Christian Science Monitor, p. 70, 168, 300

Christie, Agatha, p. 89

Ciaravino, Helene, p. 224, 314

Clinton, Bill, p. 219

Coherence, concept, p. 244

Columbus, Christopher, p. 35

Committee for Rational Inquiry, p. 133

Committee for the Scientific Investigation of Claims of the Paranormal, p. 133, 141

Compton, Arthur, p. 235

Conclusion about the research, p. 293, 294

Conn, Joseph, p. 29

Cooper, William, p. 300

Cope, Edwin, p. 315

D

Daily Sentinel, p. 103

Dallas Morning News, p. 189, 307

Daniel, p. 112, 113

Darwin, Charles, p. 161, 239, 295, 296

Davies, Paul, p. 28, 30, 99

Deal, Barbara, p. 15

Defense Department, p. 308

Defense Mechanism, concept, p. 53-55, 129, 207, 290, 291, 298, 353-357

DeHaan, M. p. 116

De La Warr, George, p. 150, 151

Delicious Living, p. 37, 38

Dell, Michael, p. 334

Demopulos, Demetr, p. 318

Denver Post, p. 103, 108

Displacement Effect, concept, p. 275

Dossey, Larry, back cover, p. 11-14, 15, 20, 26, 34, 40, 120, 166, 173, 183, 189, 299, 367

Duckro, Paul, p. 315

Dunne, Brenda, p. 187, 214, 330

Durant, Will, p. 352

E

Eddy, Mary Baker, p. 70, 72, 73, 81, 87, 98, 111, 117, 123,152, 189, 213, 221, 236, 300, 302, 314, 344

Edison, Thomas, p. 35, 107

Einstein, Albert, p. 37, 51, 73, 110, 111, 231, 331, 332, 333, 355

Elijah, p. 113, 219

Elisha, p. 74, 112, 113

Emoto, Masaru, p. 118

Episcopal, p. 57, 307

Erlichman, John, p. 219

Evans, Lara, p. 37

F

Fairfax, Samantha, p. 15

FASE Notices, Center for Faith And Science Exchange, p. 310, 318

Ferrini, Paul, p. 144

Ft. Worth Star Telegram, p. 107

Fortson, Leigh, p. 15

Foster, Vince, p. 219

Free Inquiry, p. 169, 306

Frost, Robert, p. 373

G

Galileo, Galilei, p. 13

Gardner, Martin, p. 146

Garner, James, p. 34

Gaylor, Annie Laurie, p. 29, 169

Gershwin, Ira, p. 36, 297

Gideon, p. 111

God and the New Physics, p. 28

Goodfellow, Karl, p. 15, 214, 311

Goss, Richard, p. 169

Groundhog Day, p. 338

Guidepost, p. 157, 158

Guiley, Rosemary Ellen, p. 37, 150, 329

H

Hansen, George, p. 6, 15, 132, 206, 207

Harker, Kent, p. 105

Harrington, Anne, p. 307

Harris, Sidney, p. 311

Harvard Divinity School's Tillich—Archives, p. 307

Harvey, Paul, p. 26

Healer, p. 21, 96, 162, 163, 305

Hefner, Philip, p. 21

Heraclitus, p. 123

Herbert, Nick, p. 103, 302

Hitler, Adolph, p. 61, 62, 64, 220

Hoffman, Abby, p. 331

Holman, Eugene, p. 19

Home Catacomb, p. 155, 158, 300, 304, 305, 312
Hussein, Saddam, p. 307, 308
Huxley, Thomas, p. 31
Hyman, Ray, p. 134, 135

I
Imich, Alexander, p. 15
In The Zone, p. 129
Ivins, Molly, p. 107

J
Jablonski, David, p. 315
Jahn, Robert, p. 187
Jain, Manoj, p. 364
Jobs, Steve, p. 77, 349
Josephson, Brian, p. 20
Journal of the American Society of Psychical Research, p. 205, 214
Judas, p. 117, 219

K
Kalb, Claudia, p. 31
Kappeler, Max, p. 20
Katra, Jane, p. 119, 235
Kevorkian, Jack, p. 212
King David, p. 220
King Elah, p. 220
King Saul, p. 220
Klee, Paul, p. 337
Klingbeil, Bruce, key places, p. 12, 14, 17, 18, 21, 24, 28, 38, 42, 43, 46, 48, 50, 62, 76-79, 82, 83, 110, 119, 142, 143, 173-183, 190, 191, 238, 296, 306, 333, 335, 370
Klingbeil, Deborah, p. 24, 79, 156, 158, 195, 197, 198, 201, 212, 213, 312
Klingbeil, Gloria, p. 23, 24, 79
Klingbeil, John, key places, p. 12, 14, 17, 18, 21, 28, 32, 33, 38, 43, 69, 75-78, 136, 137, 160-162, 173-183, 222, 233
Klingbeil, Mary, p. 24, 75, 79
Koch, Christof, p. 130
Koppel, Ted, p. 16
Kotulak, Ronald, p. 130
Kowolik, John, p. 198, 200
Krucoff, Mitchell, p. 366

L
Law of the Conceptual Whole, p. 179
Law of Unintended Consequences, p. 124
Lazar, Tex, p. 108
Leonardo da Vinci, p. 128
Levin, Jeff, p. 328
Lewis, C. S., p. 132
Life, p. 359
List of Consequences of Research, p. 191, 192
Luther, Martin, p. 165, 225
Lutheran Center, p. 307, 310
Lynn, Barry, p. 29

M

Magaletta, Philip, p. 115
Marconi, Guglielmo, p. 36
Martinis, Cheryl, p. 311
Matrix, the movie, p. 126
Matthews, Dale, p. 26
Matthias, p. 117
McComas, William, p. 304
McDonnell, Douglas, p. 138
McDougall, William, p. 241
McGuire, W. J., p. 183
Mead, Margaret, p. 101
Miller, John, p. 328
Miller, William, p. 29
Mims, Forrest M., p. 302, 303
Miracles of Mind, p. 10, 119, 235
Mold Test, p. 58
Monad, Gauchos, p. 69
Moore, James, p. 360
Morehouse, David, p. 308
Morse, Melvin, p. 15
Moses, p. 48, 219
Mozart, p. 128,
Mung Bean Test, p. 105, 243
Murphy, Michael, p. 129
Musgrave, Story, p. 59
Myers, Bart, p. 94
Myers, Gerald, p. 20
Myers, Gladys, p. 4, 15, 26, 94, 97, 159, 211, 288, 295, 304, 310

N

Nash, Carrol, p. 316
National Basketball Association, p. 129
National Federation of Musicians, p. 221
National Institutes of Health, p. 222
Nelson, Roger, p. 336
Newberg, Andrew, p. 228
New English Bible, p. 111, 298
New Republic, p. 302
New York Times, p. 103
Newsweek, p. 31, 32
Nixon, Richard, p. 102, 219
Nocebo Effect, concept, p. 114, 363, 368
Noetic Sciences, p. 15, 119, 215
Northwestern University, p. 25, 80, 206, 232

O

Oakes, Richard, p. 305
O'Keeffe, Mike, p. 302
O'Leary, Brian, p. 214, 309
Oprah Winfrey Show, p. 189
Order, concept, p. 62-64
Out on the Limb Test, concepts, p. 185-187

P

Palmer, Thomas, p. 198
Parapsychological Association, p. 108, 194, 316
PBS Television, p. 108, 109, 216, 313
Pearsall, Paul, p. 214, 311
Peel, Robert, p. 72, 300, 309
Penn, William, p. 223

Perry, Canon Michael, p. 327

Persig, Robert M., p. 51, 52, 297

Phillips, Peter, p. 138

Picasso, Pablo, p. 350

Placebo Effect, p. 19, 306, 307

Placebo Effect, concept, p. 83, 84, 174-177, 242, 246, 252, 253

Planck, Max Karl, p. 196

Plato, p. 220

Politically Correct, concept, p. 28, 29, 95, 302, 303

Powell, Lyman, p. 309

Prayer, concepts, p. 42, 60, 61, 66, 67, 240, 366

Presbyterian, p. 307

Princeton Engineering Anomalies Research Laboratory, p. 214, 330

Proust, Marcel, p. 17

Q

Qualitative Thought, concept, p. 51, 52, 297 (Chapter 2 endnote 4), 300 (endnote 14), 345-346, 369-370

Quantum Physics, p. 55, 62, 67, 100, 103, 110, 130, 229, 239, 240, 278, 302 (endnote 3), 308 (endnote 4), 340

Quiet Revolution, p. 159, 171, 172, 301, 305, 318

Quimby, Phineas, p. 72, 344

R

Radin, Dean, back cover, p. 15, 19, 128, 202, 206, 303, 310

Randi, James, p. 132, 133, 134, 138, 171, 229

Random Number Tests, p. 39, 63, 77, 185, 186, 309, 334

Reader's Digest, p. 299

ReDiscovering Cosmos Conference, p. 181, 228, 307

Remote Viewing, p. 187, 235, 276, 308 (endnote 3)

Resistance and Roadblocks, concept, p. 38, 93, 94, 138, 146, 152, 163, 169, 198, 201

Richard Garret, p. 126

Roberts, Frederick, p. 71

Rockford Files, p. 34

Rockwell, Teed, p. 131

Rockwell, Theodore, p. 15, 16, 55, 164, 194, 195, 298, 364, 365

Rolling Stones , p. 372

Rommel, George, p. 220

Roosevelt, Teddy, p. 27

Rubik, Beverly, p. 301, 329

Rukeyser, Louis, p. 27
Runbeck, Margaret, p. 309
Russell, Robert, p. 181

S
Sagan, Carl, p. 223, 314
St. Louis Medical Center, p. 235, 315
St. Peter, p. 74
Saltus, Richard, p. 318
Samson, p. 219
Schaefer, Glen, p. 305
Schlitz, Marilyn, p. 119, 222
Schnabel, Jim, p. 308
Schneider, Pauline, p. 299
Schunk, Laura, p. 195, 201, 312
Schwartz, Stephan, p. 367
Schweitzer, Albert, p. 145, 146, 236, 304
Science & Spirit, p. 310
Scientific American, p. 302, 303
Secret Life of Plants, p. 15, 172, 204, 311
Seely, Paul, p. 300
Semmelweis, Ignaz, p. 219, 314
Shakespeare, William, p. 373
Sheldrake, Rupert, p. 355
Shumsky, Susan, p. 329
Simpson, James, p. 148
Simpson, O. J., p. 35
Sinclair, Upton, p. 355
Sixty Minutes, p. 107

Skolnick, Andrew, p. 132, 133
Sloan, Richard, p. 31, 32
Smith, Sister Justa, p. 90, 301
Society for Psychical Research, p. 193
Socrates, p. 220, 237
Solivan, Samuel, p. 169
Soybean Test, p. 58, 244-247
Spence, Gerry, p. 224
Spindrift in Review, p. 289
Stanford University, p. 302
Stapp, Henry, p. 131
Stein, Gordon, p. 169
Steinmetz, Charles, p. 72, 73, 309
Stillings, Dennis, p. 187, 188
Sweet, Alice, p. 15
Sweet, Charles, p. 15
Sweet, Cody, p. 15

T
Targ, Russell, p. 10, 119, 235
Tart, Charles, p. 55
Teamsters, p. 221
Templeton, John, p. 29, 30, 31, 99, 213, 310
Terrorism and Prayer, p. 19, 35, 101, 124, 126 (science fiction reference), 143, 236, 237, 359, 360, 361
Thoreau, Henry David, p. 119
Three R's, concept, p. 339
Tillich, Paul, p. 184, 307
Time, p. 51

Triangle Symbol, concept, p. 180

Triticale Test, p. 258, 259

Trotsky, Leon, p. 357

Twain, Mark, p. 72, 300

U

Unconscious Thought, concept, p. 45, 88, 89, 145, 146, 291, 292

USA Weekend, p. 25

U. S. News & World Report, p. 20

United States Psychotronics Association, p. 187, 188, 278

Unity Church, p. 189, 237

University of Southern California, p. 304

V

Virtue, concept, p. 50-51

Virtue, Doreen, p. 328

W

Wall Street Journal, p. 168, 169, 170

Washington, George, p. 342

Washington Post, p. 103

Wesch, Jerry, p. 327

Westin, Walter, p. 305, 306

Westword, p. 103, 302

White, Rhea, p. 15, 129, 205, 214

Who's Who in Theology and Science, p. 310

Williamson, Marianne, p. 102

Wiseman, Richard, p. 119

Wolf, Fred Allen, p. 62

Wozniak, Steve, p. 77

Wright, Wilbur, p. 36

X

X Files, p. 18, 121, 196

Xlibris, publisher of book, p. 4

Y

Yancey, Philip, p. 20, 101, 346

Yeast Test, p. 57, 259, 283, 316

Yogananda, Paramahansa, p. 309

Yutang, Lin, p. 224

Z

Zen and the Art of Motorcycle Maintenance: An Inquiry into Values, p. 52, 297

Zimri, p. 220

Zone, in the zone concept, p. 128-130

Zygon, p. 21, 310

WHAT OTHERS SAY ABOUT
A JOURNEY INTO PRAYER

"Bill Sweet has given the world a deep, enlightening, and disturbing look into a tragic and profound struggle to bring together science, healing, and religion. His book is a 'must read' for everyone interested in the science and politics of religion, prayer, alternative therapies, and healing. It is a sobering story. Bruce and John Klingbeil, the Spindrift prayer and healing researchers, were true heroes. Unappreciated by virtually everyone—the church they sought to serve and protect, the skeptics who taunted them, and the public—they strove for 20 years to do the meticulous work necessary to scientifically explore and document the gift of healing. This book is their story. Read it and weep for what we might have learned from them. This is a true story you won't be able to put down."

—Jerry E. Wesch, Ph.D., President,
International Society for the Study
of Subtle Energies and Energy Medicine

"Science is a method of finding out *how* the world works. Religion is a way of finding out *why* the world works. Healing is a way of ensuring *that* the world works. Spindrift's experiments on the physical effects of prayer are an exciting example of trying to forge links between science, religion, and healing. All power to their elbow!"

—Canon Michael Perry,
Editor, *The Christian Parapsychologist*

"Bill Sweet's *Journey Into Prayer* is filled with dynamic discoveries of the effects of thought on plants from the Klingbeil research team, whom I enjoyed knowing."

—Cleve Backster,
Author, *Primary Perception*

"*A Journey Into Prayer* is a saga of researchers in the new field of prayer research, who, like paradigm-breaking explorers before them, met with disappointment and frustration, disapproval and rejection. The implications of their work, however, namely the effect of mind on matter, and consciousness in healing, are certainly as potentially revolutionary as those of Copernicus and Galileo, Newton and Einstein."

—John F. Miller, III, Ph.D.,
President, The Academy of Religion
and Psychical Research

"The Spindrift research is fascinating, original work and an important contribution to the healing research literature. It suggests that our consciousness interacts intimately with our environment, and that prayer and other forms of healing can be potent influences in our lives. Its implications are profound and will take many years to be digested, replicated, and absorbed."

—Daniel J. Benor, M.D.,
Author, *Healing Research:*
Holistic Energy Medicine and Spirituality

"Bill Sweet's *A Journey Into Prayer* is an answered prayer in itself. After reading the story of the Klingbeils' Spindrift Research, you'll understand how prayer exceeds humanity's healing boundaries."

—Doreen Virtue, Ph.D.,
Author, *Divine Guidance* and *Healing with the Angels*

"The Spindrift story has been well known only to those relatively few people at the center of the consciousness, spirituality, and healing research community. Thanks to Bill Sweet's marvelous book, the Klingbeils can finally get the credit they deserve as scientific pioneers."

—Jeff Levin, Ph.D., M.P.H.,
Author, *God, Faith, and Health*

"*A Journey Into Prayer* presents the clearest explanation of the scientific basis of prayer that I have ever read. Bill Sweet shows how prayer can bring together science and religion in a meaningful dialog that will help us understand and apply our own powers to heal."

—Rosemary Ellen Guiley, Ph.D.,
Author, *The Miracle of Prayer* and
Breakthrough Intuition

"*A Journey Into Prayer* sparkles with flashes of brilliance. The unique experiments with prayer explore the wonders and mysteries of prayer-healing, positive-blessing, and negative-cursing through mental choices. Bill Sweet's book helps us understand subtle agendas deep in our prayers that can ultimately help or hurt others."

—Dr. Susan G. Shumsky,
Author, *Divine Revelation*

"Few people know of Spindrift, the research team who conducted groundbreaking grass-roots experiments on healing and prayer a few decades ago when it was quite taboo. Their inventive work was rejected by their own church and by other churches, as well as by the mainstream scientific community. Now, the world can read about Spindrift's pioneering journey in the book, *A Journey Into Prayer*, by Bill Sweet. This maverick book documents the founders' discoveries, Bill Sweet's personal interactions with Spindrift, and the impact of this work now and for the future. This book also contributes to the ongoing deliberation on the experimental design issues for studies on prayer and healing, while it is immensely readable and enjoyable for all."

—Beverly Rubik, Ph.D.,
Author, *Life at the Edge of Science*,
President and Founder, Institute for Frontier Science,
Emeryville, CA

"The Spindrift story is a contemporary rendition of the archetypal Hero's Journey, the heroic tragedy of the human spirit struggling to surmount the dogmas erected against the unknown and unpredictable. Whether these obstacles consist of pseudo-religious or pseudo-scientific intimidations, the accusations of non-conformist 'heresies' actually reveal more about the unacknowledged fears and uncertainties of the accusers than of the accused. Those who challenge the entrenched authorities always do so at considerable risk, as the Spindrift story confirms.

"The irrational recalcitrance stimulated by the monumental implications of the Spindrift studies is not an isolated case. Our own Princeton Engineering Anomalies Research (PEAR) program has frequently encountered similar reactions, as exemplified in a recent letter that reads in part: 'My point of view was and remains: the deductions drawn from the PEAR experiments are impossible. So, the experimental methods must have been defective . . . . How could it possibly be otherwise in the REAL world?' One eventually comes to realize that any attempt at rational response to this kind of challenge is futile.

"True faith and true science both stem from the yearning of human consciousness to transcend its apparent limitations, whether of the spirit or of the mind, and on its willingness to accept responsibility for the unknowable and unpredictable outcomes of its choices. And, fortunately, the Hero's Journey never ends with physical death. The example of Bruce and John Klingbeil's courageous battle, so vividly depicted in this book, will continue to inspire future heroes as long as the human spirit thrives."

—Brenda Dunne, Manager, PEAR Laboratory

THE SPINDRIFT FILES

It's my conjecture that consciousness is the single most powerful force in the universe . . . . I can't recall ever else in my career when I walked into something as powerful as these consciousness experiments . . . .

The Klingbeils were involved in very controversial work . . . . Perhaps the Klingbeils did one consciousness experiment too many . . . . They might have opened a door they did not intend to open . . . . Where do you go when the government and the mob are after you?

Art Bell on his radio show Coast to Coast A.M. (4/17/05)

We got to stop science and scientific progress. Facts separate people.

Abby Hoffman

Albert Einstein was a visiting lecturer at Princeton in 1952. A Princeton doctoral student asked him, "What is there left in the world for original dissertation research?"

Einstein answered, "Find out about prayer. Somebody must find out about prayer."*

In 1983, an open-minded friend of mine met Bruce and John Klingbeil and watched several prayer tests in action. He witnessed an electronic random number test. John's thought on random zeros and ones changed them into a non-random pattern of zeros and ones. In another test, my friend saw the slow relentless beat of stressed soybeans moving toward a healing point. Next he inspected the computer tracking of stressed yeast cells in two pots, one of which John prayed over. Two streams of yeast data were gathered into two columns and were compared. The comparison showed that the yeast that received John's prayer had less stress in it than the yeast that received no prayer.

The yeast test was in full swing. A lady volunteer rang the doorbell. She came into the Klingbeils' living room, now their laboratory, and prayed for the yeast test for over two hours with promising results.

My friend also saw a visual presentation about science, religion, and consciousness that Bruce had recently finished programming on his Apple II computer. As part of the presentation, Bruce programmed Albert Einstein's $E = MC^2$ being written by a bodiless hand. John narrated an audiotape he played that synchronized with the computer program.

My friend said, "This is the beginning of something good."

Was it "the beginning of something good?"

A week later, my friend called with a report. Given a little writer's liberty for recollection, he essentially said, "Bill, I told people what you and the Klingbeils were doing. They said testing prayer was unnecessary and would never work. It's heresy and 'tempting the Lord' to test prayer at all. They said you are being deceived by aggressive malicious suggestion into doing the Devil's deeds, and here's how: the Devil has manipulated the test findings to look good, when the findings are actually forms of evil pretending to be good."

I was encouraged (sarcasm). So I guess it isn't enough that the Devil and God are fighting over the souls of men. They are fighting over random numbers, soybeans, and yeast, too.

Later a church friend with a scientific background who showed zero interest in the tests said to me, "Bill, it's the Science of Being, not the Science of Beans."

In 1989, Bruce said, "It's amazing! We have found out that there is this enormous interest in healing-prayer. And people believe statistics about prayer, but we're wrong to take it so seriously that we test it."

In 2005, a Spindrift supporter traveled from another state to visit her hometown. As she drove by her hometown church, she said, "I kind of feel nostalgic about that church because it was the first one I was kicked out of."

So much has changed since then. It's difficult to believe that religious folks, skeptics, and others for reasons not clear, opposed the Klingbeils' efforts to explore thought and prayer.

Broaching the subject of why scientific skeptics opposed paranormal exploration, Bruce surmised:

> There seems to be a fear among many scientists, there certainly seems to be among the skeptics . . . . That if we should be right, we are opening a Pandora's Box . . . . All of a sudden the kooks will be on the streets, the New Age people would be flooding into the world, and we would be back into some pre-scientific era . . . .
>
> We don't happen to feel that way. We believe that the tests have the [potential] to quantify the world of the paranormal: . . . to clean it up without sweeping it all under the rug, locking it into a box, and saying it doesn't exist, which seems to be the skeptics' approach . . . . (1989 tape)
>
> * The Albert Einstein quote is recorded in the *Leadership Journal*, Winter 1983, page 43.

In the next section, the organizing effects of thought and prayer on randomness will be discussed.

The only thing faster than a computer chip is telepathy.
Michael Dell

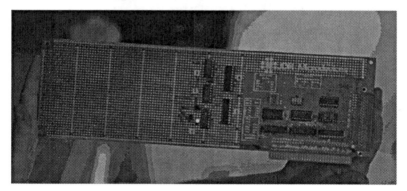

A random event generator card is imprinted
with the Klingbeils' thoughts and prayers.

Random event generators are picking up psychic activity in
the environment as you read. These responsive generators are
also called random number generators. Scientists have discovered
that random zeros and ones form into patterns when people
give attention to a situation. This discovery of randomness being
modified is gaining credibility as data is collected and analyzed.

It's remarkable. When thought is applied to random binary numbers, the numbers start to form into recognizable patterns. Bruce and John experimented with four random event generators. The first one was plugged into their Apple II in 1977.

In 1989, Bruce spoke about what was noticed when his prayer and his unconscious associations of thought imprinted a random event generator or R.E.G.

Bruce said:

> We've done a number of tests that are based on randomness, basically random flow. Some of our tests involve the calling of the turn of a card. Other tests involve the throwing of dice. Some of our tests involve electronically generated randomness . . . .
>
> It doesn't have to be prayer [to produce a recognizable pattern of zeros and ones where there should be random zeros and ones]. This [outcome] was a surprise of these tests. The only [added] effect that prayer has on these tests is to make the circuit perform a little more perfectly . . . . We find that the same qualitative thought which produces an **orderliness in an organic pattern** will also tend to produce **orderliness in an inorganic pattern,** and will tend to actually affect the oscillator producing randomness in terms of causing it to produce a more perfect pattern than it would otherwise produce . . . . [Which means that prayer helps to improve the conditions of soybeans and yeast. Prayer also helps to improve the output of a random event generator to produce a better flow of true randomness, which is the generator's identity and purpose within its ecosystem.]

The Klingbeils' tests occasioned two psychic effects.

1. A conscious effort of qualitative thought from prayer helped an R.E.G. to perform a better random flow of zeros and ones.

2. A less directed unconscious effort of thought on an R.E.G. helped randomized zeros and ones to form patterns.

Sometimes the computer would do double duty. During a prayer test, when a volunteer prayed for the benefit of a plant with data being fed into computer memory, the R.E.G. in a computer would casually pick up the rapt attention or resonating focus or bonding with a plant or loving atmosphere of the volunteer, and a pattern would form out of the randomness.

While Princeton scientist Roger Nelson visited sacred historical sites, he wasn't alone when soaking in the experiences. Nelson wondered if sacred sites emitted signals that could be picked up by a random event generator. Nelson's portable R.E.G. stayed with him and recorded every special moment.

A standout experience occurred when Roger Nelson entered the Egyptian pyramid of Khufu located on the Giza plateau. As Nelson walked through the Queen's chamber, the R.E.G. drew a line ascending at an angle. While walking through the King's chamber, his R.E.G. pocket companion drew a line descending at an angle.

Later Nelson analyzed the data from his electronic companion. He affixed the correct times in the two chamber locations, and noted that people praying, meditating, and chanting accompanied the chamber visits. The data drew a graph the shape of a sizeable pyramid. Apparently Roger Nelson's inorganic R.E.G. device responded to special resonating events at sacred historical locations. Probably the R.E.G. also responded to his human experiences. **Now, not only do skeptics have human believers to debunk, they have circuit cards!**

(*Journal of Scientific Exploration*, Vol. 12, No. 3, pages 425-454, 1998, FieldREG II, Consciousness Field Effects: Replications and Explorations, R. D. Nelson, R. G. Jahn, B. J. Dunne, Y. H. Dobyns, and G. J. Bradish.)

Khufu pyramid on Giza plateau

When you can do the common things of life in an uncommon way, you will command the attention of the world.
George W. Carver

In the next section, getting beyond literalism opens the mind to conceptualize the invisible interactions of intercessory prayer.

Art does not reproduce the visible; rather, it makes visible.
Paul Klee

THEME WEAVER

Much is made of taking an event literally in place of interpreting the **meaning** of an event. One example is the movie *Groundhog Day*. This elegant story is not fixed in linear time. The past, present, and future are interlaced.

Some literalists have trouble with movies like *Groundhog Day* because they believe these movies teach lies about how the world works. The literalist reminds us that the world does not fly backward in time and then fly forward in time. The literalist gets hung up on the illogic of the movie rather than the moral of the story. Ironically, I heard a social scientist say that *Groundhog Day* would become an enduring movie because of its universal moral message.

Yet literalists of the Bible would be the first to tell us that the world stood still for a day. (See Joshua 10:13.) Some of us know people who believe literally every word and description in the Bible and the Koran. Literalist Muslims read in the Koran that people who are not of the Islamic faith or Muslims who tolerate liberal practices are infidels, potential fodder for assassins. (See Koran 9:73.) For Muslim fundamentalists, caricature art is a literal representation of

Mohammedan. Cartoons drawn with pencils have ignited violent riots. Ironically, in the U.S. prison in Cuba holding Muslim fighters, *Harry Potter* books are the most popular.

Having talked about literalism, the following 3 R's are not to have a literal meaning. These concepts are figurative. The 3 R's are a guide. They form a mental template for the imagination, so we can visualize what inconspicuously happens during the interactions between intercessory prayer and the object being observed by prayer.

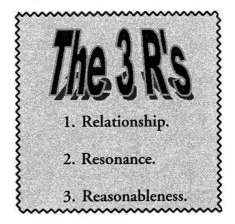

The 3 R's

1. Relationship.

2. Resonance.

3. Reasonableness.

1. When a person prays or thinks of a person, an animal, a plant, a place, a **relationship** is fashioned. We can thank **entanglement** from quantum physics for some back up on this relationship by <u>associational linkage</u>, which is defined on page 249. It reminds one of the SBC television ad **"We can't always see the things that connect us most."**

2. When a relationship is given attention, this focus of consciousness occasions a **resonance**, an entangled connected circuit, maybe a new family tie. How the quality of attention-thought is subjectively exchanged and entangled determines the quality of the effect, the improvement, the uplift of consciousness for another.

Quantum physicists may not yet agree with the above, but quantum physics would say that interactions between subjects do take place outside of time and space. Quantum physics also says that there is no such thing as a passive thought when thinking of someone else. A subtle field of effect is established. "No man is an island."

If no man is an island and a subtle field of effect does resonate out to other folks, then human beings can begin to accept that their prayers and thoughts do affect others. As an analogy, in a dark room, when one person opens the curtains, everyone in the room sees the light. Likewise, a quality prayer of a person may pull back the curtains and let the light flood on everyone in its path. By extension, prayer and meditation may resonate fields of light, which could subtly tip the delicate balance or tipping point of world consciousness.

3. When a **relationship** and **resonance** is set-up, attention is giving out a field. Does this field of good effect have a cloudless road ahead of it? Not very often. Mostly this field of good effect is affirmed in the face of the reactionary defense mechanisms in the subconscious mind, and our cultural education often has us not hear psi, and if we do hear it, we distrust the promptings from psi. Our ascending affirmations about what a field effect from prayer is enlisted to do, often hits a firewall of defense mechanisms. This firewall in the subconscious mind chimes forth and sings in sync with the conscious mind's educated resistance to psi, and the prayer request is discredited as **unreasonable.**

Other agendas in the mind want to believe what is affirmed in prayer is possible. But there are numerous competing agendas in the mind. One area of the mind believes in prayer and the mystical. A different area of the mind believes something quite contrary. When we center our attention, the mind is battling and pushing its own agendas. Another reason life is so confusing!

The third R is to open the flow of our thought to healing possibilities beyond what's **reasonable** which expands the unreasonable to become reasonable. It is to be open to the unusual, even though one might not know what that will bring. It's this openness to the impossible so that the impossible may happen. We should cast a thought beyond our collective belief systems. **Goal-free prayer operates best when it is free to liberate, conceive, expect the unexpected.**

Troops of comedians apply improvisation to birth new ideas. As long as the word "**yes**" is the response to do some improvisation, the comedic energy flows from person to person. An unreasonable request to improvise doesn't stop the flow. The improvisation will keep flowing as long as the word "**no**" is never spoken. This "**yes**" hints at how one can expand his creative attention to accept that sometimes the unreasonable can migrate over to the reasonable. George Bernard Shaw wrote "The reasonable man adapts himself to the world. The unreasonable man persists in trying to adapt the world to himself. Therefore, all progress depends upon the unreasonable man."

For similar themes supporting the 3 R's, see the Law of the Conceptual Whole on page 179 and the Triangle Symbol on page 180.

May the Father of all mercies scatter light, and
not darkness, upon our paths, and make us all
in our several vocations useful here.
George Washington, 1790, to the
Hebrew Congregation in Newport, Road Island

In the next section, our **perceptions** of phenomena and persuasive personalities will be discussed.

PERCEPTION

Most folks appreciate seeing a circus where exciting events are happening all around them. The Barnum and Bailey Circus has "something for everyone."

There is a psychological effect named after circus showman P. T. Barnum. It's the *Barnum effect*. The Barnum effect means that sometimes a human being experiences a psychic, psychological, or spiritual epiphany that tantalizes him into thinking the information in those moments were "the greatest show on earth" and zoomed in on him individually. The subconscious mind of the believer affirms the spectacular show, when actually what was experienced overwhelmed the man. He became convinced his psychic revelation or miraculous healing was personal, clear, and undeniable, when the experience had only a **general** meaning that the informed man would take more casually.

We humans find we believe the oddest affirmations. Deliberate or not, for good or evil, many magicians, psychics, faith healers, showmen, and con artists know how to get human beings to believe. These experts know that the subconscious mind of a believer will go along with their flashy ceremonies and confident mannerisms. Some showmen are born with the ability to spot a believer's weaknesses and exploit them. The roar of showmanship, charisma, and promises get a believer to suspend his suspicions and doubts, while deep down the voices of his defense mechanisms scream at him to be suspicious, but he refuses to listen.

Once a believer is convinced something has happened, the showman can get a person to believe the next level of outlandish revelations or claims. "The fish is caught in the net." The subconscious mind reinforces the spectacular experience by reassuring the conscious mind, "Since what we witnessed was true in the first example, then what we are now witnessing in the second example has to be true also, even though it is outlandish." The subconscious mind lets us see what we believe. New England healer Phineas Quimby wrote "If I really believe a thing, the effect would follow whether I am thinking of it or not."

The Klingbeils' tests of consciousness on healing didn't elicit the Barnum effect. The Klingbeils' tests were not showy but subtle. A woman came to me with a boatload of enthusiasm for Spindrift. She anticipated that the tests were dazzling to watch. When she looked closely at what the experiments involved, she ran out the door as fast as she could to get away from Spindrift. Next thing I knew, she was off to India chasing a guru.

In the next section, a subtle test finding about **purpose** will be discussed.

> Wait patiently for divine Love to move upon
> the waters of mortal mind, and form
> the perfect concept.
> Mary Baker Eddy

PURPOSE

What did some tests subtly show? Bruce answered by showing how prayer **which supported identity** provided the order and purpose needed for an identity.

Bruce explained:

> As our concepts percolate, people will begin to grasp how the holiness and compassion of an individual affects the order coming out of purpose driven prayer . . . . How divine order unfolds the poignancy of purpose of an identity. How the harmonizing effects of order exist to clarify the purpose of an identity. How an identity as a system relates itself to the conceptual whole ecosystem of its surrounding environment. [To prayerfully recognize a system's identity unearths its human function and its spiritual purpose, thus wholeness.]

> That we have a comparison between [loving quality thought that empathizes with an identity and promotes order, identity, and purpose] and [ego thought that pushes its wants, willpower, and belief] gives scientists, healers, and parapsychologists something in human consciousness to measure . . . . That is new. (1989 conversation)

If experiments can show that **the patterning power of purpose clarifies the identity of a system,** scientists can compare that pattern of identity with a pattern produced by **hit-or-miss willpower and belief.** Test results should tell us that willpower and belief **rarely** promote the order and purpose of a system's identity. Willpower and belief push a system around indifferent to the order and purpose needed. In contrast, a loving quality flow of prayerful thought **does** promote the order and purpose needed.

The power of purpose gives a sense of going somewhere, of meaning, of hope that not all effects of consciousness and the earthly activities of mankind are by chance or helter-skelter. If an implicit divine ordering-force in consciousness could be recognized both intuitively and experimentally, mankind has a crack at understanding life on a deeper level than just the random dance of electrons and bloodless dots and dashes, particles and waves. There is purpose.

> **The most important purpose of prayer may be to let our true selves be loved of God.**
> Philip Yancey, *Prayer*, p. 44

PURPOSE PERMEATES PRAYER

**We are what we repeatedly do. Excellence, then,
is not an act, but a habit.**
Aristotle

The following might get a laugh from the skeptic, but it might help the rest of us to conceptualize the actions of qualitative holy prayer to fill a situation with purpose and meaning. It's been the conjecture of the Christian Science practitioners I have known that to know better who you are *assists* the healing process.

How strange sounding is this question? Can we see who we are beyond who we are? I theorize that if we could talk to the divine motivations in prayer, they would tell us their **Prime Directive** is to bring out to us who we are. How does prayer do that for us? By giving us small glimpses of our "other" identity beyond the physical senses.

A human being may know himself as a material self, as a DNA inherited contrivance of molecules. This person may not know anything about himself in regard to his spiritual identity.

The way to **spiritually identify himself** may be unknown to the person. He may not know a way to find out who he is. It's like an orphan who, if he could find his parents, could find out who he is. Some of us are spiritual orphans, not aware who we are, that our "spiritual self" has parents, in a singular God.

What is an advantage to purpose driven prayer? With purpose driven prayer, we are no longer cutoff from our Divine Parental Source. We begin to see we are connected to a Divine Family Relationship. We are anchored to a knowing which begins a creative process in consciousness. We find our relationship to the small picture, our unique identity, brings our awareness of how we fit into the big picture, our unique purpose.

Our identity and purpose often have a correspondence with the circumstances. For example, I heard a general say that for him and many who become soldiers, one doesn't exhibit bravery until the circumstances dictated it. People who can't figure out who they are may find, within a given a set of circumstances, that they can see they have a purpose. For example, the arrival of children brings purpose for some people within their ecosystem of home and neighborhood. He who uncovers a promising purpose emboldens himself to become less a victim and more a victor.

It may be tricky to expound in words what prayer does with purpose, but with many things in life, when we catch the vision that others have caught, we click in that we are on to something bigger than the physical self. By experiencing the comfort of prayer, we interpret more **meaning** to events, we try to learn **compassion,** we try to savor an **epiphany,** and we take notice of those **in the zone moments**, which convey purpose to us.

Our spiritual identity is here to be **individual and creative.** A glimpse of our spiritual individuality may be the WD-40 for encouraging our creativity and purpose. Sometimes we can sense our individuality recognizing psi consciousness during creative moments. In those moments, we may get a burst of insight that our purpose is to find our individuality, not to become a robot. The little picture of our **identity** and the bigger picture of our **purpose** develop an awareness of our creative possibilities of what to do now and next.

An "identity crisis" is when we let "groupthink" define purpose for us. Steve Jobs of Apple Computer said, "Don't let the **noise** of others' opinions drown out your inner voice. Have the courage to follow your heart and intuition. They somehow already know what you truly want to become." If we are in a group, a church, or a society where everyone thinks the same way, **then we're not a symphony of different instruments any more. "Send in the Clones."**

A book about the significance of individuality within the diversity of an ecosystem is *The Wisdom of Crowds* by James Surowiecki. He wrote on page 77 "Everything we know about decision making suggests that the more diverse the available perspectives on a problem, the more likely it is that the final decision will be smart."

Perhaps when Jesus Christ advised that we should close the door behind us when we pray, he meant that, unless group thinking was shut out, we cannot hear God's communication **to our individual identity.** Jesus said, "When you pray, go into a room by yourself, shut the door, and pray to your Father who is there in the secret place; and your Father who sees what is secret will reward you." (NEB, Matthew 6:6) We need our individuality. Shutting the door behind our spiritual self helps us to **safeguard against identity theft.**

Just as a car or piano benefits from a tune-up, we may occasionally need **a spiritual tune-up** that affirms who we are as a spiritual identity or self. Disturbances and distractions occur to us in our daily lives, but **retuning** our spiritual identity gets us back to our purpose.

Spiritual identity implies purpose. By identifying who we are, we find our purpose. The focus of prayer is steadier when we have our purpose. Our purpose rings in us that the universe beyond space/time is this vast lighted Cathedral of the Mind. Our spiritual self has a purpose to play by directing slivers of light from this vast Cathedral of the Mind on our human circumstances.

A metaphor of "an island in the mirror" may help to illustrate our spiritual self or identity. Imagine an island that is seen only in a mirror. But this island isn't seen in the space in front of the mirror. Similarly imagine that our spiritual identity is seen only in a mirror. Our spiritual identity or self appears in the mirror, but it's not seen in space/time. Spiritual identity is reflected in the mirror from beyond space/time.

Each of us has a personal mission that can be spiritually discerned which only we can accomplish. Perhaps the next frontier beyond space/time might be to find our purpose through our circumstances. Jesus Christ said he was in two locations at the same time. He was on earth and in heaven. That amounts to bi-location—being two places simultaneously. (John 3:13) **Like "coincidental lines" overlapping,** two locations as one location suggests that our physical self is here in space/time and our spiritual self is here beyond space/time.

In the next section, radio signals interfering with natural states of mind will be discussed.

Everything is a miracle. It is a miracle that one does not dissolve in one's bath like a lump of sugar.
Pablo Picasso

CAVE DWELLER

The Scottish believe that the stories we tell about our lives define who we are. Spindrift feels that prayer is similar. What people pray for tells a story and defines who they are. Stories and prayers edify. The reformative purpose of prayer is to promote growth out of a stagnate circumstance. In the movie *The Natural,* Robert Redford said, "We live two lives. The life we learn from and the life we live after that." Results from prayer are comfort, reformed lives, and healing moments.

Stories of the **paranormal** and **prayer-anormal** suggest that our common laws of time and space aren't securely moored 100% of the time. The **function** of stories, prayer, forgiveness, and psi consciousness are being taken seriously by some scientific thinkers. The soft sciences and the hard sciences are beginning to agree that they are observing the same light at the end of the tunnel. There is a progressive melding of spirituality and scientific concepts.

A juxtaposition is posited by the Klingbeils. People used to be attuned to the Earth and Nature. Most people are now attuned to the technological. Scientific progress has brought a continual increase in the electromagnetic waves traveling through the Earth and atmosphere. Men and woman are bombarded with an infinite unrelenting barrage of electromagnetic signals that go through their bodies and minds. These ubiquitous signals are silent noises in our heads. These signals tincture us when we are awake and asleep. There is no getting away from them.

The staggering presence of radio, television, digital, satellite, and radar emissions going through the air weren't here in the Nineteenth Century. (Before the United States' entrance into World War II, the Massachusetts Institute of Technology bounced **the first radar signals off the dome** of the Mother Church of Christian Science in Boston. MIT personnel shot off a telegram to England which decoded was—Mary Baker Eddy made a hit.)

The Spindrift Team pondered the question of electromagnetic emissions causing mental interference. **Could too much electromagnetism hinder** the clarity of individual spiritual consciousness?

Bruce speculated:

> It used to be that someone could go out to the countryside to get away from it all. You do carry

your thoughts with you, but getting away from
the urban life can help. Going out in Nature helps
one get attuned to oneself to think more clearly.
That sense of peace which quiets one's thought
may clear one's thought. [Jesus Christ went up to
the mountains to refresh his thoughts, for
example.]

That type of isolation and natural renewal of
mental perspective is becoming less possible to
encounter in Nature. Signals find a path to people
everywhere. From what I have seen and
experienced, it seems reasonable that the plethora
of electromagnetic waves coming at us interferes
with our thinking and the quality of our prayers.

Then Bruce talked about a **Faraday Cage, which is a
safe room of copper or lead** that blocks electromagnetic radio
frequency interference called RF. Bruce continued:

The idea of trying a Faraday Cage around different
healers while they pray would be a way to test
this theory of mental interference. If through
electrical isolation prayers improved by being more
effective, this result would imply that the
interference was sufficiently knocked out to permit
the normal human functioning of the mind and
body of the healer.

Praying inside **a cave** is another way to block RF. A Sony
experiment beamed radio waves at the brain that activated sight,
sound, and smell. Apparently this Sony experiment suggests a
reason to go into a cave or copper cage and annul RF.

Every science begins as philosophy and ends as art.
Will Durant

CONSPIRING MINDS WANT TO KNOW

We all want to fulfill our full potential. But we often experience being thrown off-track. Our focus of attention drifts. Our mind doesn't keep **an eye on the ball**, which prevents a breakthrough in a situation. Why? Our education, our ego, choices, and biases are partially what get us off-track. *More deceptive* is the diversion of our defense mechanisms to forestall our "looking in the right places."

Apparently, when we experience the paranormal, our "**defense mechanisms,**" our **DMs**, immediately start to change the details. If we are brave fools and share our experience, we may become inarticulate about what really happened. When someone reminds us of our psi experience, we may have changed the details enough, so that the experience isn't accurate, or we deny the psi experience ever happened. Soon we might feel foolish for telling what happened or even become scared of our experience. We may tell our questioners, "Drop the subject. I want my life to go back to normal." Our DMs succeeded to distort the experience and raise doubt and distrust.

Spindrift speculates that there is a conspiracy of our collective DMs to undermine a flawless accounting of psi experience. This way the psi experience can stay hidden from an accurate human remembrance.

During the June 2004 Congressional Hearings investigating "9/11," a detail stood out. The Federal Aviation Agency and the Air Controllers focused on the first hijacked airplane, and they missed seeing the second hijacked airplane in front of their eyes on their radar screens. This focus of attention on one plane provides an analogy of how defense mechanisms displace our best efforts to notice other facts. It's like a magician who creates intense focus on what is straight ahead instead of the margin where the trick takes place.

Have you noticed that sometimes a stray thought sends us into productive territory? The human mind likes some novelty, but not novelty that moves too far from the status quo of everyday living. When we experience too much unusual phenomena, our psi natures will be exposed to us. Then our DMs fret "How do we keep them down on the farm, once they have seen Paree?" So the defense strategy is to *rarely* let the fun of "Paree" or "psi phenomena" be enjoyed by our conscious minds. We are privileged when we witness our intuition at work. To have consciously "seen Paree" is beating the odds.

Our memories of the paranormal live in the mind, but so do the defense mechanisms. Inaccurate accounts of psi caused by DMs was only one challenge for the Klingbeils.

Bruce and John Klingbeil anticipated that future skeptics would explain religion and psi as beliefs necessary only for the evolution of the brain. Religion and psi would become impotent and dismissed as crazy beliefs compared to the discoveries of science. In 1970, in anticipation of the advances in material science and medicine, the Klingbeils said of their plans for their research, "If you are going to be in a **circular** firing squad, it's better if you fire first." Otherwise, flimsy examples of psi and failed examples of prayer will heighten and grow the assertion that psi is fun to daydream about, but psi is a fantasy that doesn't exist. So the Klingbeils wanted to get out front with their speculations about how the mind treats psi.

The memory is no more in the brain than the picture coming from a television studio is in the television receiver.
Rupert Sheldrake

SABOTEURS OF PSI JUST MIGHT LIVE IN OUR OWN MINDS

When a person's belief system is challenged, the defense mechanisms may jump in to belittle and brush off the event as a coincidence, not a psychic or spiritual experience. A person apparently has to reject a psychic experience or change his belief system. Even for a believer, if an event is outside of his selective acceptance of psychic experience, his mind tends to reject it.

For example, author Upton Sinclair and his wife Mary Craig wrote a book on psychic experiments. The book is *Mental Radio*. Albert Einstein wrote the preface. Sinclair writes on page four "The evidence in support of telepathy came to seem to me conclusive, yet it never quite became real to me. The consequences of belief would be so tremendous, the changes it would make in my view of the universe so revolutionary, that I didn't believe, even when I said I did."

PSI BECOMES SHY

Other subconscious actions of the mind assist the defense mechanisms to knock out the conscious awareness of the paranormal. One example. While a person is being tested, his spontaneity, inspiration, and novelty of doing the test wear down. His psi intuition becomes bored with what it's doing. Psi data drops down to chance levels.

Another example. Many actors, models, and athletes are able to perform on demand. Participants in psi tests rarely perform well on demand. Perhaps subconscious demands on psychics and pray-ers, are why, when they are tested under controlled conditions, they don't perform too well. **Test participants become shy.**

The **"shy effect"** occurs when a participant is pressured to be spontaneous and accountable for his gifts. **The shy effect is like a photographer who sees an expression on a child's face and clicks his camera. When the photographer tries to get that same expression again for the final professional picture, the child becomes shy and can't reproduce the expression.**

Perhaps the pressure on a researcher to get results spawns the shy effect. For example, a researcher notices intriguing effects which he records during pilot runs of a test. During a more definitive test, the effects aren't there.

Do the collective mind fields of everyone consciously aware of a test "imprint" a test? Yes. Apparently all folks affect a test. Then there are the "negative expectations" projected by a skeptical mind on a test. (See page 119.)

The shy effect is disparaged by debunkers of psi. Skeptical debunkers complained that if psi is real, psi should occur on demand. The Klingbeils countered that what is first needed, is to discover "how" psi and prayer operate in the subconscious mind, so there is a level playing field about observing the effects of consciousness.

The mind acts as if it has many moving parts. The Klingbeils' novel idea was to monitor the functions of the defense mechanisms, the shy effect, (plus the related concepts of pushback and psi decline.) A family meeting of these subterranean mind effects may be to practice strategies so that no experience of psi is definitive enough to be fixed firmly as fact by mere mortals.

Mortals are *potent input receptors* of phenomena, but belief systems, mental filters, and defense mechanisms hinder our objectivity about the *output* of the phenomena. When we experience an extraordinary incident, we should write down our impressions of the incident as soon as possible. Why? Our mind may almost immediately take what we experienced and convert key facts into fiction. If we are interested in pinning down psi, we are in a war between our perceptions and our defense mechanisms.

You may not be interested in war, but war
is interested in you.
Leon Trotsky, Russian revolutionary theoretician

A DELICATE BALANCE OF CONTRASTS

One man's spiritual transformation is another man's cognitive uplift. People's lives are so varied from their upbringings and brains going through such diverse educational processes to interpret reality, that different versions of reality are likely to be clashing. What one hears, processes, and accepts as true and false, good and bad, is determined by one's make-up: the way he is wired, the amount of creativity he expresses, maybe experiments with mind altering drugs, how he utilizes qualitative thought (the holy ingredient in thought) guiding his ideas about reality. Genes, parents, environment, experiences, gifts, talents, empathies, chance, and an awareness of a context one is in, etc., conjures up how one decides what is closest to the truth. In 2005, research suggests that a gene may influence if one is a conservative or a liberal thinker. (How scary is that?) Another study suggests that nighttime sleep patterns are shorter and slightly more agitated for liberals than conservatives.

What are we hearing? One person has a terrible time in life with painful memories. Yet he believes in a Higher Power.

Another person is an atheist who has everything go pain free in his life. Yet bring up the subject of God, and the atheist may go into a cursing tirade about how the mammoth problems in the world are derived from believing in God and practicing religion. Unfortunately, the atheist can legitimately point to dreadful and gruesome activities occurring in the name of God and religion. These activities support that religions can be dangerous.

Some people practice the **prayer of disorder.** They pray for the failure of a competitor's project or promotion. A *Life* magazine poll cited that 5% who answered said they prayed toxic prayer purposely to hurt others. (March issue, 1994) Terrorists mix words of slashing, anarchy, and murder into their prayers. Before they kill, suicide bombers kiss the Koran and pray.

Extremist Muslims have shown the world that their version of religion worships terrorism. If there is a difference between Nazi fascists as savages and extremist Muslims as savages, it's that Muslim terrorists torture and kill to honor Allah.

"One man's heaven is another man's hell" **is a twist that fits** when we hear extremist Muslims proclaim that a democratic government replacing Islamic rule is against God. In fact extremist Muslims give no option to non-Muslims when it's about Islam. Extremist Muslims act like **the Borg in *Star Trek*.** The Borg civilization gobbled up every civilization it encountered. The Borg told everyone not Borg "Assimilate or die!"

When one thinks of Mormons, what pops into mind? Polygamy. When some non-Catholics see a priest, what do they think? Unfairly or not, they wonder if the priest is a child molester. When one meets a Christian Scientist, what emerges in the mind? Does he go to a doctor? When one thinks of Muslims, what image is in our mind? Terrorists scream, "Allah is great!"

Some of us have a tendency to internalize a few preconceptions about various religions and leave it there. The point is that religions are often misunderstood. The Mormon can't totally succeed in convincing many people that polygamy is no longer a tenant of the church. A Christian Scientist can't convince many people that he is free to do whatever he wants with medical methods. Catholics can't sway the opinion of the public about priests molesting children. Few moderate Muslims can convey a balanced view of themselves to the West.

Spiritually minded Muslims have the added problem of the West's ignorance of Islamic culture. Admittedly, for example, the clothing that women wear does spook some of us out in the West. After 9/11, Muslims have the hazy educational task of untangling, of separating the moderate and fair Muslims from the militant and fanatic Muslims. The folks of the West and East have to learn who are the forces of light and darkness. Here is why.

The West sees Osama bin Laden as a mass murderer. Millions of Muslims see bin Laden as a holy man and hero. *The 9/11 Commission Report* includes a statement that claims the following about dark prayers. " . . . in a speech at the al-Faruq training camp in Afghanistan, bin Laden specifically urged trainees to pray for the success of an upcoming attack involving twenty martyrs." (2004 Commission Staff Statement titled "Outline of 9/11 Plot," p. 19.)

On June 19, 2006, the *Associated Press* reported that Islamic gunmen kidnapped "four Russian diplomats near their embassy in Baghdad . . . killing one embassy employee. 'God has enabled the lions of **monotheism** to arrest four Russian diplomats in Iraq and kill the fifth,' said a statement from the group . . . ." On May 26, 2006, Sunni Islamic terrorists killed Iraq's Olympic tennis team coach and two tennis players because they were wearing shorts.

James Moore, Jr., refers to 9/11 in his book *One Nation Under God: The History of Prayer in America.* Moore writes on page 443 "Beyond the wrenching horror of the attacks themselves and the lives that changed forever that day came the unsettling realization that the men who inflicted such carnage on innocent men, women, and children of every color, national origin, and religious persuasion had used **prayer** to validate their cause."

The evidence builds that Muslim terrorists pray to express hate, not love. On August 10, 2006, an Al Qaeda plot was thwarted to blowup ten airplanes over the Atlantic Ocean. The plot may have involved mothers filling their babies' milk bottles with liquid explosives.

If the meek wish to inherit the Earth, they should become mindful that humanity is in the fight for its life with small groups of militant political religionists who can leverage technologies that could bring a catastrophic end to all human beings on the Earth.

In contrast, Tibetan Buddhists turn written prayers around on **a prayer wheel.** The turning of the wheel is supposed to activate the written prayers to begin blessing. A devout Buddhist man in Nepal made **a prayer wheel and a water wheel into one wheel.** As the wheel turns it transmits **prayers of harmony and peace** into the environment twenty-four hours a day. St. Paul said to "pray without ceasing." Perhaps this devout Nepali has discovered his way to pray without ceasing. (1st Thessalonians 5:17)

Skeptics point to **the war with the world's weather**—for example, hurricane Katrina which devastated New Orleans—as proof that there is no God. "How could God allow Katrina to happen," they say. Like on many episodes of *The Twilight Zone,* the veneer on civilization was torn off when tranquil neighborhoods shifted to anarchy during the flood. Skeptics turned "love thy neighbor" on its head by pointing out that the outpouring of love and money by citizens of the world was the brain's selfish instinct to help others survive, because helping others survive reciprocally guarantees the givers' survival.

With such contrasts, it's a miracle the world works at all!

We should be like the Mona Lisa. She keeps
smiling while her back is to the wall.
unknown author

EBB AND FLOW OF SUCCESS AND FAILURE

What is the forecast? The explanations of reality by scientific skeptics are challenging. The skeptics make a case that our lucky lives are the result of winning a cosmic lottery. Skeptics and atheists would agree that believers have the right to exist, but not that we are here for a purpose. Scientific skeptics maintain that the practice of psi and primitive Christian healing are anachronisms. The skeptics point out that the fakers of psi, the failures to heal, the frauds of research, the effects of placebos, and the hypocrisies of religion confirm that believers are delusional.

Psi researcher, Daniel Wirth, went to prison for perpetuating financial fraud. Wirth's participation in millions of dollars of fraud has raised questions about his honesty and his worth as a data collector for the studies he did of prayer and healing. Wirth and his research assistant and coconspirator in fraud, Joseph Horvath, who was previously in jail for arson and embezzlement, probably never did any scientific prayer studies at all.

A scary omen for anyone thinking of delving into consciousness is the death of Elisabeth Targ, M.D. While doing a scientific study of prayer on healing brain disease, Dr. Targ developed the same brain disease and died.

The argument that compassionate intention in prayer has been the most widely applied alternative therapy on the planet Earth reinforces the analysis of many a skeptic and atheist that mankind is crazed, believes in superstition, and is in danger. (Skeptics might be right about the "danger" of prayer when considering how some people pray with hatred toward their victims.)

What is neuroscience or cognitive science or brain science telling us about our spiritual experiences? It depends on your viewpoint. Discoveries of the brain can be used to show that spirituality and prayer are delusions or that there is a higher purpose for spirituality and prayer, or both.

Neuroscience discovering the existence of nonlocal prayer and psi is a larger quest than neuroscience discovering the hard wiring of spirituality, prayer, and the DNA God-gene, which influence one's beliefs and biology. Why is seeking psi a larger quest? Neuroscience supports the *internal* neurological effects in the body of what meditation does but not the *external* intercessory effects outside the body of what prayer does. That is, so far, meditation has more evidence for its activities in a human body than prayer has for its activities at a distance.

Meditation reminds me of *The Wizard of Oz*; "You just need a brain." You don't need God or psi in meditation. Some neuroscientists are taking the position that religion, prayer, and psi are cultural beliefs ingrained on the brain. "Such beliefs are no longer necessary and should be abandoned for the evolved man and woman" as one neuroscientist put it.

The neurologically intertwined communication within a body responds to attitudes, placebo effects, and nocebo (negative) effects. Internal communication in the body is not controversial. What is controversial is that entangled minds and bodies *communicate with each other at a distance.* Does hearing about entangled minds communicating bring prayer up on our radar screen? Yes, since prayer often creates healing communication at a distance.

Every question about faith, spirituality, and God can't be answered by science. The Klingbeils' work suggested that, if one starts with simple subjects to test and learns from them, then one has more know-how to test more complex subjects later on. Bruce and John couldn't figure out how to test human beings because of the complexities and variables involved.

What is an example of a variable? One catch-22 theory is that when increasing numbers of people know about a test and give attention to a test, their thoughts involuntarily interfere with a test. So how do lots of folks know about a test, but not think about it? The Klingbeils expected that future scientists would creatively solve the tricky problem of knowing about a test, so human beings as test subjects would be adequately isolated from interference from outside minds.

That outside minds interfere with the minds and bodies of human test subjects might have been a variable in a prayer study published in 2006. This *Study of the Therapeutic Effects of Intercessory Prayer* (STEP) stated that the patients who were prayed for healed no better than the patients not prayed for. Co-author of the STEP study, Manoj Jain, M.D., of the Baptist Memorial Hospital, Memphis, Tennessee, said, "One caveat is that with so many individuals receiving prayer from friends and family, as well as personal prayer, it may be impossible to disentangle the effects of study prayer from background prayer."

Ted Rockwell reviewed a news report of the STEP study that claimed to demonstrate that intercessory prayer from third parties didn't have a beneficial effect on patients. He noted that:

Dr. Jain correctly cites a problem that could cloud the effects of an otherwise-positive study. But if a study, properly carried out, demonstrated, despite this problem, that prayer was effective, then that conclusion would have to be taken as valid support for the idea.

If the study of prayer was accurately described, it did not follow proper scientific protocol. Informing one group that you were praying for them, while the other group was not so informed, could stir up all sorts of concerns: "Why pray for me, and not that guy? I must be dying." Or "Why are they using prayer on me? Does that mean the doc has given up on me?" In other words, they deliberately introduced an important confounding factor, which means that the two groups were not the same. This confounding factor was apparently not random but was actually applied to one group and not the other.

The effects of worry on physiology are well known—e.g. "White Coat Blood Pressure Artifact." The study therefore violates the most basic principle of epidemiology: that the test group and the control group must be as nearly identical as possible, except for the variable being tested. Such a defect has invalidated many other studies.

In addition, it was not a "blind study": that is, the participants and the experimenters were informed as to which group the individual patients were in, which introduces another research no-no. For these reasons alone, this report would not be publishable in most credible scientific journals.

However, the study did produce results of an unexpected nature raising new questions to be investigated about prayer.

The STEP study and an editorial response were published in the *American Heart Journal.** In the response, Duke University's Mitchell Krucoff, M.D., and his colleagues suggested that everyone STEP back and notice that the study *did show unanticipated results*, namely, that prayer can convey bad effects. " . . . researchers must be vigilant in asking the question of whether a well intentioned, loving, heartfelt healing prayer might inadvertently harm or kill vulnerable patients in certain circumstances."

Here is what the Klingbeils deduced about bad effects.

❖ At times goal-directed prayers, full of benign intentions, can do more harm than good by pushing a patient in an unnatural direction.

❖ At times our conscious minds pray one way, and our subconscious minds pray with another agenda. I remember *consciously* forgiving someone in prayer, but *unconsciously* I was seething in unforgiveness. Which thought conveyed my truth? My unconscious thought. I was consciously thinking forgiveness, but I was transmitting fuming prayer, cursing instead of blessing.

❖ At times we pray with "groupthink" (what others think) instead of with inspiration (with original creative thinking). When we pray with groupthink, we potentially reinforce a fear or fix solidly a negative on a person or a situation. We unwittingly parrot in prayer what we hear from others and what our culture convinces us to repeat. This tumbling prayer is the opposite of what we intended to do.

Stephan Schwartz, current director of the Rhine Research Center, and Larry Dossey, M.D., have written a paper that chronicles nineteen prayer studies on human beings. Of the eleven successful prayer studies, one study was published four months prior to the STEP study. (See the "Evidence for Correlations between Distant Intentionality and Brain Function in Recipients: A Functional Magnetic Resonance Imaging Analysis" in the *Journal of Alternative and Complementary Medicine* December 2005, Vol. 11, No. 6: 965-971.)

* The STEP articles are in the *American Heart Journal* April 2006, Vol. 151, No. 4: 934-942, 762-764.

~~~~~~

To give intercessory prayer a better opportunity to succeed generally, Bruce and John Klingbeil suggested the following. Perform pre-tests to find individuals in the population who appear to show at least modest healing results. Ask these individuals to be the healers tested in the experiments. The better *the input* from the healers, the better the possibility that *the output* of a test will produce healing signals above the noise and chance that compel a test to fail. (See page 55.)

In designing a study, it might be wise to acknowledge that various types of thought produce different patterns. If holy thoughts occasion quality and ordering-effects that can be distinguished from goal-directed, placebo, and nocebo effects, then patterns of thought should be considered in designing a study.

> The experimental investigation of psi and quality psi acting on targets distantly is the scientific challenge to work out between opponents and proponents. Because of the illusive behavior of thought and the failures and flaws found in research, Bruce and John predicted that it would take a gargantuan effort into the future, like the way NASA plans missions to the moon and beyond, to demonstrate evidence effective enough to establish that quantum fields and spiritual fields of psi and quality do exist in man and creation.

Concerning the existence of psi, skeptics and believers will endlessly disagree. The believers argue that skeptics have convinced themselves to dismiss a wide spectrum of quality experiences in life. The skeptics argue, "If you can't quantify quality, don't trust those unusual experiences you have." (See page 33.)

Debates will abound. Tests of prayer and psi will cycle plus and minus, with a success followed by a failure. Winners of the contest about the existence of God, of prayer, and psi will take their turns as "King of the hill." (See page 124.)

In the future, the debate over prayer given for children in school settings probably will have to be settled scientifically, not religiously. Dropping religion from the debate releases the Constitutional conflicts, which leaves science to study the benefits or not of children praying in school. (See page 186.) Ironically, public high schools in the Washington D.C. area, with elevated populations of Muslims, have set aside prayer rooms for students to prostrate and direct their prayers toward Mecca.

The happiness of your life depends upon the quality of your thoughts . . . therefore, guard them accordingly.
Roman Emperor Marcus Aurelius (270-275 A.D.)

If science can discover an acceptable method to distinguish holy thoughts from human thoughts, can we test for holy persons? We should try since quality people are the hope for the Earth.

In 1986, John Klingbeil said:

> Aside from the charge a lot of us will get by seeing how the universe is really put together, I believe that the experiments will radically change the value system of mankind. I believe the tests will get people both to think about holiness and to understand its relationship to their well being.

How can we obtain evidence that effects of creativity, purpose, and spirituality are from a Divine Ordering-Force and not made up by the human mind alone? Bruce began by distinguishing *patterns of order* for divine effects and *patterns of less order* for human effects. That is, by utilizing human thoughts imbued with holy qualitative (quality) thought and human thoughts apparently not imbued with holy quality thought, two different types of order are projected on our human experiences.

Bruce Klingbeil addressed the questions, "Is it necessary to have God in the prayer loop? Is it necessary to be aware of the existence of a Divine Ordering-Force influencing our human experiences?"

Bruce wrote:

> This question is going to be the heart of the argument over qualitative research in the years ahead. Perhaps it will only be answered on the basis of experience. By this I mean that if *measurable* qualitative healing power can only be attained through "the way of holiness" in a religious sense, that is, through a God-centered life, this, then, speaks for itself.
>
> Since objective tests only measure the effects of thought and don't tell us much about thought directly, anyone can postulate anything they like about the thought that produces the effects. On the other hand, if only a certain mental outlook leads to the ability to produce the effects, that carries some weight. And, on this, the evidence isn't in.
>
> We have demonstrated that *some* Christian Science practitioners and *some* other religious individuals produce *measurable* qualitative healing power. We have yet to find atheists who can do this. (See page 181.)

Possibly the future logic of human events may furnish good reasons for psi and prayer to advance in a technological age. (See pages 191-192.)

John Klingbeil said, "Prayer is an ordering-mechanism that changes physical systems . . . . We have to first shift the paradigm to shift society to consider investigating prayer scientifically."

If society shifted to investigate prayer in the laboratory, Bruce Klingbeil felt that this initial window of opportunity would last about a decade wherein to perform preliminary experiments that might build a case for quality psi as the vector behind normalizing prayer. Then interest would cycle wane, and the skeptics would organize new ways to counterpunch many scientific claims about psi including nonlocal prayer.

A quick answer to prayer happens so seldom that its spontaneous nature can't possibly be relied upon to pique the curiosity of a scientist.

If prayer works for someone, it often works incrementally. The recipient of prayer usually notices the effects in retrospect. Telling the story of what prayer did doesn't help a scientist understand what happened. A suitable middle ground to observe prayer should be reached. (See page 296.)

The natural born healer, the student of healing who learns he can improve his talents, the person surprised he has the potential to become a healer, and the person who may be disappointed that his talents probably lie somewhere else than healing, all these people will be tested in the future. Psychics will be tested, too, when society raises the bar of credibility for the business of the paranormal. The Klingbeils' foresight that healers and psychics will be tested and categorized for psi and prayer boiled tempers. (See page 164.)

Bruce and John predicted that future controversies surrounding psi and prayer would involve the following questions.

1. Can science determine when psi and prayer are delusions or reality?

2. Can the reach of consciousness be measured?

3. Is there evidence of consciousness extending a field of quality effect addressing needs across distance?

4. Can spiritual science keep pace with breakthroughs in medicine, genetics, brain science, and science in general where human beings can create and do just about whatever they want?

5. Can subconscious saboteurs of spirituality and psi be trapped in the act as they launch distortion, displacement, and the vanishing effect when human beings seek evidence of psi?

6. When computers, robots, and the Internet come alive with consciousness, will their enhanced speed and superior intelligence ratchet up their psi abilities, prayer power, psychological techniques, and spirituality leaving men to wonder what is man and where is his place in this enhanced frontier? (See pages 125-128.)

For *A Conclusion* about the Klingbeils' research, see page 293. For *Spindrift in Review*, see page 289.

You can't always get what you want,
but you might get what you need.

The Rolling Stones

Happiness makes up in height for what it lacks in length.
Robert Frost

The experiencer of psi and prayer has a momentary peek on the soul of reality. It's been said, "If you can't say it in words, say it in music. If you can't say it in music, say it in dance." The believer who experiences psi is sympathetic to the **music**, the singular rhythm, and dance steps of his experience that **he seems incapable of describing, but few skeptics catch the soul of it,** steeped in their enlightenment about **the beat of the rhythm** pulsing the dance steps. In the *Merchant of Venice*, Shakespeare inked "Trust no man who hath no music in his soul."

The threats of nuclear and biological murder promised by negative believers in religion and the deployment of supernatural powers promised by positive believers in religion suggest the future. It's no longer a question of, if it's right or wrong to build bridges between science, religion, and consciousness. It's a question of, do we have any choice? The future remains invisible.

*****X*****

About the Author

Bill Sweet has always been interested in how consciousness and prayer relate to science and religion. A natural connection between like-thinking people resulted in his involvement in the research of prayer and consciousness at Spindrift. Bill became a president of Spindrift, Inc.

Brought up on the North Shore of Chicago, Bill graduated from New Trier High School and Illinois State University with a major in communications. Bill founded and was president of an entertainment booking agency in Chicagoland. Bill's avocations include being an investor, an audiophile, and a ham radio operator. He resides in Mount Prospect, Illinois.

A favorite quote of Bill's is by Charles Steinmetz, the father of modern electricity. "Someday . . . the scientists of the world will turn their laboratories over to the study of God and prayer and the spiritual forces which as yet have hardly been scratched."

CPSIA information can be obtained at www.ICGtesting.com
Printed in the USA
LVOW10s1503250813

349502LV00001B/128/A